# Methods in Buddhist Studies

Also available from Bloomsbury:

*Adaptation and Developments in Western Buddhism*, Phil Henry
*Buddhism and Iconoclasm in East Asia*, Fabio Rambelli and Eric Reinders
*Buddhism in America*, Scott A. Mitchell
*A Critique of Western Buddhism*, Glenn Wallis
*Language in the Buddhist Tantra of Japan*, Richard K. Payne

# Methods in Buddhist Studies

*Essays in Honor of Richard K. Payne*

Edited by Scott A. Mitchell and Natalie Fisk Quli

BLOOMSBURY
NEW DELHI • LONDON • OXFORD • NEW YORK • SYDNEY

BLOOMSBURY INDIA
Bloomsbury Publishing India Pvt. Ltd
Second Floor, LSC Building No. 4, DDA Complex, Pocket C–6&7,
Vasant Kunj, New Delhi 110070

BLOOMSBURY, BLOOMSBURY ACADEMIC INDIA and the Diana logo are trademarks of Bloomsbury Publishing Plc

**First published in India 2024**
First published in Great Britain 2019


Cover design: Maria Rajka

This edition published with permission from Bloomsbury Publishing Plc,
50 Bedford Square, London, WC1B3DP, UK



A catalogue record for this book is available from the British Library.
A catalog record for this book is available from the Library of Congress.

ISBN: 978-93-61318-63-4

Typeset by Deanta Global Publishing Services, Chennai, India

Printed and bound by Manipal Technologies Limited, Manipal

To find out more about our authors and books
visit www.bloomsbury.com and sign up for our newsletters

*Richard K. Payne has played so many roles in my academic and professional career. I am grateful for his scholarship, teaching, mentoring, scolding, administering, editing, etc. I am also grateful for his humor, kindness, and skillfulness.*

*May this work produce merit for the benefit of all beings.*

N.F.Q.

*For Richard: mentor, ācārya, kalyāṇamitra, friend.*

S.A.M.

# Contents

# Contributors

**Judith Berling** is Professor Emerita of Chinese Religions, past dean and vice president of the Graduate Theological Union, Berkeley, and past president of the American Academy of Religion. Her research interests include interreligious learning and Chinese spirituality. Her publications include *Understanding Other Religious Worlds: A Guide for Interreligious Education* (2004) and *A Pilgrim in Chinese Culture: Negotiating Religious Diversity* (1997).

**Courtney Bruntz** is Assistant Professor of Asian Religions, Doane University. Her primary research focuses on Buddhist teachings and practices in contemporary China, taking place in both urban and rural settings. This includes an emphasis on Buddhist tourism and missionization. She is coeditor of the forthcoming volume *Buddhist Tourism in Asia: Imagining, Secularizing, and Commodifying the Sacred.*

**Lisa Grumbach** is an adjunct faculty member of Ryukoku University, Kyoto, Japan, and the Institute of Buddhist Studies, Berkeley. Her research focuses on interactions between Buddhism and local *kami* traditions in medieval Japan. Her publications include "The Creation of Ritual Meat Avoidance by Japanese State Systems," in *Sacred Matters, Stately Concerns: Faith and Politics in Asia, Past and Present*, edited by John M. Thompson (2014).

**Chenxing Han** is a graduate of the Graduate Theological Union, Berkeley, California. Her research interests include Buddhism in the West, Asian American studies, and Buddhist chaplaincy. She has published in the *Journal of Global Buddhism*, *Pacific World: Journal of the Institute of Buddhist Studies*, and *Buddhadharma: The Practitioner's Quarterly.*

**Takuya Hino** is a lecturer at Komazawa University, Tokyo, Japan. His research interests include Japanese Buddhism, Japanese history, Japanese literature, and linguistics. Recent publications include "Ocean of Suffering, Boat of Compassion" in the *Journal of the American Academy of Religion* (2012) and "The Daoist Facet of Kinpusen and Sugawara no Michizane Worship in the *Dōken Shōnin Meidoki*: A Translation of the *Dōken Shōnin Meidoki*" in *Pacific World* (2009).

**Charles B. Jones** is Associate Professor in the School of Theology and Religious Studies at the Catholic University of America, Washington, DC. His research interests include Chinese Pure Land Buddhism and the history of Buddhism in Taiwan. Recent publications include *The View from Mars Hill: Christianity in the Landscape of World Religions* (2005).

**Scott A. Mitchell** is the Dean of Students and Faculty Affairs at the Institute of Buddhist Studies, Berkeley. His research interests include Buddhism in the West, modern Buddhism, media, and ritual. His publications include *Buddhism in America* (2016) and *Buddhism Beyond Borders* (2015), coedited with Natalie E.F. Quli.

**Franz Metcalf** is an instructor, California State University, Los Angeles. His research interests include contemporary Buddhisms, depth psychology, and Buddhist experience. In addition to numerous popular books on the application of Buddhism to everyday life, he has contributed to many edited volumes, encyclopedias, and bibliographies, most recently "Buddhist Views of Childhood" for Oxford Bibliographies Online.

**Victoria R. Montrose** is a doctoral candidate in the Department of East Asian Languages and Cultures, University of Southern California, Los Angeles. Her research interests include Japanese Buddhism, Buddhism and modernity, Buddhist education, and religion and higher education. Her publications include "Floating Prayer: Localization, Globalization, and Tradition in the Shinnyo-en Hawaii Lantern Floating" in the *Journal of Religion in Japan* (2014), and "Shinnyoen" in the *Brill Handbook of East Asian New Religious Movements* (2018).

**Charles D. Orzech** is Professor of Religious Studies at Colby College, Waterville, Maine. His research interests include late Mahayana and tantric Buddhism, semiotics and visual culture, museums and religion. Recent publications include "Tantric Subjects: Liturgy and Vision in Chinese Esoteric Ritual Manuals," in Yael Bentor and Meir Shahar, eds., *Chinese and Tibetan Esoteric Buddhism* (2017) and "Ritual Subjects: Homa in Chinese Translations and Manuals from the Sixth through Eighth Centuries," in Richard K. Payne and Michael Witzel, eds., *Homa Variations: The Study of Ritual Change across the Longue Durée* (2015).

**Aaron P. Proffitt** is Assistant Professor of Japanese Studies, University at Albany-SUNY. His research interests include medieval Japanese Buddhism in the context of broader East Asian and Mahayana theories of ritual speech, the afterlife, and debates about the relationship between Buddhist practice and the attainment of enlightenment. His publications include "Dohan no himitsu nenbutsu shiso: Kenmitsu bunka to mikkyo jodokyo [The Esoteric Nenbutsu Thought of Dohan: Kenmitsu Culture and Esoteric Pure Land Buddhism]" in the *Journal of World Buddhist Cultures* (2018), and a forthcoming monograph, *Esoteric Pure Land Buddhism in Early Medieval Japan*.

**Natalie Fisk Quli** is a research fellow at the Institute of Buddhist Studies, Berkeley, and Executive Editor of *Pacific World*. Her research interests include Theravada Buddhisms in America and Buddhist modernism. Her publications include *Buddhism beyond Borders* (2015), coedited with Scott A. Mitchell, and "Western Self, Asian Other: Modernity, Authenticity, and Nostalgia for 'Tradition' in Buddhist Studies," in the *Journal of Buddhist Ethics* (2009).

**Charles Willemen** is Rector and a professor at International Buddhist College, Thailand. His research interests include Sarvāstivāda and both Chinese Buddhism and Japanese Buddhism. His publications include a translation of a version of the *Dhammapada, The Scriptural Text: Verses of the Doctrine with Parables* (1999), and *A Collection of Important Odes of the Law: The Chinese Udānavarga* (2013).

# Preface

One of the joys of academic life is finding a colleague who is not only a stimulating and challenging conversation partner but who embodies the finest virtues of the scholarly profession. Richard Payne has been such a colleague—a treasure—in my life. Richard and I have shared the challenge of trying to do it all: administrating, teaching and advising, mentoring young scholars, serving professional organizations, researching, and publishing for academic and broader audiences. His success in all these ventures and his prodigious output have made him a model as well as a colleague. It is indeed a pleasure and an honor to pay tribute to him in this festschrift.

Richard served for many years as the energetic dean of the Institute of Buddhist Studies (IBS), which is situated (for the most part, comfortably so) between the Buddhist Churches of America, for which it educates ministerial leaders, and the Graduate Theological Union (GTU) in Berkeley, a consortium of Christian (Western and Eastern), Buddhist, Unitarian, Jewish, Muslim, and Hindu partners that together offer a PhD in religious studies as well as various forms of interreligious engagement. For eight of Richard's years as dean of IBS, I was dean of GTU, that is, of the consortium as a whole. As fellow deans, we collaborated on developing policies and understandings that would enable these very diverse schools and centers to collaborate academically. I valued Richard highly as a reliable source of keen analysis, constructive criticism, and sound ideas, and I deeply respected his steady hand on the tiller of his institution.

Richard and I were also colleagues in the GTU Doctoral Area of Cultural and Historical Studies of Religions. In a consortium dominated by Christian theological schools, Richard, himself a graduate of the GTU doctoral program, consistently championed rigorous historical, textual, and social scientific research, and emphasized the importance of making a clear distinction between that work and the work of theology and the practical disciplines. I had the pleasure of co-teaching with Richard a doctoral methods seminar, "Issues in the Study of Religions." He insisted that students critically engage readings that exposed the unconscious biases that can distort the study of religion, and that they develop clear and critical understandings of method and methodology. Although the material was always challenging, his pedagogical approach made full use of his dry wit and vivid examples, helping students sink their teeth into challenging ideas.

Over almost three decades in the doctoral program, I have served with Richard on more student committees than I can count. He is quite simply a superb mentor. He asks probing questions, challenges unexamined assumptions, makes students defend their theoretical choices until they are very clear about their entailments, and always demands scholarly coherence. He has been a helpful second reader to my advisees, and to his own he is a challenging but supportive mentor, encouraging and requiring that they take full responsibility for their scholarly choices.

More than any colleague I have known, Richard also mentors students into the activities of the profession. His advisees help organize conferences and they edit papers and conference volumes. They also coauthor articles with him, honing their skills for creating publishable work. The students I have known have relished their work with and for him, and some have continued to be active in the work of editing volumes after graduation. Not only does this contribute to the students' professional development, but it also helps to account for Richard's astonishing scholarly production—by engaging his students in collaboration he was able to accomplish far more than he could have on his own.

In fall 2016 I was acting dean of GTU for a semester while we awaited the arrival of our newly appointed dean, Uriah Kim. During that time, Richard came up for review as a member of the Core Doctoral Faculty. Faculty under review send copies of their publications since the prior review (normally seven years). In Richard's case, the file of recent publications was so vast that I could only sample it, which I did with great delight. Not only the quantity but the range and quality of the work were truly remarkable. As a scholar of Chinese religions I am well aware that many scholars choose an extremely narrow and specialized path in the vast fields of Eastern religions. Not so with Richard. While he has done extensive work on tantric texts and rituals, the scope of his work—the range of Buddhist texts, the range of theoretical issues, and the range of scholarly conversations he has addressed—was stunning. This was also exemplified in the many conferences that he hosted at IBS, inviting speakers to offer papers on important and emerging issues in the study of Buddhism and religion.

I have not spoken with Richard about his retirement plans but I suspect that retirement for him will simply mean less multitasking and more attention to whatever projects he chooses to pursue. I cannot envision him "at rest," though perhaps he has hidden sides unknown to me.

I do know that he has broader interests than Buddhist studies and publishing. I once almost literally ran into Richard and his wife at the Metropolitan Museum of Art in New York. We were both moving in to view a Rembrandt painting, though from different directions, and were suddenly shocked to find ourselves cheek by jowl with someone we knew from Berkeley. I hope that Richard's retirement will allow many more Rembrandts, or whatever other treasures he might savor. Whatever he chooses, he has certainly earned it, and he leaves us with a truly distinguished legacy of published scholarship and a rich legacy of former students and mentees to advance scholarship in religious studies.

Judith Berling
Professor Emerita of Chinese Religions,
Past Dean and Vice President of the Graduate Theological Union

# Introduction: On Maps, Elephants, and Buddhists

Scott A. Mitchell

On numerous occasions, Richard Payne has written about the influence of Western psychology on or the psychologization of Buddhism—a key facet of Buddhist modernism. This body of work has been, at turns, both exploratory and critical, revealing both the historical trajectories of this influence and the pitfalls and dangers of assuming that the Buddhist path is, at the end of the day, little more than an individual exercise in personal growth. For example, in his contribution to David McMahan's *Buddhism in the Modern World*, Payne writes, "Buddhism has not just been interpreted psychologically. Rather, psychotherapy, modern occultism, and Buddhist modernism arise within the same cultural milieu, and the ease with which Buddhism is interpreted as psychotherapeutic is a consequence of that common background."[1] This historical sketch goes on to trace the intersecting discourses that converged in the period between the US Civil War and the First World War, discourses that gave rise to these three phenomena. In his contribution to Mark Unno's *Buddhism and Psychology*, Payne begins with a reflection on how he had, at one time, assumed that there was a natural consonance between the Jungian concept of individuation and the Buddhist concept of awakening. He argues, however, that this is not the case, that the modern psychotherapeutic process is indebted to a Romantic/Protestant Christian atonement narrative—beginning with an original spiritual purity, followed by a fall, and finally a return to that purity. The Buddhist path functions on a wholly different narrative structure—from ignorance, to intent to awaken, to awakening. Essentially, modern interpreters project onto Buddhism what they are looking for, a path toward individuation, and thus find it: "The atonement narrative stands behind both individuation and the psychologized interpretation of awakening, thus creating the illusory appearance that individuation and awakening are the same."[2]

Commenting on this critical stance, Ann Gleig has noted that "Payne decries the common assimilation of Buddhism into the Jungian narrative," suggesting that Payne's stance is simply this—a rejection of modernist rearticulations of the Buddhist path.[3] And yet, at the same time, in his contribution to Michael Aune and Valerie DeMarinis's *Religious and Social Ritual*, Payne takes quite a different approach—and an explicitly etic one at that. His study here is on ritual, specifically "the way in which ritual can provide for personal, that is, intrapsychic, transformation."[4] Rather than translating a tantra and discussing its ritual (which Payne has done), rather than discussing ritual's efficacy in the social realm (which Payne has also done), and rather than critiquing or "decrying" the amalgamation of modern psychology and modern Buddhism, here Payne is approaching the question of ritual's effective power from a point of view outside the tradition, a specifically psychological one. Why? Payne writes, "I believe that intellectual efforts should be driven by problems rather than methodology, and that the methodology should follow the formulation of the problem. The question of ritual as an effective means of self-transformation, that is, as a means of intrapsychic change, leads me first to think in psychological terms."[5]

This is the crux of the issue: questions determine method, not the other way around. The question put before Payne in *Religious and Social Ritual* was the personal efficacy of ritual—not how does one perform a ritual, not what is the symbolic meaning of a ritual, not what is the history of a ritual, but how does ritual change one's interiority? This is a psychological question, one thus requiring a method built to answer such a question. Moreover, the question asked will reveal something about the ritual, and by extension Buddhism, but it will not reveal everything. Again, it might tell us something about personal or intrapsychic change, but it won't tell us very much about the historical development of the ritual under study or how the ritual is understood or performed in various, specific cultural contexts. It is a limited view, a limited revelation of Buddhism's far more complex and nuanced totality.

We might say that scholars in the field of Buddhist studies are engaged in a single project—an answer to the question: What is Buddhism? Put another way, we are collectively engaged in the project of defining our subject, a subject with a two-and-a-half millennia history and roots covering half the globe (and now, arguably, everywhere). Such a subject, vast and diverse, cannot be defined simply, will always have fuzzy and contested borders, and resists a totalizing and essentializing Theory of Everything. Buddhism can be defined historically, sociologically, philosophically, anthropologically, via art and material culture, commerce, and economics, with various etic tools from psychology to media studies, and with its own emic tools, including, to use Payne's word, *praxis*.[6] This vast array of scholarly tools at our disposal is one reason that Buddhist studies is best defined as a field, not a discipline, and that each of these methods reveal parts of our subject, but never the whole.[7] If Buddhist studies is a field, and I can be forgiven for using an obvious, even trite, metaphor, it is a field still being charted, a field whose map has yet to be completed. And just as a topographical map tells you one thing about a field and a political map tells you something very different about that same physical space, so too do different methods tell us different things about the same object of our studies, Buddhism.

This volume—dedicated to Payne's large contribution to this field, his own travels and cartography over the past four decades—takes method as its starting point. And to follow Payne's dictum above, that problems (questions) ought to drive method, the question that animates the chapters of this book is simply: how does method change what we think we know of our subject? Put another way, what do different methods reveal about Buddhism? The objective in the following volume is not to argue for the primacy or value of one particular method over another, nor is it merely self-reflexive scholarship on theory and method in our field. The objective is to demonstrate how what Buddhism "is" changes by the questions we ask and the methods we use to answer them. As Chenxing Han (in this volume) reminds us, there may be no "there there"; Buddhism resists totalizing and essentializing definitions. Nevertheless, our collective work as scholars still serves the valuable function of revealing parts of an ever-changing, ever-shifting whole, a project Payne has contributed to in innumerable ways.

## Mapping the field

Buddhist studies is a field insofar as it has no single method, which is a prerequisite for a discipline. Whereas a rising generation of scholars has a dizzying array of methods to choose from, this was not always so.

The modern academic study of Buddhism emerged in two locations—philology and area studies. Colonial civil servants in the eighteenth and nineteenth centuries were not only collecting texts to be dispatched to Europe for translation by eminent scholars such as Eugène Burnouf, they were also setting up their own translation projects in the colonies, such as the Pali Text Society. These collections of manuscripts have been and continue to be the foundation upon which Western academic translations of Buddhist texts are based. Such studies are invaluable, providing us with a wealth of knowledge about Buddhism's doctrines, teachings, practices, and historical and cultural locations wherein those teachings and practices developed. The discovery of new caches of texts allows us to learn even more about this historical development as new versions of texts, text fragments, and texts in multiple languages are brought together and comparatively studied. As Paul Harrison has noted, "Reports of the death of Buddhist philology have been greatly exaggerated," owing in no small part to the discovery of new texts, particularly in Afghanistan and Pakistan, as well as manuscript collections in both Europe and Asia which have more to reveal to contemporary scholars.[8]

In addition to the study of texts, and by extension history and philosophy, Buddhist studies also came of age in twentieth-century area studies. Before the Second World War, but increasing greatly during the Cold War and the postcolonial period, European and American universities and scholarly societies became increasingly organized around area studies, intentionally interdisciplinary fields of knowledge dedicated to specific geopolitical regions. Arguably, many of these regions were defined by the collapse of empire and the desire of "the West" to continue the maintenance of "the Orient," as is particularly evident in Middle East studies.[9] Early Buddhist studies was similarly focused on specific parts of the Buddhist world, carved up along modern political lines, and whose vestiges remain in our field, reinforced by university departments and scholarly societies, the locations where our work is done. Scholars, thus, routinely specialize in either South or East Asia, Central Asia, or Southeast Asia, Japan but not China, and so forth. And while teaching demands may require some to become dilettantes in a related subfield (via the dreaded World Religions class), one's CV will nevertheless betray a particular focus on a particular part of the world.

As the saying goes, when you only have a hammer, everything looks like a nail—and if the only tool at the disposal of Buddhist studies were philology, then Buddhism looks like a text. This is to say that methods shape what we know about the subject insofar as they are only able to give us certain kinds of answers. This is not to argue that Buddhist studies, as a field, should abandon or reject any particular method; it is to suggest that we benefit from interdisciplinarity and that we should continue to engage in critical self-reflection. In the case of area studies, Payne writes that such an orientation "mold[s] the field of Buddhist studies in profound ways and shouldn't be employed uncritically. It is through critical self-reflection on the established field that new research and insights become possible."[10] Because area studies takes modern geopolitical borders as a given, it may be unable to see transnational crossings or cultural phenomena not easily confined to the nation-state. Critical self-reflection on area studies, indeed on the field as a whole since the 1990s, has pushed the boundaries of Buddhist studies and allowed for the development of new theoretical and methodological perspectives. Such developments complement rather than supplant preexisting methods and orientations, which is as it should be. To paraphrase Thomas Tweed, methods are mere sightings of religion from specific vantage points and, as such, are limited.[11] The more tools one has at one's disposal, the more one is able to see.

Oliver Freiberger, building on the work of David Shumway and Ellen Messer-Davidow, suggests that disciplines engage in "boundary work," wherein a discipline is rhetorically constructed, its borders policed or expanded, and what counts as appropriate scholarship within the discipline is defined.[12] In many ways, Buddhist studies engages in such boundary work as well, but because it is interdisciplinary, a certain amount of intra-field boundary work also occurs wherein scholars debate the appropriateness of different methods, subfields, subjects, or theories for inclusion in the field.[13] Such debates have consequences, in part, because they define our subject. By claiming that one subfield or method is not appropriate for inclusion in the field, it is implied (sometimes explicitly stated) that the subject is not *Buddhist*. Payne has written on the importance of such definitional questions, specifically in regard to defining religion, which can as easily be applied to the question of defining Buddhism: "The definition of what a religion is . . . is not an incidental question, but rather it is central to any contemporary discussion of religion. The question of how religion is defined is important because the definition implicitly legitimates certain aspects of a religion and de-legitimates others."[14] Thus, critical self-reflection on the field, intra-field infighting about proper methods or disciplines, and the definitional work of Buddhist studies are questions that should not go unexamined. As a field, we should resist the urge to treat some forms of knowledge as superior or more authentic than others and instead acknowledge that different forms of knowledge are just that—different—and that the field benefits from multiple tools at its disposal in its attempt to provide a full accounting of Buddhism.

Reflecting on a symposium, "Buddhist Studies Today," held at the University of British Columbia in 2015, Donald Lopez quotes Holmes Welch writing about the state of Buddhist studies half a century earlier: "Obviously, the philologist, the philosopher, the student of comparative religion, and the social scientist, each remaining what he [*sic*] is, must try to understand the others' approach to Buddhism, study the others' discipline, and collaborate in a concrete way so that the results of research may suffer less from the shortcomings that each now finds in the work of the other."[15] Lopez, in summarizing the 2015 symposium, goes on to note,

> Perhaps the largest question to emerge from the workshop was the nature of the boundaries that have long defined the field of Buddhist Studies, boundaries of language, period, region, genre, and sect and dichotomies between doctrine and social history, textual analysis and devotional cult and root text and commentary. Over the course of three days, many of these boundaries were expanded, crossed and blurred. By the end, it was clear to all participants—both the Fellows and the senior scholars—that a plurality of approaches is not only desirable but essential for the field of Buddhist Studies to grow, not only in the scope of its study but also in its audience.[16]

## Methods in Buddhist studies

The present volume is a specific type of edited volume—a *festschrift*—and we are conscious of the liability many edited volumes suffer; namely, a lack of coherence. One might assume that organizing an edited volume around a specific scholar's work and contribution to the field would provide a focal point around which all the contributors could rally, thus providing coherence. In the case of Richard Payne's contributions to Buddhist studies, (thankfully) this is not the case.

Payne's work, albeit focused in large part on ritual and Japan, has enormous breadth. Richard has been interested in, has written and published on, has taught graduate seminars and organized symposia and conferences on topics from ritual to translation, psychology to history, the premodern and the modern, institutions and economics. He has been as concerned with Kamakura-era Buddhism in Japan as with the contemporary popularity of mindfulness meditation in the United States, Indian tantric Pure Land texts to contemporary Chinese *homa* rituals in California. As editor of numerous volumes himself, as well as the Institute of Buddhist Studies' academic journal, *Pacific World*, he has worked with dozens of scholars across multiple subfields and disciplines. As a teacher, over nearly three decades at the Institute, he has advised countless students and followed their research interests across time and space. If we were looking for a singular scholarly approach, a scholar who has steadfastly focused his or her attention on a single research topic or method, Payne is not that scholar. And we, the beneficiaries of his work, are all the better for it.

This breadth of interest—while a potential liability for an edited volume—is perfectly appropriate and in keeping with the central question; again, intellectual endeavors should be problem-driven, and method follows from the question. Buddhist studies scholars, collectively, are engaged in a project to learn everything there is to know about the object of our study, Buddhism, and that "everything" cannot be captured by a single method. Payne's interests have taken him far across the field of Buddhist studies, following questions, crossing boundaries, and charting territory other scholars fear to tread. To push this cartographical metaphor, the map of the terrain enriched by Payne's travels has benefited all of us in our own travels through his various roles as editor, scholar, and teacher.

Thus, it was only appropriate that we chose methods as the theme for this volume and invited a wide array of scholars—some colleagues, some former students—to contribute in honor of Payne's work. Divided into four parts, the following chapters reveal a broad view of the tradition both historically and in the contemporary world, both in Asia and the West.

We open with the past, in a trio of historical studies of Japanese Buddhism. The chapters in Part 1 point to the intersection of religion, culture, politics, and economics. Lisa Grumbach's study, "When Food becomes Trespass," focuses on local Japanese food customs historically tied to hunting and fishing. Offerings of meat were routinely made to local *kami*, but by the Kamakura period (1192–1333), the Japanese political landscape had become "Buddhisized," and the authorities began passing laws banning the killing of animals. As Grumbach asks, "What happens, then, when a community's daily food becomes defined as sin, as illegal, as trespass of both religious morality and secular law?" In a comparative study of three temples, Grumbach discloses how local economies shaped each temple's responses to the bans, from effectively allowing for meat offerings to continue, to substituting rice for meat, or making exceptions to the new laws. Such comparative studies reveal the larger social and economic contexts within which Buddhism develops and adapts to larger political and cultural forces, refining and reframing Buddhism in the process.

Victoria Montrose's chapter takes us to the modern period, and specifically the development during the Meiji period (1868–1912) of Buddhist universities. Whereas scholars of Japanese Buddhism have taken a self-reflective look at the role imperial Japanese universities played in the formation of modern Buddhist studies, little attention has been paid to sectarian Buddhist universities in the same period. Montrose demonstrates that the majority of universities officially recognized by the Meiji government were related to one of the "Kamakura schools" of Buddhism (Zen, Pure Land, Nichiren, etc.), and "thus, we are left to wonder what, if anything, the Buddhist universities contributed to the nascent field of modern Buddhist studies." Montrose's study is focused on the Ōtani Jōdo Shinshū proto-university, the Gohōjō (Institute for the Protection of the Dharma). Informed by modern critical scholarship, students at the Gohōjō began campaigning the sect's main temple to reform its doctrines and practices, a campaign that was initially rejected but later incorporated into the denomination. Montrose thus argues that universities emerged during the Meiji period as a third center of power in Japanese Buddhism, augmenting main temples as centers of doctrine and practice and administrative temples that acted as intercessors with the government.

History, of course, tells us as much about the past as it does the present, a point argued by Aaron Proffitt in his contribution. Based on his larger study of the thirteenth-century Shingon monk Dōhan, Proffitt begins his study by noting the ways in which contemporary sectarian understandings of Japanese Buddhism easily break down both in contemporary practice and historically, when viewed free of anachronistic presumptions. In sum, Proffitt argues for an "Esoteric Pure Land," a way of understanding how practices assumed to be located solely in one tradition or another are, in fact, commonly found in both. Historically, as in the case of Dōhan and others, practices to Amitābha are not at all uncommon even in an "esoteric" tradition such as Shingon. Contemporarily, one finds living Buddhist communities easily transgressing such sectarian boundaries. The seeming oddness of such transgressions is the result of our modern presumption that sectarian divisions are, in fact, normative. They are not, nor have they ever been.

Part 2, "Ritual in Translation," concerns itself with textual studies. Charles Willemen's contribution is a translation and study focused on a single text and driven by a seemingly simple question: "When did Aśvaghoṣa's text and its ritual use find its way into the Kṣudrakavastu of the traditional Sarvāstivādins, known as Mūlasarvāstivādins, at the end of the seventh century?" The work under study here, "A Scriptural Text about Impermanence" (*T*. 801) will eventually be used ritually both in praise of the Buddha as well as to be chanted during cremation ceremonies for monastics. It contains ideas that are a good fit for later Mūlasarvāstivādins but has Aśvaghoṣa's pedigree. How did this come to pass? This is a question about textual and ritual development over time, a question philology is well equipped to answer. And, even in this short text and short study, we see the transgressive nature of texts and practices, the ease with which they transcend our contemporary scholarly and sectarian categories.

Similarly, Takuya Hino focuses on one specific text, a Japanese Confucian tale, the *Oni no Shikogusa*. The tale features a pair of brothers mourning the loss of their parents. One, a court official, is distracted from his duties and tries to forget; the other becomes obsessed with remembering and visits the parents' grave daily. While the story features the familiar Confucian concern for filial piety, Hino's analysis demonstrates how the text was promulgated by esoteric Buddhist poet-monks. Their efforts in popularizing the story thus had the twofold effect of spreading certain Confucian ideas while simultaneously reimagining those ideas in the context of Japanese Buddhist ideology. Moreover, as diseases spread in Japan, specific rites developed to counter what was believed to be their cause — malevolent spirits — rites that can be traced back to tales such as the *Oni no Shikogusa*. As Hino argues, while the work has garnered significant study in the field of Japanese literature, when examined from the point of view of Japanese religion, other meanings emerge confounding our attachment to anachronistic modern categorizations. As mentioned earlier in Proffitt's contribution, making plain modern and/or sectarian biases in our scholarship has been a central feature of Payne's body of work. His discovery of the *Aparimitāyuḥ-sūtra* during his graduate studies struck him as "delightfully transgressive" precisely because the text included both esoteric and Pure Land practices, practices which modern/sectarian scholarship tended to treat exclusively, a presumption not often shared by the authors of these texts in their own historical times and locations.[17]

Whereas Willemen and Hino are focused on single texts, their studies expanding our view of Buddhism in the process, Charles Orzech's study expands our view even further by looking at a specific practice (or, rather, examining something *as* practice) and searching for it across multiple texts. The practice in question is meditation on the thirty-two major and eighty minor marks of a buddha. Often understood as having a purely iconographical basis and function in the tradition, Orzech argues that they are linked to specific devotional and meditation practices. His study ranges far and wide across both Mahayana and Theravada texts and is reminiscent of Payne's recent volume, *Homa Variations*—specifically the *longue durée* and the processes by which rituals change over time. Orzech's initial inquiries into (possible) rituals of seeing a buddha's marks cannot compare with the detailed studies of the *homa* ritual (which is supported by a large collection of canonical texts, ritual manuals, and anthropological studies); nevertheless, this expanded textual view, one in which the researcher seeks multiple instances of a particular practices across texts and traditions, is a rich field of research.

Whereas textual studies of ritual may be methodologically problematic—because we only have access to the text and not the practice itself[18]—Buddhist studies need not limit itself to textual and historical studies. And so, in Part 3 we turn our attention to ethnography.

The definitional and legitimizing work of Buddhists and Buddhist studies, as well as ethnography focused on younger Buddhists often overlooked in contemporary scholarship, is the focus of Courtney Bruntz's contribution, "Buddhism, Consumerism, and the Chinese Millennial." In contemporary mainland China, as Buddhism sees significant growth, a popular narrative has emerged that juxtaposes "real" Buddhism and a Buddhism corrupted by modernity and money. Bruntz skillfully argues that, while there are certainly charlatans that use Buddhism to deceive others for personal gain, there are also savvy monks using contemporary media to spread the dharma. This activity happens within the "gray market" of Chinese religion, a space where private enterprise profits off tourism to Buddhist sites, and Buddhists must navigate indirect economic and state support of religion. Furthermore, a young generation of Chinese millennials, much like millennials in other modern locales, is searching for meaning in a rapidly changing world. It is in this space that monastics at the Longquan Monastery digitize Buddhism in the form of animated videos, microblogs, WeChat, and websites to spread the dharma to young Chinese. Bruntz builds on Payne's critique of a "rhetoric of rupture"[19] that posits a premodern Buddhism as embedded within society and modern Buddhism as disembedded, needing reintegration. She argues that modern adaptations are not a result of this rupture, a desire to become "re-embedded" as it were, but are in fact a continuation of the centuries-old practice of Buddhists making the practice relevant for changing times.

As Natalie Quli has argued, Buddhist studies was slow to accept "the West" as a legitimate field site, a situation that has slowly changed over the past two decades.[20] Nevertheless, ethnographies of contemporary Western and American Buddhism are few and far between, a point taken up by Chenxing Han in her contribution, "Describing the (Nonexistent?) Elephant." She reflects on the use and non-use of ethnography in the study of American Buddhism and suggests that augmenting historical studies with on-the-ground research would help reveal "the elephant"—the totality of American Buddhism—or its absence. Drawing on her previous scholarship, she further reveals voices overlooked or silenced in the study of American Buddhism, specifically young adult Asian Americans, who navigate shifting terrain between and among different traditions of heritage and convert Buddhists. Han's contribution is appropriately self-reflective, noting the importance for scholars to reevaluate their methods, their blind spots, and their positionality toward their subject. She rightly notes that in conducting her research she is asking her subjects to define their identities as young adult Asian American Buddhists in ways they may not have done before. This work may "bias" the results; however, it also points to the role scholars play in defining our subject for our subject. Buddhists and Buddhist scholars cocreate Buddhism, and in this act may unintentionally legitimate some forms of the tradition and silence others.

The critical self-reflective turn in Buddhist studies compels the scholar to examine theoretical frameworks that guide scholarship. This work includes questioning terms borrowed from different disciplines, such as Payne argues in his essay "Why 'Buddhist Theology' Is Not a Good Idea,"[21] and leads us to our final section on theory and method. In his contribution to this volume, Charles Jones asks "Is a *Dazang jing* a Canon?" He details how the term "canon" is itself an etic category, one that comes from outside the Buddhist tradition, and wonders if it is the most applicable term for collections of Buddhist texts. In his analysis, he traces the historical development of Buddhist "canons," and notes how intertwined these projects are with politics and technology, constructed at specific points in history by specific persons. In the modern era, not only are canons transformed by new technologies, but Buddhist *relationships* to canons and texts change. Jones asks, "Can one circumambulate a DVD-ROM or place it on a high seat and reverence it?" And, it may go without saying, scholarly activity is now inextricably linked to canon formation. We are implicated in this process as we go about our business collecting and translating Buddhist texts.

The relationship between scholarly work and the Buddhist tradition is taken up in Franz Metcalf's "Our *Buddhadharma*, Our Buddhist Dharma." Here, Metcalf asks two seemingly simple questions: "First, who *is* (a) Buddhist? Second, what should be a Buddhist's *relation* to Buddhism?" On the face of it, Metcalf argues for a definition of Buddhism, and by extension Buddhists, and suggests that such a project is possible. This position may run counter to Han's assertion that there is no "elephant," that Buddhism is more a chimera than a pachyderm. However, the more fundamental concern of Metcalf's contribution, the true insight of his work, is to point toward the *relationship* between scholars and practitioners (who sometimes inhabit the same body) and argue that we as scholars (even those of us who are not simultaneously practitioners) have an ethical responsibility toward Buddhism. One may or may not agree with his ultimate definition of either "Buddhism" or "Buddhist," but the self-reflective exercise of thinking through categories is both profoundly important and well in line with Payne's larger oeuvre, which similarly thinks through the consequences of the choices we make in how we formulate both questions and answers.

A self-reflective and critical appraisal of scholars' relationship to Buddhism (regardless of the personal identity of the scholar in question) lies at the heart of Natalie Quli's contribution, "On Authenticity: Scholarship, the Insight Movement, and White Authority." Quli skillfully weaves together three interrelated problematics: the construction of authentic Buddhism vis-à-vis the Orientalism of such figures as Henry Steel Olcott and Buddhist studies; the sectarian identity formation of the Insight movement based, in part, on that earlier construction and the subsequent denigration of non-white Theravada Buddhist traditions; and, crucially, how whiteness informs these discourses of authenticity, lifting up some forms of Buddhism while dismissing others. Such discourses manifest in the Buddhist world as sectarian polemics against rival Buddhist traditions, but these discourses manifest in academe as well—and especially in Buddhist studies, a field marked by scarce resources, competitiveness, and more than a little "assholery."[22] Such discourses shape not only what we know about our subject, they shape what we are *allowed* to know through grants, faculty appointments, and so forth; and these discourses shape what is known of Buddhism outside the academy. Thus, the project of critical self-reflection on theory and method, of continually reexamining our (ethical) relationship to Buddhists and Buddhist traditions, and our role as scholars, practitioners, or both is a project not to be taken lightly.

This volume's eleven chapters gesture toward the complexity and nuance of the Buddhist tradition writ large. Buddhism, a vast and diverse global phenomenon with fuzzy boundaries, can be nothing less than complex and nuanced, and any one scholar (or Buddhist) can only play a small role in constructing the entire picture. Scholars approaching the subject from a historical view can shed light on past developments that played important roles in how the tradition has come to us in the modern period. These events can be understood on their own terms, but can also shed light on our contemporary assumptions and blind spots. Textual analyses reveal the intersection of doctrine and practice, but when we approach texts we thought we knew from new perspectives, different aspects of the tradition and its intersections with politics and culture are revealed. When researchers are curious about Buddhism as a living religion, when scholars spend time with Buddhists, further insights are revealed; Buddhism becomes a religion deeply intertwined with the fullness of people's lives, a continuation of the past rather than a rupture from a premodern purity. Such sightings of the religion compel us to be continually self-reflective, questioning the use of theoretical frameworks and metaphors that may have worked for other religions or other times but obscure our vision of the fullness of the tradition. Each of these essays, thus, reveals different aspects of Buddhism, each set of question-driven methods adding to what we know of Buddhism or challenging what we once held as obvious, allowing us to slowly, gradually, approach an answer to the central question: what is Buddhism? Our collective work as scholars can do no more than this; each of us can only chart part of the territory, and through mutual respect and understanding of each other's work, learn from our colleagues' travels.

## Personal note

It seems appropriate to end this introduction on something of a personal note. I have known Richard Payne for twenty years. In that time, he has served as my graduate advisor, as my mentor, as my dean, and as my fellow faculty member. It is hard for me to separate these roles, but through all of these, I have come to rely on his expertise, his experience, his wisdom, his wit, and his compassionate commitment both to the study of Buddhism and to the Institute of Buddhist Studies. Richard is a brilliant scholar, an adept administrator, and a reluctant politician who steered the oft-times rudderless IBS ship through difficult waters over the course of his twenty-five years as dean. This knowledge has been passed to me as his student, as his "replacement" (though no one could replace him in fullness) as dean, and so it is difficult to parse out what I've learned from him as scholar from what I've learned as friend and colleague. To this day, when I struggle with a piece of writing, when I am grappling with an idea, I trust that I can turn to Richard for advice, that I can send him a draft of what I'm working on, and his generous spirit will manifest in insightful and incisive feedback. I am sure I have written some version of the obligatory "I am indebted to Richard Payne for this idea" footnote more times than I can recall, and much of this indebtedness came long after he was obligated to respond to my emails as my advisor. I am profoundly thankful for his continued guidance, the foundational role he has played in my intellectual and professional development. The only appropriate response, of course, is gratitude.

# Part One

# Historical Studies

Part 1 consists of three historical studies, a tried and true method in Buddhist studies. Together, these three chapters look at history in Buddhist Japan and point us toward the intersection of religion, culture, politics, and economics.

Lisa Grumbach's "When Food Becomes Trespass: Buddhism and the *Kami* in Local Economies" examines what happens to a culture wherein hunting, fishing, and meat offerings to local *kami* are impacted by Buddhist prohibitions against the taking of life. Demonstrating the utility of multi-site comparative approaches, her study of three shrines reveals how differing economic contexts shaped adaptations in local customs to meet new religious and social realities. Such an approach guards against essentializing thirteenth-century Japan by revealing a varying topography, one of the strengths of a multi-site method.

Using a single case-study approach, Victoria Montrose moves us to the Meiji period and the rise of modern Japanese universities. Whereas the impact of Western-influenced critical scholarship in state universities has been well researched in recent scholarship, developments in sectarian Buddhist universities are less well studied. Montrose explores both how modern critical scholarship affected the development of Buddhist universities and, by extension, their root traditions, as well as how these sectarian universities interacted with cultural and political movements at large.

Aaron Proffitt makes connections between past and present in his "Taking the Vajrayana to Sukhāvatī." His paper shows how contemporary studies and historical studies can mutually inform one another. Rather than viewing contemporary Japanese Buddhist praxis as a postmodern mixture of disparate sectarian practices, he argues that an "Esoteric Pure Land" practice has a historical provenance in Japanese Buddhism that has been obscured by modern essentialist and sectarian readings of the tradition.

All three chapters point to the messy and boundary-transgressing reality of Buddhism as a lived tradition, one in which culture, practice, and economics pay scant attention to academic categories or sectarian identities.

1

# When Food Becomes Trespass: Buddhism and the *Kami* in Local Economies

Lisa Grumbach

*Give us this day our daily bread*
*and forgive us our trespasses . . .*

By the middle of the Kamakura period, arguments in Japan about the morality of killing animals for food, especially as offerings to the *kami*, began to reach all levels of society in ways that would affect people's daily lives. These arguments had come from multiple sources. Buddhist preachers made appeals for people to stop hunting and fishing, and some had great success convincing aristocratic landholders to enforce "killing bans" (*sesshō kindan* 殺生禁断) on their properties. Buddhist *honji suijaku* 本地垂迹 doctrines, teaching that local gods were manifestations of buddhas or bodhisattvas, also questioned the propriety of offering meat or fish to *kami* who, as "really" Buddhist, would rather have things like flowers or incense. The military government (*bakufu*) was also concerned about hunting. As men of warrior status increasingly became government officials with obligations to perform shrine duties, they needed to avoid actions like killing that incurred defilement (*kegare* 穢), which barred one from participating in shrine rituals.[1] The Kamakura *bakufu* therefore enacted laws to prevent its retainers from hunting. Landholders, both aristocrats and Buddhist temples, also used *sesshō kindan* rules in broader ways to limit the activities of the people who lived on or near their estates. Local people had previously freely entered forested areas and mountains to hunt, gather other food items, and collect wood, but estate owners came to see these activities as poaching and illegal logging.[2]

From the perspective of the local people, however, killing animals was a significant part of everyday food habits and local economic practices. Hunting and fishing were the primary ways people in medieval Japan obtained meat. Meat and fish, as representative of the community's food, were used as food offerings to the local *kami*. What happens, then, when a community's daily food becomes defined as sin, as illegal, as trespass of both religious morality and secular law? How did local communities react to suggestions that these standard food items be removed from the offering tables for their gods? This chapter focuses on this latter question, examining how three different communities reacted to calls to eliminate meat and fish offerings from their rituals. The starting point for this examination is a well-known passage from Mujū Ichien's *Shasekishū*, which he composed during the years 1278–1283, at the time when bans against hunting and calls to eliminate meat offerings to *kami* had become normative in society. Mujū relates this episode about fish offerings for the deity of the famous Itsukushima Shrine:

> While inspecting the premises [of Itsukushima Shrine], a certain venerable priest who had confined himself to the shrine on retreat saw countless numbers of fish from the sea donated as offerings to the gods. Now the Original Ground of the gods who soften their light are the buddhas and bodhisattvas, who, placing compassion before all else, admonish men not to take life. This custom of making offerings of fish was so utterly questionable that the monk prayed to the gods especially that they might resolve his doubts about the matter.
>
> This is what the deities revealed to him: "Indeed, it is a strange business! Unaware of the nature of moral causality, wantonly taking life and unable to rid themselves of delusion, there are those who hope to serve us by offerings of living beings. Because we transfer the responsibility for this to ourselves, their guilt is light. The creatures whom they kill use this as a 'skillful means' to enter into the Way of the Buddha, since their lives are wantonly cast away and offered up to us, their days numbered by past karma now being exhausted. Accordingly, we gather to us those fish whose numbered days of retribution are spent." When he had heard this, the priest's doubts were immediately resolved.
>
> This is perhaps the reason that offerings of deer and birds are made at Suwa in Nagano province, and at Utsunomiya in Tochigi province, where there is much hunting. Ordinary people cannot understand the "skillful means" of the provisional manifestations of the buddha.[3]

For Buddhist monk Mujū, grounded in *honji suijaku* thinking, offering fish or meat to a *kami* is "utterly questionable." How is it to be explained? Surprisingly, rather than a rejection of the offerings, the god announces a Buddhist doctrinal backing for them. The *kami* accepts the offerings because only fish that were destined to die anyway are caught. This combination of Buddhist notions of skillful means and karma allow the god to receive the offerings. Mujū notes that this may be the reason why hunting is allowed at Suwa and Utsunomiya, two shrines famous for their meat offerings. Although here this Buddhist idea that justifies killing is associated with Itsukushima, later it would become associated almost exclusively with Suwa. Suwa would become famous for continuing to allow hunting and meat offerings, while Itsukushima and Utsunomiya would give up their ritual meat and fish offerings.

At least this is the usual assumption. In fact, no one has attempted to investigate what happened at all of the shrines. The case of Suwa has been well researched since ample documents attesting to the shrine's practices are still extant. A lack of sources for Itsukushima and Utsunomiya seems to be the reason why no one has bothered to look at them. Certainly, there are fewer available materials for these two shrines, especially sources that explicitly talk about hunting or fishing in relation to shrine ritual. Yet, while there are fewer sources, documents are not nonexistent, and when taken together with considerations of local economic and political developments, we can get a fair picture of the role of hunting or fishing at these shrines and how practices changed over time.

This chapter employs a two-pronged methodology in order to reconsider assumptions about the fate of meat and fish offerings at these three shrines. First, by placing shrine ritual within the context of local economies, it suggests that ritual practices were necessarily connected to the local economy; thus, any changes in ritual should be considered in relationship to changes in the economic and political situation of the region. That is, if a shrine were to change its ritual customs, this action would impact its relationship with the local community, either aligning the shrine more closely with changing political and economic realities, or distancing it from the community if the change did not support or match the actual realities of community life. The chapter thus examines how the success or failure of attempts to change rituals based on hunting and fishing were also linked to larger economic and political considerations at Suwa, Itsukushima, and Utsunomiya.

Second, this chapter uses a comparative approach to bring a broader view to the issue of meat and fish offerings at shrines in medieval Japan. Studies of religious sites in Japan tend to focus on a single institution. This has long been the case within Japanese scholarship, and within Western studies as well this has been the trend over the past two decades. While single-site studies are highly valuable for understanding the development of a specific shrine or temple—and we need more of them—such a focus can inadvertently lead to blind spots or a too narrow understanding of developments. By comparing

Suwa with Itsukushima and Utsunomiya, we can see how responses to hunting bans developed differently within each particular local context, giving us a more nuanced view of the impact of Buddhist teachings as they met with practices for local *kami*.

It will not be possible to present a full history of each shrine or its ritual systems, so I will focus on elements that provide information about food offerings. As food offerings are directly connected to the local economy, I will also provide a brief overview of the economic situation at each site and its connections to food practices. Additionally, given the fact that economy is often connected to politics, I will indicate how the changing political environment may also have factored in each shrine's development. The chapter first introduces Suwa Shrine and the development there of doctrines that responded to Buddhist pressures to abandon meat offerings. In particular, how did local economic circumstances factor into Suwa Shrine's ability to resist Buddhist demands to stop hunting animals for meat offerings? The chapter then examines Itsukushima Shrine. Located in a dramatic setting on the ocean, this shrine was defined by sea-based concerns: fishing, but also its considerable importance in protecting and fostering sea trade within the Japanese archipelago and beyond to the continent, particularly Korea. How were these economic factors connected with the fish offerings famously referenced above by Mujū Ichien? How did fish offerings at Itsukushima change when economic and political forces changed? Finally, the chapter considers Utsunomiya, nestled in the mountains of Tochigi and, like Suwa, famous for meat offerings. Utsunomiya also faced the pressures of anti-hunting measures. How did the shrine react to those pressures, and how did changing economic and political fortunes in the region work to support or suppress shrine rituals and the lives of local people? In finding answers to these questions, we will see that the degree to which economic and political changes were also at play in each region helps us to understand why and in what form religious rituals survived or were abandoned.

## Suwa: Meat offerings and the agricultural cycle

Suwa Taisha is a shrine complex composed of the Upper Suwa Shrine (*Kami* Suwa Jinja 上諏訪神社) to the southeast of Lake Suwa and the Lower Suwa Shrine (Shimo Suwa Jinja 下諏訪神社) to the northwest of the lake. The Japanese Buddhism scholar Miyasaka Yūshō has suggested that this southeast-northwest alignment inspired the selection of the *honji* figures for the shrines' *kami*: Fugen for the Upper Shrine's deity, Takeminakata 建御名方, and Kannon for the Lower Shrine's *kami,* Yasakatome 八坂刀売, as Fugen and Kannon are found in the southeast and northwest positions, respectively, in the Womb Mandala.[4] Whatever the reason for associating these bodhisattvas with the site, Suwa was increasingly coming under the sway of Buddhist influences by the middle of the Kamakura period, as were shrines around the nation.

The influx of Buddhist thinking brought a wave of new concerns at Suwa, particularly related to the ritual presentation of meat in offerings for the gods. As demands to stop the killing of animals became a normative part of Buddhist doctrine and preaching during the Kamakura period, Suwa's rituals were put into the spotlight for rethinking—or better yet, eradication. However, at Suwa, calls for eliminating hunting and meat offerings were met with resistance. Suwa Shrine priests, for their part, stressed the centrality of the practices to the cult; we shall see that local people also expressed concern. The hunting traditions of the shrine were intimately linked with the area's agricultural practices, so a change to one part of the shrine ritual held the potential to adversely affect the entire system.

The Suwa Shrines are located at the base of the mountains that surround the plains encircling Lake Suwa and act as conduits for channeling the *kami* and their power from the mountains to the fields. Many of the shrines' rituals occur in the mountains, including the hunts and the felling of the trees for Suwa's other famous rite, the Onbashira 御柱 festival, in which the sacred poles demarcating the shrine precincts are renewed and replaced. The mountain pastures of the region were also famous for the breeding of horses, which were sent as a tribute to the central Yamato government and were important to the medieval warriors. These activities—hunting, logging, and raising horses—formed a significant part of the local economy.

Since hunting occurs in the mountains, the practice is often associated with mountain worship. Indeed, worship of the *kami* as the master of the mountain and its animals is central to rituals conducted by the shrine priests and by the hunters themselves. But the shrine's ritual hunts were undertaken primarily to insure the success of the community's agricultural work. Hunts were held several times a year from the fifth through ninth months in conjunction with the agricultural cycle.[5] The *misakuta mikari*, for example, was a hunt conducted at the time of planting rice and other crops (*sakuta* 作田). The largest of the hunts, the seventh-month *Misayama mikari*, is described in an early source as a wind festival (*kazematsuri* 風祭) for protecting the crops from damage by late summer storms.[6] Hunting was thus integrated into community farming practices, and meat offerings served both to petition the gods for fertility and to thank them for abundance. From the perspective of the local people, it would be difficult to simply eliminate these many rites from the annual ritual calendar, as to do so would risk a collapse of the crops. Hunting and the killing of animals was performed for the sake of making the community's food. Thus attempts to eliminate hunting could not be taken lightly. A Kamakura-period document states flatly that Suwa's "rituals cannot be held without deer" (*shika nakute ha mikamigota ha subekarazu sōrō* 鹿なくては御神事はすべからず候).[7]

From the early medieval period, Suwa's hunting rituals were already well-known, even outside of Shinano province. In 1212, when the *bakufu* wanted to ban hawk hunting among its warriors, it singled out only Suwa for exception:

> 8th month, 19th day: It is ordered to [all] *shugo* and *jitō* that hawk hunting is banned. However, the *mi-nie* hawks of the Suwa *daimyōjin* in Shinano province are pardoned [from the ban].[8]

Mujū Ichien, writing in the mid-Kamakura period, also mentions Suwa as famous for hunting, and hunting and meat offerings feature prominently in Suwa-related documents. One shrine document, the *Suwa Kamisha monoimirei* 諏訪上社物忌令, dated 1317, states that "those who are the *otō* 御頭 (annual ritual sponsors) of the shrine have hunting as their basic [duty] and should use the *mi-nie* hawks to obtain offerings."[9]

How, then, did Suwa react as calls to stop hunting and eliminate meat offerings intensified over the course of the Kamakura period? The earliest source that shows the local Suwa reaction to this problem is in fact not a shrine document but a lengthy tract, the *Kōgizuiketsu-shū* 廣疑瑞決集, authored in 1256 by Shinzui 信瑞 (d. 1279), a Pure Land preacher active in the Suwa area. The text consists of Shinzui's responses to twenty-five questions asked by the Suwa warrior Atsuhiro 敦廣 about the Pure Land teaching, focusing on both doctrine and practice. Many of the questions reveal that Atsuhiro is concerned about the ramifications of his being a warrior and hunter for his possible rebirth in the Pure Land, and about the implications that the Buddhist call to stop hunting hold for his worship of the Suwa deity.

A sampling of Atsuhiro's questions indicates the range of his concerns on these issues. First, on the problem of killing and its karmic effects Atsuhiro asks:

> If a person does not stop taking life, will he not be able to attain *ōjō* no matter how much he recites the *nembutsu*? Or is that, even if he takes life, as long as he recites the *nembutsu* he can achieve *ōjō*?[10]

A similar issue is raised in another question:

> A certain person does not fear taking life at all, nor does he practice [making] very many good roots. If . . . his body is unclean, even if he says the *nembutsu* will he be able to attain *ōjō* or not?"[11]

In these questions a concern about the possible limits of the power of the *nembutsu* for a person like Atsuhiro, who was a warrior and hunter, is apparent. Does the power of the *nembutsu* guarantee that even a person who kills, does not perform Buddhist practices, and engages in defiling actions can attain birth in the Pure Land?

Another set of questions relates specifically to the Suwa rituals:

> A certain person takes the lives of animals without limit, and there is none who can equal his exquisite offerings to the *kami*. Yet he also makes [Buddhist] halls (*dōtō* 堂塔), recites the *nembutsu*, always enters into karmic bonds, copies the *Daihannya* sutra for the sake of his present life, has himself made one thousand Kannon statues, and has even caused others to make one thousand Jizō statues. What do you think of such a person?[12]

Here the question shifts to consider the case of a person who participates in rituals for the *kami* by hunting animals, as at Suwa, but who is also a "good Buddhist." Can such a person enter the Pure Land? Finally, the questions turn to a defense of the Suwa practices against the newly arrived Buddhist teachings:

> From the past until now, in order to gain good fortune (*fuku* 福), we have worshiped the god by killing living beings. Isn't this something we should continue to do?[13]

Atsuhiro asks even more forcefully:

> If one goes against the proper [offerings] of a *kami* who has long been worshiped by taking life and instead uses things like incense and flowers, the *kami* will not accept such improper offerings and it is as if one has not worshiped at all. In order not to provoke the god's anger, one should all the more accept the god's punishment. No matter what one says, one should not question this matter.[14]

Taking Atsuhiro as a representative voice, it seems that the local Suwa people considered Buddhist attempts to remove hunting from the shrine's ritual practices as a drastic move fraught with the potential danger of incurring the wrath of the god.

Shinzui responds to each of Atsuhiro's questions, but the answers mostly follow a set pattern: one should not hunt or kill, and should entrust in the *nembutsu*. To the question about the power of the *nembutsu* to insure *ōjō* for those who take life, Shinzui instructs that only by reciting the *nembutsu* and repenting of the past evil of taking life will one be able to attain birth in the Pure Land, noting that in Buddhist texts there are many examples of "evil people" (*akunin* 悪人) who butchered domestic animals or hunted wild game but who achieved *ōjō* by repenting of their past actions.[15] In response to the question about someone who kills animals and makes exquisite offerings to the gods, but who also does many good Buddhist deeds (building halls, saying the *nembutsu*, making Buddhist statues, etc.), Shinzui answers that, even having done such good acts, someone who kills is still probably destined for hell; however, if this person stops killing and concentrates his efforts on saying the *nembutsu*, then his birth in the Pure Land will be assured.[16] Shinzui's responses emphasize two trends that were important to him: the general Buddhist notion that one should refrain from killing and repent of past transgressions; and the specific Pure Land practice of saying the *nembutsu* and entrusting in Amida.

We see from this exchange that as Suwa's hunting practices and meat offerings met with criticism from the outside, the people of Suwa were not quickly convinced that their customs should be abandoned. Instead, a traditional view dominated, and Suwa's practices continued. However, the *Kōgizuiketsu-shū* makes no reference to the idea seen in Mujū Ichien's *Shasekishū* that the god purposefully brings to itself the animals to be killed. This idea first appears at Suwa in the aforementioned *Suwa Kamisha monoimirei*, composed in 1317 to rectify and redefine many of the shrine's practices as new Buddhist ideas and *honji suijaku* associations became accepted. In a section of the document dealing with meat offerings (*minie* 御贄) for the deity, the hunting of animals is configured as "compassionate killing" (*jihi no gosesshō* 慈悲の御殺生). The text directs that "people who act as the ritual sponsors (*otō* 御頭) can hunt any animal, keep *minie* hawks, and make animal offerings," and instructs hunters to recite a specific phrase when carrying out the hunt:

> If [you] intone [the phrase] *gōjin ushō suihō fushō koshuku ninchū dōshō bukka* 業尽有情雖放不生故宿人中同證仏果 in your mind, the animals that have been taken will immediately achieve buddhahood and attain the path (*jōbutsu tokudō* 成仏得道).[17]

This phrase is nothing other than the doctrine met with in Muju Ichien's *Shasekishū*, that the *kami* compassionately bring to themselves only animals whose karma has ended and are destined to die. In the *Monoimirei*, the idea has been reworked into a four-phrase *gātha*-style verse, most commonly known in this version:[18]

| | |
|---|---|
| *gōjin ushō* | 業尽有情 |
| *suihō fushō* | 雖放不生 |
| *koshuku ninten* | 故宿人天 |
| *dōshō bukka* | 同證仏果 |

> Having exhausted their karma, these living beings even if released would not live [for long]; by abiding in people and the god, they likewise achieve buddhahood.

Approximately forty years after the *Monoimirei*, in another Suwa document, the *Suwa daimyōjin ekotoba* 諏訪大明神絵詞, this phrase is referred to as the deity's "original vow" (*hongan* 本願). The *Ekotoba*, written in 1356 by the Suwa Shrine monk Enchū 円柱, records the shrine's purported history and describes its major rituals. The hunting rituals remained popular, and Enchū's description of the seventh-month Misayama hunting rite paints a lively scene of the mountain filled with shrine priests, *kagura* performers, *miko*, the community members (*ujibito* 氏人), as well as throngs of people there just to watch.[19] After the main priest opens the mountain for the hunt, the hunters go forth into the brush.

> The grasses are grown so tall that they hide the men and horses. Only the tips of their bows and the tops of their hats can be seen. At this time the wild animals fly out and run, and a wild struggle ensues with the hunters. Although the several hundred mounted warriors, who [must] avoid fallen trees and rocky terrain, line up their horses to prevent [the prey from] escaping into the mountains, only two or three animals are hit by the arrows. The phrase revealed by the deity, which is [the deity's] original compassionate vow (*honsei higan* 本誓悲願), and the stories told by the village elders should be made to agree with each other.[20]

Enchū suggests that the reason only two or three animals are actually hit by the hunters' arrows is due to the god's compassionate vow. That he states at the end that the god's vow and the stories told by the village elders need to be reconciled perhaps indicates that the verse was still not well-known among locals, and they may have even resisted it. Elsewhere in the *Ekotoba*, Enchū's statements express additional concern that the local people should be made aware of the "real" reason the animals are killed—that is, as a form of skillful means employed by the god based on its original vow.[21]

By inserting this Buddhist doctrine of compassionate killing into its cultic practices, the Suwa priests were able to maintain the hunting traditions that supported the fertility of the fields and the growth of the crops. Although this idea seems to have started out in association with Itsukushima Shrine, by the mid-1300s it had been adopted at Suwa. Later, it would become associated exclusively with Suwa as the *Suwa-no-mon* 諏訪ノ文 or *Suwa-no-shingon* 諏訪ノ真言 (the "mantra of Suwa"). Suwa Shrine would also create other religious items that allowed people to eat meat. By the Muromachi period, the shrine was distributing the *kajikimen* 鹿食免 ("deer-eating license"), an amulet that allowed the holder to eat meat.[22] Another popular item was "deer-eating chopsticks" from the shrine, with the same efficacy as the *kajikimen*.

Thus, rather than trying to reform shrine rituals to fit a trend against hunting and meat offerings advocated by some Buddhist preachers as part of general Mahayana moral teachings, Suwa adopted another Buddhist doctrine, one based in *honji suijaku* ideas of the relationship between buddhas and *kami*, which took a more lenient view of such practices for the *kami*. The shrine's hunting rituals were closely linked with local agricultural practices, so eliminating them seems not to have been an option. The shrine priests stressed the importance of hunting, and local people fretted over the consequences of change. Although outside critics urged reform, there does not seem to have been enough pressure to force the shrine to change its practices. The comparison with Itsukushima and Utsunomiya will help explain why this might have been the case.

## Itsukushima: Protecting trade on sea and land

Compared to those of Suwa, records that specifically discuss food offerings within Itsukushima's history and rituals are scant. However, the small amount of material on the subject, combined with information about the shrine's economic and political connections, provides some sense of changes in shrine practice over time.

Itsukushima is located on the island of Miyajima in the Seto Inland Sea, off the coast of Hiroshima. The shrine is thus also colloquially known as Miyajima. Today the shrine is most famous for its beautiful setting and its red torii gate that stands in the water. The deer that wander the island freely, as at Nara, are also a prominent attraction. Although shrine legends place the founding of the shrine in 593, the first documentary reference to Itsukushima dates to the year 811 (Kōnin弘仁2) in a short notice in the *Nihon kōki* 日本後記, which simply states that in Saeki-gun 佐伯郡, Aki-no-kuni 安芸国, the name of the local god is Itsukushima no *kami* 伊都伎嶋神.[23] However, by 867 several new gods had been added to the pantheon, significant among them three goddesses collectively known as the Munakata 宗像 deities.[24] The Munakata goddesses came originally from Chikuzen 筑前, a western area (in present-day Fukuoka Prefecture in northern Kyushu) that at the time was not under control of the Yamato state. The Chikuzen shrines and their deities represented the Munakata clan, an immigrant kinship group with strong ties to Silla and the Korean peninsula.[25] Oki-no-shima 沖ノ島, the site of one of the Munakata shrines, lies well off the coast of Japan on the way to the Korean peninsula, and the Munakata clan controlled shipping and imports from the continent. For the Yamato court, creating and maintaining a strong relationship with this group had been an important concern since at least the early 700s.[26] The fact that the Munakata deities were also enshrined at Itsukushima, located approximately half-way on the route between Chikuzen and the Yamato ports in Naniwa and Sakai, underscores both the continuing importance of the Munakata clan and the growing role of Aki province, and the Itsukushima Shrine, in transport and commerce.

Aki province was also an important source of goods and materials for the Yamato court. The region was famous as a producer of salt, and archaeological evidence shows that as early as the *kofun* period iron ore was being mined there.[27] *Sueki* 須恵器 pottery, while not unique to this area, was another important product.[28] Moreover, producing salt, iron, and pottery necessarily required a significant amount of fuel for fires and kilns, and Aki was known for its forests and lumber production.[29] Lumber was used not only locally but was also sent to the capital—and was used to build the ships for transporting goods.[30]

Sea-based shipping of products and materials was an important element of the local Aki economy, but this was not the only way to send goods to the capital. The Sanyōdō 山陽道, a road connecting the capital to Dazaifu in Kyushu, ran through Aki province, and goods were shipped overland along this route.[31] The significance of both land and sea routes is reflected in an Itsukushima Shrine document that demonstrates the shrine's role in offering protection for local trade routes. A petitionary prayer recorded in the year 1176 (Angen 安元 2) begins by noting the presence of several visiting deities (*marōdo* 客人), confers thanks for offerings, and ends with prayers for the abundance of the five grains, peace for the people of the province, and finally

> protection in the night, protection in the day; [may there be] calm waters in the sea routes for the transport ships [so they] arrive on time at the shore; [and may there be] no illness in the [horses'] hooves on the land.

> 夜ヲ守り日ヲ守り給天、運上ノ船筏 海路浪静シテ合期ニ著岸シ、陸地乃蹄 メ無恙[32]

Another important development was the influx of aristocratic clans from the capital during the second half of the Heian period. From about the 1080s the Fujiwara family became landholders in the area, and in the mid-1100s the Minamoto clan became estate owners.[33] Most notable was Taira Kiyomori, who in 1164 became the absentee estate owner of lands managed by Itsukushima Jinja.[34] A *gammon* written in this same year by Kiyomori relates the reasons for his deep faith in the Itsukushima deity and thanks the god for benefits (*riyaku* 利益) that he had received. The document also records gifts made by Kiyomori to the shrine, including a set of sutras containing the *Hokke*, *Muryōgi*, *Kan-Fugen*, and *Amida* sutras (collected together with the *ganmon* as the *Heike nōkyō* 平家納経, still held by the shrine). With patronage from the Taira family, the shrine created close connections to the centers of power, and locally the authority of the shrine's priests, the Saeki 佐伯 family, grew. Yet the relationship with the Taira proved to be a double-edged sword, and when the Taira fell at the end of the Genpei war, so too declined the fate of the Saeki, who were then replaced at the order of Minamoto Yoritomo by a Kanto-based branch of the Fujiwara family.[35]

The early history of the shrine thus indicates that the local community had close connections to the sea, that sea-based trade was an important part of the local economy, and that the shrine had close ties to aristocratic members of the court. However, in reviewing the local history and shrine documents, two things stand out as strangely missing. First, there is a surprising lack of references to fishing in the local economy or to fish offerings at the shrine, as we might expect to see in light of Mujū Ichien's description of the shrine's practices. Later documents such as the origin stories penned during the medieval eras also give no indication that fish were an important part of shrine offerings. An early version of the origin story found in the *Genpei seisuiki* 源平盛衰記, composed in approximately the mid-Kamakura period, instead focuses on the arrival of the shrine's gods from across the sea. The story says that from the west a red-sailed ship appeared (*saihō yori kurenai no ho agetaru fune* 西方より紅の帆挙たる船). On the ship was a spear standing upright in a jar, to which red strips of cloth were attached (*senchū ni hei ari, hei no naka ni hoko wo tate, akanusa wo tsuketari* 船中に瓶あり、瓶の中に鋒を立て、 赤幣を附たり), onto which descended the three maidens who would become the Itsukushima deities. Through an oracle the maidens/deities instructed Saeki no Kuramoto 佐伯鞍職 to build the shrine.[36] This locally famous origin story of Itsukushima reiterates the importance of the goddesses who come from the west and oversee trade, yet offers no evidence of fishing or fish offerings in relation to the shrine, and neither do any other local and shrine-related sources through the Kamakura period mention fish offerings. Mujū Ichien's account is in fact the only source for this information.

Just because sources do not mention fishing or fish offerings, however, does not mean that these things did not occur or were not important at the shrine. Detailed discussions or lists of offerings made at shrines and temples are in fact relatively rare, since they seem to have been a matter of course to the local participants. At Suwa, the abundance of references to hunting and offerings represents an exception rather than the norm. Even without many specific mentions of fishing or fish offerings at Itsukushima, I think we should assume that fishing was a primary economic activity of the area and that fish offerings were made at the shrine.

Fortunately, one Itsukushima text does mention both fishing and food offerings for the deities. The *Itsukushima shidai no koto* 厳島次第事, found in the *Nagato-bon Heike monogatari* 長門本平家物語 (early Muromachi period), elaborates on the above story of the red-sailed boat, explaining that the three female deities had originally been princesses in an Indian kingdom. For our purposes, the significant part of the story is as follows: Just before encountering the goddesses, Saeki no Kuramoto shoots a golden, nine-colored deer at Inamino 印南野. But the golden deer here are considered to be deities, or manifestations of the deity (*mukashi kon-iro no shika ariki, kore gonja nari* むかし金色の鹿ありき、是権者也), and anyone who harms them would be fined and cast out to sea from the shore of Aki. Thus, in order to appease his hunger (*ue wo yasumen ga tame* 飢をやすまんがため), Kuramoto sets out on boats with nets and fish hooks and walks along the beaches to catch fish (*ami-fune tsuri-bune ni nori nado shite, kono uraura wo tsutaihi-aruku* あみ船つり船に乗などして、此浦々を傳ひあるく). Involved in such pursuits, one day he sees a boat with red sails. Approaching it, he meets the three deities who had descended onto the cloth strips set up in a jar (in this version, a lapis lazuli *tsubo* 壺). The deities announce that they are hungry after their long journey, and they ask Kuramoto to give them some food. Kuramoto asks them what they will eat; they reply that they will have "a little bit of white rice" (*hakumai koso sukoshi sōrō* 白米こそ少し候). He asks them how much, and they reply five *masu* 升. After feeding them, he receives instructions on how to build the shrine. The deities then announce that they will now live in this place to appease their hunger (*ima ha ue wo yamenu to te ware kono tokoro ni suman to omou* 今は飢をやめぬとてわれ此所に住まんと思う), and they send Kuramoto to scout out a location to build the shrine. Finally, the deities, now speaking as the essentially singular *daimyōjin*, reveal to Kuramoto, "Your coming here was [due to] my working. The manifestation of the golden deer at Inamino was also me." (大明神のたまはく、汝を是へ下すもわがはからひなり、印南野に金色の鹿に現ぜしもわれ也).[37]

In this story, a man has engaged in both hunting and fishing, and yet, when confronted by hungry goddesses, he is requested to offer white rice! In other words, a hierarchy of appropriate food practices is being established here. First, the text makes clear that the sacred deer of the area are off limits for human consumption. Fishing, not hunting, is deemed the appropriate way for people to obtain their food. The goddesses' request implies a rejection of both meat and fish while emphasizing that white rice is the proper food of the gods. The development of the story neatly encapsulates changing views of food practices over time. From early in the shrine's history, killing the deer of Miyajima had been prohibited. Instead of eating deer meat "to appease their hunger," local people ate fish, and they undoubtedly made offerings of fish to the deity, as attested in the *Shasekishū*. But this text suggests that by the early Muromachi period the deity would no longer accept fish and instead required rice. We should perhaps surmise that at this time the ritual offerings had already been changed, and the *Itsukushima shidai no koto* revises the origin story to back up the new ritual practice. Thus, while sources that describe fish offerings are not to be found, this narrative creates a basis for rejecting fish offerings.

The second prominent absence in the sources is the idea of the god's compassionate killing, which in the *Shasekishū* is associated with Itsukushima. Nowhere in shrine-related sources is there any knowledge of this doctrine. At Suwa, the idea was reformulated into a four-phrase *gātha* said to be the god's original vow. In the *Itsukushima shidai no koto*, a four-phrase *gātha* is included, but with a different content. The phrase reads:

| | |
|---|---|
| *Ichido sankei shoshujō* | 一度参詣諸衆生 |
| *Sanzu hachinan eiriku* | 三途八難永離苦 |
| *Wakō dōjin kechiensha* | 和光同塵結縁者 |
| *Hassō jōdō jōsakubutsu* | 八相成道常作佛[38] |

Those beings who have worshiped here even once
Will eternally be spared from the suffering of [encountering] the River of Hell and the eight unfortunate [births]
Those who create a karmic bond with the gods who soften their light
Will complete the eight events [in the life of a buddha] to forever create a buddha

As a *gātha* created for a *kami* in the course of writing the origin story, this verse is perhaps most remarkable for how generic it is. Nothing in the wording connects the sentiments to any specific characteristic of the Itsukushima deities. The verse could be placed into any origin story for any *kami*. It turns the Itsukushima deity into a general "Buddhicized" *kami* who could be worshiped by anyone.

Perhaps this was the intent. Itsukushima, different from Suwa, had become closely connected to the central government in Kyoto through its important position in trade and commerce and its direct connections to powerful aristocratic families. Its character had changed from being a local shrine related to regional economic and community activities to one with national importance related to the concerns of the imperial court. In part, the Itsukushima deity lost its particular features as a god of the island of Miyajima, concerned with local trade and fishing, and was transformed into a god who protected national trade routes and offered a general Buddhist salvation to everyone. This connection of Itsukushima to these outside concerns seems to have made it more readily accepting of the larger religious trends of the day. Thus, when *honji suijaku* doctrines suggested that the *kami,* as buddhas and bodhisattvas, did not need or want offerings of meat or fish, changing the shrine's ritual offerings was more easily accomplished.

## Utsunomiya: Warriors, priests, and markets

Utsunomiya Jinja, also known by the name Futarasan 二荒山, is located in Tochigi Prefecture (formerly Shimotsuke province). It is not far from the more famous Nikkō 日光 area, which contains another shrine also called Futarasan as well as the Tōshōgu 東照宮, the shrine-mausoleum for Tokugawa Ieyasu. The fact that there are two Futarasan shrines causes some confusion in reckoning the early history of Utsunomiya, and the relationship between them has not always been clear. For our purposes, we can focus on the history of Utsunomiya in connection to the Utsunomiya family, the hereditary shrine priests. This warrior clan's genealogy traces its origins to a Buddhist monk named Sōen 宗円, said to be the grandson of Fujiwara Michikane 藤原道兼, and who was sent to Shimotsuke province at the request of Minamoto Yoshiie 源義家 to become the abbot (*zasu* 座主) of Utsunomiya. According to this story, Sōen's descendants became the Utsunomiya family of hereditary priests for the shrine.[39] However, there are many factual problems with the genealogy. The name itself first appears in 1183 in association with a man named "Nobufusa of Utsunomiya" (Utsunomiya-dokoro Nobufusa 宇都宮所信房) (per the genealogy, Nobufusa is the son of Munefusa 宗房, who is the son of Sōen). The *Azuma kagami*

吾妻鏡 indicates that Nobufusa's father had a close relationship with Minamoto Yoritomo, and Nobufusa himself fought in the Genpei war for Yoritomo.[40] From this time, Utsunomiya clan members figure as important retainers of the shogun, and their duties required that they travel to or live in Kamakura and Kyoto.[41] In 1184, another member of the lineage was appointed by Yoritomo to be the first Utsunomiya priest (Utsunomiya *shamushiki* 宇都宮社務職). This was one Yoritsuna 頼綱, also said to be a grandson of Sōen through another of Sōen's sons, Munetsuna 宗綱. This was an appointment of the *honryō ando* 本領安堵 type, which indicates that Yoritsuna was fully considered a vassal of the shogun while invested as a priest of the shrine.[42] Subsequent sources about Utsunomiya reflect both the status and obligations of the clan as warriors and their duties as shrine priests.

The relationship between the Utsunomiya family and the Kamakura *bakufu* is certainly paramount for understanding the development of the shrine and the region; however, an emphasis in scholarship on warriors and their activities has meant less investigation of other aspects of Utsunomiya life and society. It is clear that the social and economic situation of the province of Shimotsuke was similar to Suwa. Both were land-locked regions depending on agriculture and products from the nearby mountains. This area of eastern Japan has long been famous for its tradition of hunters known as *matagi* マタギ. Although *matagi* have typically been thought of as professional hunters who lived apart from agricultural communities, recent research indicates that this view has been mistaken. *Matagi* were also farmers, and they hunted when necessary for food, for offerings, and to pay their taxes.[43] This fact again indicates the close relationship between agriculture and hunting as interconnected practices in medieval Japan. Undoubtedly, due to the similar role of hunting in the local economies, Utsunomiya established loose ritual connections with Suwa. The *Utsunomiya daimyōjin no koto* 宇都宮大明神事 (found in the *Shintōshū* 神道集, comp. 1352–1360) indicates this connection by establishing a family relationship between the deities, saying, "Now, this *myōjin* [Utsunomiya] is the older brother of Suwa *daimyōjin*" (抑此明神、諏訪大明神、御舎兄).[44]

As at Suwa, hunting and meat offerings figured prominently in shrine ritual. The *Utsunomiya daimyōjin daidai kizui no koto* 宇都宮大明神代々奇瑞之事, dating to 1484 (Bunmei 16), for example, relates several gifts of meat offerings (*ikenie* 生贄) made to the god in gratitude for miraculous aid. The text records that in the Kōhei 康平 era (1058–65), the god is said to have aided Minamoto Yoshiie in the defeat of Abe no Sadato 安倍貞任, and being grateful Yoshiie made a meat offering (*ikenie*) to the god.[45] In Bunji 5 (1189), the deity aided

Minamoto Yoritomo in defeating Fujiwara no Yasuhira 藤原泰衡, and in thanks Yoritomo also made a meat offering. Even further, he granted five villages (*gō* 郷) within the Nasu-no-shō 那須庄 estate as places dedicated to hunting for the meat offerings for the shrine (那須庄内五箇郷 . . . 被充置生贄狩料所).[46] As the incidents described in the text purportedly occurred several centuries earlier, we may wish to question the historical accuracy of the accounts; but the point is that the Utsunomiya tradition understands these offerings to be the best and most honorable type for the god.

Hunting to obtain meat offerings for the shrine's regular ritual observances was one of the main duties of the Utsunomiya clan members. An important source providing a glimpse into these religious activities is the clan's house rules, the *Utsunomiya Kōan shikijō* 宇都宮弘安式条 (hereafter, *Shikijō*), dating to 1283 (Kōan 6). During the medieval period, many warrior clans codified house rules that formally laid out the duties and responsibilities of clan members. The Utsunomiya clan rules is one of the earliest examples. Since the family was the priestly lineage for the shrine, perhaps it is not surprising that twenty-four of the total seventy regulations concern religious activities. Broadly, the document describes activities for clan members who acted as shrine priests (*shinkan* 神官), Buddhist priests (*sōto* 僧徒), and shrine workers (*miyaji* 宮仕). Higher-ranking members of the family served as shrine priests, sponsoring and conducting rituals for the Utsunomiya *daimyōjin*. Those charged with Buddhist duties worked as shrine-monks (*shasō* 社僧) and "offering monks" (*kyōsō* 供僧) at the *jingūji*. The shrine workers were members of the family and their retainers who performed various other shrine duties.

The Utsunomiya house rules show that the shrine's hunting rituals were similar to Suwa's. Like Suwa, Utsunomiya also held a fifth-month Satsuki hunt. As at Suwa, when hunting was banned, the shrine acted to preserve its rituals. A rule that specifies the parameters of hunting bans (*sesshō kindan no koto* 殺生禁断事) states that

> on the *rokusai-nichi* 六斎日, this law should be strictly enforced and it [hunting] should be stopped. If [someone] ignores the ban, [he] will be subject to a fine. However, those who are performing official duties (*tōyaku* 頭役) for this shrine are not subject to the ban.[47]

It seems that as far as the shrine was concerned, *sesshō kindan* bans were operative only on the six days of the month devoted to Buddhist observances, and even on these days people working for the shrine in the capacity of *tōyaku* were excepted. Another important similarity between Suwa and Utsunomiya were the responsibilities expected of family members in respect to their duties at the shrine versus work for the Kamakura *bakufu*. The Utsunomiya house rules show that, as at Suwa, the shrine rituals were generally of greater importance than work in Kamakura. The *Shikijō* states that those working as shrine officiants of various sorts must perform their duties for the shrine's largest annual observances and events, even if they were resident in Kamakura; only Kamakura *ōban* 大番 duties, or business in Kyoto, took precedence over the shrine rituals.[48]

The *Shikijō* also provides information about commercial activities in the Utsunomiya area in regard to "markets within the landholdings" (*ryōnai ichiichi* 領内市々) and discusses their regulation. The house rules stipulate that house members and retainers should not be involved in *mukae-gai* 迎買—forcing merchants to sell them products at a cheap price before the market opened and then reselling the items at a higher price for a profit—and that they should not coerce people to buy goods (*oshigai* 押買).[49] House members working at the shrine as *miyaji* and lower-level workers were forbidden to engage in commercial activities at the market.[50] The *Shikijō* also mentions a *kuramoto* 倉下, a person in charge of financial matters and money lending.[51] These activities suggest that markets were becoming an important source of income for at least some of the Utsunomiya house members.

The overall picture of religious tradition, political connections, and new economic opportunities at Utsunomiya sets the scene for understanding attitudes to hunting. Hunting bans that were directives of the Kamakura *bakufu* were to be enforced. However, hunting connected to shrine ritual should be protected. The Utsunomiya clan, as both retainers of the *bakufu* and shrine priests, sought to balance their obligations to the warrior government while maintaining the traditions of the shrine. Furthermore, while hunting was important in the food practices of the area, it had not been elevated to the level of representing an essential doctrinal feature of the deity, as at Suwa. As the local economy changed, the Utsunomiya family took an interest in participating in and regulating the new economy. So long as the minimal requirements of shrine ritual were met, they need not be overly concerned with protecting one economic practice—hunting—over any other. Utsunomiya did not adopt special doctrines or ideas to protect hunting, and, unlike Suwa, it never became famous for its rituals. But nor did the shrine completely abandon hunting rituals at any point in its history. In 1617 Hayashi Razan, discussing the relationship between Utsunomiya (Futarasan) and the other Futarasan

Jinja in his *Futarasan shinden* 二荒山神傳, comments on the identity of the shrines despite an obvious difference:

> Although it is said that Futarasan and Utsunomiya are not different, nevertheless at Futarasan one does not offer birds and fish, while at Utsunomiya one offers birds, fish, and deer. (二荒山・宇都宮、雖不異、而二荒不供鳥魚、宇都宮供鳥魚鹿)[52]

Today meat offerings are still used in rituals at Utsunomiya.

## Conclusion

Suwa, Itsukushima, and Utsunomiya each in their own way met Buddhist teachings that defined meat and fish offerings for the gods as based in the sin of killing and no longer desired by the deities. Suwa opposed suggestions to change their practices and carried on as before, albeit with a new Buddhist doctrine to account for the god's rituals and hunting by local people. Itsukushima seems to have gradually given up their fish offerings, perhaps with little concern from the local priests or people. Utsunomiya took a middle road on the problem of *sesshō kindan* and *honji suijaku*-based objections to meat offerings, following the government's bans on hunting but quietly continuing hunts for meat offerings for the *kami*.

Looking at the economic and political situations of each region has provided a larger context for understanding why each site developed as it did. Given the small number of sources in some cases, we have had to take a wide view of the history of each place; even so, we have seen that the linkage between the local economy and the ritual system that sought to sustain that economy formed the basis for responding to a new situation. At Suwa, the local economy was based on agriculture and hunting, with the latter seen as supporting the former. Suwa Shrine's ritual hunts and the offering of meat to the deity were intended to insure the success of the crops. To stop the hunts was thus considered something that could potentially harm the crops, and the economy. Additionally, at Suwa there were no outside political factors or significant changes in the economy at this time to make forgoing the rituals a viable option. Although Suwa had some ties to the *bakufu* government and some access to markets, these were not as significant as at Utsunomiya. The fact that Suwa was more isolated from the central government and market changes meant that agriculture remained the basis of its economy. There was no local reason to change the rituals, even if pressured by Buddhist preachers. Instead, the local people and priests found it fit to adapt Buddhism to their needs.

At Itsukushima, where, according to Mujū Ichien, "countless numbers of fish from the sea" were offered to the gods, a different set of religious, economic, and political factors were at play. For this site we have the fewest available sources, and unfortunately none of them from any time period seems to support Mujū's story that Itsukushima was famous for its fish offerings. Rather, the sources point in a different direction. For the shrine, the most important local industry was not fishing but trading. Sources from the shrine and those related to the Aki region indicate that shipping routes for sending local products to the capital, and connecting the capital to the continent, were at the top of the local economy. As noted above, this does not mean that fishing was not also part of the economy, or not important to the local people. Nor does it mean that fish were not offered at Itsukushima. It rather indicates that the Aki economy was based on multiple industries. For the shrine, at least, the most important industry was not fishing but rather trading and commerce that connected the shrine to the centers of power. If offerings of fish were to be reduced or ended—replaced by offerings of white rice—this may not have been a terrible change for the priests.

The case of Utsunomiya is quite similar to Suwa in terms of its ritual system, but its reaction to calls to end meat offerings was more muted. The shrine priests, as warriors, had closer ties to the bakufu in Kamakura, making them obligated to follow orders that came from the shogun. They must then necessarily follow bakufu orders to limit or ban hunting. This they did, yet they also carved out special exceptions for the shrine's hunting practices. As at Suwa, Utsunomiya too preserved its hunting rituals—Suwa was not unique. But, since the shrine did uphold hunting bans, Utsunomiya did not function as a place that could license anyone to hunt anywhere. That particular fame went to Suwa. Political contingencies from the outside were thus sufficient at Utsunomiya to force some change. Additionally, with the development of markets at Utsunomiya, new economic possibilities may have emerged to broaden the economic base of the region from relying only on agriculture and hunting to include trade and business.

The site of Suwa has been well studied, and it is rightly famous within studies of hunting and religion in Japan for developing the *Suwa-no-mon*. But comparing Suwa with these other two sites, even in this admittedly limited way, puts the developments at Suwa in new light. Research on Suwa tends to stop with a reiteration of the *Suwa-no-mon* as a new and unique feature of the Suwa cult. It is certainly an important development in the *honji suijaku* discourse that began to change shrine practices as more *kami* were identified as manifestations of buddhas and bodhisattvas. But in refusing to give up hunting and meat offerings in the face of Buddhist demands, Suwa's response was not only based on concerns of maintaining a ritual tradition. If tradition were the only issue, then all other shrines in Japan could also have argued to retain their meat and fish offerings. But we know, as at Itsukushima, that most in fact gave them up. Suwa was able to maintain its traditional offerings in part because hunting was still an important part of the agricultural economy. The Suwa warrior Atsuhiro doesn't spell out the connection between hunting and agriculture, but his concerns about the wrath of the god were surely this: that in changing the offerings, the god would become angry, and the crops would be decimated. Without any other economic or political incentive to change, the status quo was the safest option.

In this respect, then, Itsukushima was the shrine with the most incentive to change. Although conclusions about this shrine are the most speculative since the sources are so scanty, the trajectory of the documents suggest that sea-based trade had always been a major part of the regional economy and an important focus of shrine ritual. Even though Mujū says the shrine used countless fish in its offerings, ironically that is the aspect of this sea-side shrine that today we must assume to be true, since the shrine sources make no mention of it. As the region drew the attention of the central government for its control of trade, and as influential groups like the Fujiwara, Minamoto and Taira created ties to the shrine, Itsukushima fell subject to influences and trends from outside its immediate surroundings. Mujū attests that fish were still being offered in the late 1200s. By the mid-1300s (early Muromachi), the *Itsukushima shidai no koto* suggests that fish offerings had been replaced by rice. Unlike at Suwa, we have nothing that records what local people thought of such a change. But switching to "pure" Buddhist offerings may have met with little resistance at a shrine where the commercial economy was already as important as the food economy.

Examining the history of Utsunomiya together with Suwa has revealed something else about the latter shrine. Suwa was not unique in maintaining its hunting rituals. The general notion that Japan's shrines altogether gave up meat and fish offerings, with the notable exception of Suwa, is overstated. But this idea has persisted because those who study Suwa look at that shrine alone, without reference to other shrines. A lack of comparative work in this way hinders understanding of the development of shrine ritual. With the knowledge that Utsunomiya too continued to perform its hunting rituals, the survival of

Suwa's rituals becomes less exceptional. This fact forces us to reconsider why *both* Suwa and Utsunomiya—and undoubtedly other places—were able to continue their hunting rituals. As noted above, the place of meat offerings as related to the local food economy then comes to the fore. At both Suwa and Utsunomiya, meat offerings were retained because they continued to be important in the local agricultural economy as supported by shrine ritual. But in regard to hunting in general, the shrines' responses diverged. Suwa's idea of religious hunting as essential to its *kami* (and local economy) was codified into a Buddhist doctrine specific to the shrine but which could be used by anyone who learned it (typically through initiation in a hunting tradition) or who bought a "license" from the shrine. Utsunomiya, in contrast, maintained the importance of its hunting rituals, but, with strong ties to the *bakufu,* otherwise conformed to national (*bakufu*-ordered) laws limiting hunting.

The connections between local economies and the worship of a region's *kami* are one factor that allow us to understand how shrines develop. The religion called Shintō—the broad umbrella term for the worship of local gods in Japan—to a large degree can be qualified as being a religion of local economies. Local people, priests, and patrons both near and far worshiped deities for protection and aid in the things that sustained their daily lives: agriculture, hunting, fishing, commerce. Today, as inheritors of the rapidly changing economic environment of the past one hundred years, those shrines that have been able to forge connections to the modern economy—such as Fushimi Inari in Kyoto as a shrine of business success and Nishinomiya Shrine in Kobe as a shrine for the worship of Ebisu, the god of merchants—are the ones that continue to attract worshipers and remain vibrant presences in their communities.

2

# Making the Modern Priest: The Ōtani Denomination's Proto-University and Debates about Clerical Education in the Early Meiji Period

Victoria R. Montrose

Meiji-period (1868–1912) Buddhism has garnered increased scholarly attention in recent years due to its significance in reconceptualizing the Buddhist tradition both in Japan and globally. Japanese Buddhism lost its hegemony with the end of the *tera-uke* system (state-mandated temple registration system for all citizens) and endured a period of persecution during the *shinbutsu bunri* and *haibutsu kishaku* campaigns of the early Meiji regime. Increased interaction with other major traditions also led Japanese Buddhists to grapple with their role in modernity and the place of Japanese Buddhism within the "world religions." A crisis of identity ensued, and during this period many Japanese Buddhists questioned Buddhism's compatibility with modernity and the nation-state, its status as a foreign or indigenous religion, and deliberated whether Buddhism could compete with Christianity globally.

High-stakes debates emerged over reforms to Buddhist education as Buddhists grappled with these questions of modernity. In response to the perceived threat from the rise of groups like Christian missionaries and Shintō nationalists, Buddhists in Jōdo Shinshū's Ōtani denomination generally fell into one of two camps. The progressive camp believed the best way forward was to embrace the increasingly pluralizing religious landscape through engagement with and education in non-Buddhist teachings, while the conservatives felt it was better to return to sectarian fundamentals by reinforcing traditional values and practices.

Ōtani's proto-university, the Gohōjō (護法場, Institute for the Protection of the Dharma), and its more traditional counterpart, the Gakuryō (学寮, often translated as "academy"), were the main stages for debates over the objectives and direction of clerical education in the Ōtani denomination. Some of these debates turned into increasingly hostile conflicts, eventually reaching a crescendo with the assassination of the progressive reformer Senshōin Kūkaku 闡彰院空覚 (1804–1871). The perpetrators of Kūkaku's assassination were never identified, though it is believed that his conservative rivals were responsible. The fact that this conflict escalated to such a degree speaks to the significance of these issues for many in the Ōtani denomination. Though this conflict over the appropriate response to the new challenges brought on by the Meiji period was not unique to Ōtani, it was among the first to experiment with institutionalizing these reforms with the establishment of the Gohōjō. Further, several Gohōjō alumni went on to lead the sect and the nascent Ōtani University in the second half of the Meiji period, making it an instructive case study in the rising influence of higher education in modern Buddhism.

This chapter will focus on a case study of Ōtani's Gohōjō. After an introduction to previous scholarship on Buddhist education and Buddhist studies in the Meiji period, I explain the brief but dynamic history of the Gohōjō and analyze its impact on higher education within the Ōtani denomination. As the Gohōjō was an early experiment with new higher educational models in the first half of the Meiji period that eventually developed into modern Buddhist universities, I conclude with some thoughts on what this study may be able to tell us more broadly about the changing state of Buddhist education in the Meiji period.

Within Meiji Buddhist studies, scholars have also begun to take a self-reflexive look at the intellectual history of the field of Buddhist studies in Japan.[1] Japanese scholars such as Sueki Fumihiko and Hayashi Makoto, as well as Western scholars such as Jacqueline Stone, Kathleen Staggs, and Orion Klautau, offer a variety of useful observations about the use of Buddhist scholarship in Buddhist modernization projects.[2] For instance, Klautau argues that a contributing factor to the reconstruction of Buddhist identity can be found in the developments in historical writing in the late Meiji and early Taishō periods.[3] He highlights the crucial role of historical narratives in the creation of a modern Buddhist identity and argues that emerging conceptions of the nation-state as well as the drive for clerical reform shaped these narratives, namely the Kamakura New Buddhism thesis and the Edo-period Buddhist decline thesis. Buddhist studies scholars such as Tsuji Zennosuke, Klautau writes, often clung to romanticized views of earlier Buddhism, specifically Kamakura Buddhism. While scholarship like Klautau's has greatly expanded our understanding of the intellectual genealogies that led to the field of modern Buddhist studies, his work focuses almost exclusively on the activities of the imperial universities. Thus, we are left to wonder what, if anything, the Buddhist universities contributed to the nascent field of modern Buddhist studies. It would also be useful to know more about the kinds of interactions shared between scholars at the two types of universities. Further, while works by scholars such as Tanigawa Yutaka and James Ketelaar have circled around the topic of Buddhist universities, none have addressed the emergence of Buddhist universities with much detail.

The exclusion of Buddhist universities from the larger history of the field of Buddhist studies is problematic not least because Buddhist higher educational institutions, though not legally granted "university" status until the University Ordinance in 1918, have always outnumbered the imperial universities. The first imperial university opened in Tokyo in 1886, and three additional campuses, in Kyoto, Tohoku, and Kyushu, were established before the end of the Meiji period. During the same period, there were sixteen Buddhist "universities."[4] Of course, it is open to debate whether the academic missions and educational approaches of the imperial and Buddhist universities can be fairly compared, yet the sheer number of schools and alumni produced by these Buddhist universities in this time period render this topic worthy of further scholarly attention.

In this regard, Hayashi Makoto's work on the role of Buddhist universities in the birth of modern Buddhist studies is instructive. He asserts that the development of modern Buddhist studies cannot be fully understood without a serious examination of the role of religiously affiliated universities. For example, Hayashi points out that among the first schools to receive official recognition as universities under the University Ordinance of 1918, four of six represented sects had grown out of "New Kamakura Buddhism."[5] As a result, he argues, these sects generated considerably more scholarship on their seminal texts (Lotus Sutra, *Tannishō*, *Shōbōgenzō*, etc.) and founders within their own sects (Nichiren, Shinran, Dōgen, etc.) compared to the other Buddhist sects without universities.[6] Furthermore, Hayashi asserts that the participation of these Buddhist universities in early research associations, such as the Buddhist Association of Japan (Nihon Bukkyō Kyōkai 日本仏教協会) and the Japanese Association of Buddhist Studies (Nihon Bukkyō Gakkai 日本仏教学会), established influential crosscurrents between scholars at imperial and Buddhist universities. Finally, by comparing the organizational structure and early curricula of Buddhist universities with those of the imperial universities, Hayashi highlights differences in approaches to the study of religion, especially Buddhism.[7]

The 2014 publication *Kindai Nihon no Daigaku to Shūkyō* (*Universities and Religion in Modern Japan*) goes beyond the role of Buddhist universities in the development of Buddhist studies to cover a wide range of topics relating to the emergence of religious universities in Japan.[8] The contributors to this collection consider the characteristics of religious education since the introduction of universities in the Meiji period and explore the implications of religious education in the modern era that took place not only in churches and temples but also at universities. Importantly, this volume opens up a variety of avenues for further research, including the relationship between religion and modernization in Japanese thought and differences in Christian and Buddhist higher education in modern Japan. Miura Shū advocates a reexamination of the history of Buddhist studies in light of the insights brought about by postcolonial theory. Specifically, he calls for more attention to the Japanese (nationalist) and Chinese ([neo]-Confucian) influences on the development of modern Buddhist higher education. Ishida Kazuhiro's work heeds Miura's call by examining the influential role of relationships between fellow Japanese scholar-monks and the impact of their interactions during their time abroad and afterward.[9]

While the abovementioned works have made substantial progress toward a deeper understanding of the field of modern Buddhist studies and a few have contributed to our understanding of the development of Buddhist education in the Meiji period, more work is required in order to understand the full spectrum of Buddhist education in Japan. Buddhist universities remain largely overlooked within Meiji Buddhist studies and scholarship on the birth of modern Buddhist studies. I address this lacuna in my research, and the present case study of the Ōtani denomination of the Jōdo Shinshū sect of Buddhism's proto-university, the Gohōjō, emerged from my explorations into this topic.

The case study of the Gohōjō demonstrates that the new educational style practiced at the Gohōjō fostered critical thinking and led to many students' dissatisfaction with the denomination's traditional structures and conservative viewpoints. Gohōjō students criticized the state of the sect as "being left behind by the movement of time" (時代の流れに取り残されつつある).[10] Almost immediately following the Gohōjō's founding, students began a campaign demanding reforms from the Higashi Honganji, and some of these reforms were eventually enacted (though not without a fair amount of conflict). The success of the Gohōjō reformers at the Gohōjō is especially impressive when we consider the institution's relatively short life span of five years.

Even at this early stage a shifting power dynamic can be seen: the Gohōjō illustrates an example of educational institutions having direct influence on sectarian organization and leadership. Prior to the Meiji period, the main power centers of Japanese Buddhist sects were the head temple (*honzan* 本山), which served as the primary training temple, along with the various administrative temples that interacted with the shogunal government's office that regulated Buddhist temples and Shintō shrines. This dual administrative system, which distinguished between loci of spiritual authority and temporal authority, continued into the modern period in many respects. During the Meiji period, however, Buddhist (proto)-universities began to emerge as a third power center. In the next section, I turn to the memoir of a prominent alumni, the *Ōtani University One Hundred-Year History* (*Ōtani Daigaku Hyakunenshi 大谷大学100年史*, hereafter the *Hyakunenshi*), and other Gohōjō archival materials to examine its history in more detail. These documents offer insight into how new higher education institutions like the Gohōjō negotiated with earlier power centers to establish themselves as a third power center within modern Japanese Buddhism.

## Gohōjō: Ōtani's proto-university

Several Buddhist universities, including Ōtani University, claim founding dates as early as the sixteenth and seventeenth centuries; however, Buddhist universities did not begin to take on their modern forms until the mid to late Meiji period. These early founding dates refer to academies, or *gakuryō* (学寮), modeled on earlier forms of Buddhist education and influenced by Confucian and Chinese Buddhist styles of pedagogy. The academies educated a relatively small proportion of monks, and these educated "scholar-monks" (*gakusō* 学僧) enjoyed elite status. During the Meiji period, for reasons that I will elaborate on later, the major Buddhist sects gradually transitioned to a higher education model that more closely resembled that of a modern Western university. This transition bore major consequences not only for clerical education, but also the development of the field of modern Buddhist studies, and for the organization within each sect.

Monastic education in the Ōtani denomination during the Edo period was shared by two institutions: the Gakuryō 学寮 (academy) and the Ango 安居 (monastic retreat).[11] Due to a series of fires, records for these institutions are sparse, and most of the remaining records are from the late Edo period. We know that both the Gakuryō and the Ango grew throughout this time period. Records show that the Gakuryō campus enrollment reached 1,500 students in 1826 and by 1828 the campus included a total of seven buildings. Also in 1828, enrollment for the Ango reached 1,700 students. Subjects at both institutions centered on the study of sectarian ritual and text. Records show that both the Gakuryō and the Ango occasionally taught non-Buddhist topics, such as National Learning and Neo-Confucianism. The first recorded instance of this was a lecture offered in 1824 titled "Introduction to Confucianism" at the Gakuryō. In 1831 records indicate that in one course students read and discussed the *Nihonshoki* at the Ango. In 1863, during the tumultuous Bakumatsu period, the Ango offered a lecture on Christianity and heliocentrism. Aside from these sporadic offerings, neither the Gakuryō nor the Ango offered courses or lectures on non-Buddhist subjects with any regularity.

This changed in the early Meiji period when, in an effort to prepare its priests for the escalating threats posed by an increasing number of critics, the Ōtani denomination's higher education institution, the Takakura Gakuryō 高倉学寮 began in earnest to teach non-Buddhist subjects. On August 1, 1868, two lay retainers were appointed to head up the plans to establish an academy for *gaigaku* 外学 (literally translated as "outside studies" but in this case refers to "non-Buddhist studies") research and education. A suitable site was found near the Gakuryō four days later. Though *gaigaku* classes had been held in the ordinary lecture halls 講堂 prior to the Meiji period, conservatives grew critical of holding of lectures on Buddhism's critics in places designated for teaching the dharma. Just two weeks after the beginning of the search, the Gohōgakujō 護法学場 (more commonly referred to as the Gohōjō) held an opening ceremony. On that occasion, professor and then head of the Gakuryō, Kōzan-in Ryūon 香山院竜温 (1800–1885), delivered a speech in which he explained that while "*gohō*" once meant simply the preservation of the honzan and the pursuit of sectarian studies, or *shūgaku* 宗学, at the Gakuryō, the recent proliferation of evils views (*jaken* 邪見), such as Christianity, National Learning, and Western Astronomy, necessitated a response that includes research and education in *gaigaku*.[12]

Led by Ōtani priests Kōzan-in Ryūon and Senshōin Kūkaku 闡彰院空覚 (1804–1871), the Gohōjō was founded in August of 1868 as a place to study *gaigaku*, which despite its vague name, refers specifically to the teachings of four of Japanese Buddhism's most vocal critics and largest perceived threats: Christianity, Western Astronomy (particularly heliocentrism), Confucianism, and National Learning. Though their curriculum was distinct from that of the Gakuryō, instructors at the Gakuryō were expected to teach and conduct research on *gaigaku* at the Gohōjō. The Gohōjō and Gakuryō were jointly managed, and leaders were appointed from within the faculty on a rotating basis. There were no specific requirements to enroll at the Gohōjō, and students were admitted on a trial basis through recommendations. Some students were only affiliated with the Gohōjō, while others maintained affiliations with both the Gakuryō and the Gohōjō. For these reasons, perhaps, the enrollment numbers for the Gohōjō are not known.

The academy taught Western teachings, astronomy, National Learning, and Confucianism. The curriculum on Western teachings focused specifically on Protestant teachings, Catholic doctrine, and church history. National Learning instruction included Shintō texts, *waka* 和歌, and *wabun* 和文. The curriculum for Confucian teachings included various Chinese classics and economics. As previously mentioned, National Learning and Confucianism had been taught at Ōtani's Takakura Gakuryō during the Edo period, when both began producing strong criticisms of Buddhism. (Western) Astronomy, specifically heliocentrism, was an essential subject because traditional Buddhist cosmology, which centered on Mount Sumeru, was often the subject of ridicule and was commonly cited as proof of Buddhism's backwardness by its critics. Along with astronomy, mathematics and calendrical studies were also taught. Lectures and discussions on the "teachings of false doctrines" (*haja no yōmon* 破邪の要文) led by instructors from the academy were held every other day.[13]

The Gohōjō was a place for students to learn and develop responses to Buddhism's critics. For example, students were often expected to take opposing sides of an argument and debate.[14] Further, it was common practice at the Gohōjō for anyone at any level, from professor to novice, at any time to hold a form of debate-style examination called *ryūgi mondō* 立義問答 in the dining hall, where students and teachers engaged in academic discussions about a chosen topic. Among the Gohōjō's most notable alumni is Nanjō Bunyū 南条文雄 (1849–1927), who includes the following recollection in his memoir:

> With the intent of refuting false doctrine, Senshōin would set the Chinese translation of the Christian Bible on the bookstand and have us read extensively from it have us discuss and read extensively from it. Then, we students would also be divided to represent Buddhists and Christians and discuss and debate the superior points of each doctrine. It is fun to remember that time when we burned with a love of learning and above all, a lively pursuit of one's wishes.
>
> 破邪顕正という趣意から、闡彰院嗣講は漢訳した耶蘇教の聖典を見台に乗せ、大いに講読せられたことがある。したがって私たち寮生も仏·耶両教徒に分かれ、教義の優劣を討論したこともあった。なんといっても活気縦横、好学心に燃えた当時のことは思い出しても愉快なことである。[15]

Despite Nanjō's positive impression, the Gohōjō's progressiveness spurred conflict with the more conservative lay leadership of the Honzan. Almost as soon as it was founded, the Honzan moved the site of the Gohōjō several times soon after its founding, acts that were seen by the Gohōjō as meddlesome and an attempt to hinder the institution's growth.

A mere three months after opening, on the eve of the Hō'onkō 報恩講, Shinran's memorial service, the Gohōjō staff and students and the Honzan had their first major flare-up at a meeting between various representatives from the Ōtani denomination and the Gohōjō. At this meeting, the Honzan leadership gave a presentation on the denomination's large debts, explained to be a result of rebuilding the Honzan and substantial lending to the government. The lay leaders argued that because of the impoverished state of the denomination, the Gohōjō would have to remain small. Upon hearing this, a number of outraged Gohōjō novices demanded an explanation from the Honzan leadership, who attempted to leave without answering the novices. The *Hyakunenshi* paints a rather dramatic scene of the Gohōjō novices chasing after the Honzan leadership, who eventually burst through shoji doors to escape the angry novices.[16]

Though the Honzan always insisted on the inseparability of the Gakuryō and the Gohōjō, opinions on the true nature of their relationship fell into two distinct camps.[17] As time went on, factions between pro-reform and anti-reform students continued to deepen. In a heated debate on December 11, 1868, students sympathetic to the more progressive Gohōjō wore black robes, while students sympathetic to the more conservative Gakuryō wore blue robes. In spite of or perhaps because of these philosophical disputes, the Honzan often sent mixed messages about the proper place and value of *gaigaku* within the sect; while taking steps to hinder the growth and power of the Gohōjō, it also recruited *gaigaku* researchers from its branch temples.

In March 1869, three Gohōjō students went directly to the Honzan and submitted the following letter:

> Since the founding of the Gohōjō, young volunteers from various regions have gathered. The objective is researching subjects suitable to the times such as the classics of Shintō, Confucianism, and other Non-Buddhist teachings, but at its core it is about the renewal of imperial rule. The misgovernment of the Honzan must be reformed and we students submit various plans.
>
> 護法場開設己来、諸国有志の青年これに集まり、主に神·儒および外教の典籍等、事に適切なる学科を研究する目的なりしが、中には王政御一新の趣にもとづき、御本の弊政を改革せんとて、種々の計画をめぐらす徒もこれあり。[18]

Though the exact plans for reform are not included in my source materials, one major component is often stated in secondary sources: the call for the resignation of the lay leadership and the placement of priests in their former roles. Upon receiving the letter, the Honzan attempted to seize the three students, but they were narrowly able to evade apprehension and sought refuge in the Gohōjō. Although several students, teachers, and staff at the Gohōjō were punished by the denomination, their actions did eventually lead to a number of reforms, including the removal of lay member administrators and the appointment of priests in their place. Another reform was the establishment of a Public Discussion Hall/Forum 衆議所, a place for clergy, laity, and students to openly express their opinions. In the *Hyakunenshi*, the students are praised for having learned the importance of looking at the sect from the outside in, while the Honzan is referred to as "closed" (閉鎖的).[19] The way things are "remembered" in historical writing is important, and this assessment indicates the current (as of the volume's writing), "official" understanding of the Gohōjō's place in Ōtani's history as a place for progressive reform that is valued over the conservative Honzan leadership.

Despite these developments, the conservative faction maintained that any shift in scholarly attention away from the sect's teachings was a dangerous diversion. Consider the following statement by conservative Gakuryō instructor, Genjuin Tokujū 賢殊院得住:

> The power to destroy the dharma is in the hands of Śākyamuni's disciples. Just as if you work to eradicate Buddhism's enemies, more enemies will grow in their place, it naturally follows that if you willingly [work to] eradicate Christianity, more Christians will grow in its place. Throw away the "self-power"-driven efforts to destroy non-Buddhist teachings and entrust in the divine power of Śākyamuni.
>
> 仏法破滅するは釈尊の御弟子の力なり。勤めて排仏を排すれば、排仏いよいよ多くり、勇んで耶蘇いよいよ多くなるは自然の道理。外教を破するには自力を捨てて、釈尊の神力をかるには如かず。[20]

Here, Tokujū cautioned against studying for the purpose of expelling other teachings and advocated studying for the purpose of learning about Buddhism. The fear and sense of crisis shared by both the progressive student-priests and the conservative sectarian leaders elicited opposite responses; while the progressives felt the only way to effectively counter Buddhism's critics was to have an intimate knowledge of their critics' philosophy and teachings, the conservatives felt that the best defense was to strengthen their commitment to Buddhist teachings.

These two perspectives were at the core of the struggle over Buddhist education, and the sustained conflict between the two led to significant structural reorganization within the Ōtani denomination during the Meiji period.

This struggle was manifested perhaps most memorably with the assassination of a prominent instructor at the Gohōjō and Gakuryō, a reformer named Senshōin Kūkaku (1804–1871). Kūkaku was born in 1804, resided at Kyoto's Fushimi Saihōji 伏見西方寺, and trained at Nara's Tokuganji 徳願寺. Little else is known about his early life. We know he was ordained at Saihōji in 1835. Later he was known as Tōei 東瀛, Eishū 瀛洲, and ultimately Senshōin. He studied under Ungein Daigan 雲華院大含, a prolific Buddhist poet, painter, and instructor at the Gakuryō. Daigan retired in 1849 and Kūkaku became an assistant lecturer at the age of forty-five. Two years later, in 1851, he was involved in a heresy (異安心) incident known as the Tonjo Jiken, which is notorious within the Ōtani denomination.[21] His involvement in the incident led to his expulsion from the priesthood until his reinstatement in 1863. He became an instructor at the Gakuryō in 1865 and was a leader in the establishment of the Gohōjō three years later.

During Kūkaku's tenure at the Gohōjō his areas of instruction were quite varied, from Christianity to the Chinese Bible (as recalled in Nanjō's memoirs, quoted above), John Bunyan's *The Pilgrim's Progress* (in Japanese『天路歴程』), and Shinran's *Nishujinshin*『二種深信』, *igyōbon sanzengi* 易行品·散善義, *Shakkyō Shōmyū* 『釈教正謬』, *Gengibun*『玄義分』, *Shinkoku ketsugihen* 『神国決疑編』, *Hajakenshōshō* 『破邪顕正鈔』. He was influenced by the work of Kōzan-in Ryūon and mentored many future leaders within the denomination. He was assassinated in 1871 and no one was charged with his murder, though it is largely believed to have been committed by a lay member of the sectarian leadership who had been ousted under the sectarian reforms Kūkaku had helped establish.

Kūkaku's life and death fit perfectly into Ketelaar's heretic-martyr framework. Once painted as a radical and dangerous heretic by the conservative leadership, Kūkaku was later redeemed as a visionary reformer who helped usher the Ōtani denomination into the modern era. The straw raincoat he wore every day became a symbol for the academic pursuits of Ōtani University, is held in the Ōtani archives, and is periodically exhibited in Ōtani University's museum. Ōtani's history places Kūkaku's life and the history of the Gohōjō as reflections of the larger dilemmas of sectarian education that persist into the present day: that of doctrine versus practice, or the traditional sectarian approach to learning versus a more practical approach to learning that incorporates the perspectives of the nation and society.[22]

After his death, two of Kūkaku's disciples, Ishikawa Shuntai 石川舜台 (1842-1931) and Atsumi Kaien 渥美契縁 (1840-1906), became denominational leaders. The two colleagues, however, fell on opposite sides of the debate over the proper direction to take the Ōtani denomination, eventually becoming fierce rivals. While Ishikawa planned inspection tours abroad, established a Translation Bureau (*honyaku kyoku* 翻訳局), and created a scholarship program to train and educate exceptionally gifted students within the denomination, Atsumi prioritized eliminating the group's massive debt and oversaw large-scale construction projects with the rebuilding of the Founder's Hall and Amida Hall. The different approaches of these two figures illustrate the schism between conservative and progressive responses to the challenges of a rapidly globalizing and modernizing society.[23]

Though the Gohōjō did not officially close until 1873 (the Gakuryō's name was changed to the Kanrenjō 貫練場 that same year), few historical documents concerning the Gohōjō remain after 1871. The *Hyakunenshi* explains that the absence of sources may be understood as a sign that the Gohōjō had already achieved many of its goals for sectarian reform. Though they were not completely successful in opening the sect to the degree that many at the Gohōjō originally envisioned, by 1871, priests at the Gohōjō and allied priests from local branch temples had replaced many of the powerful conservative lay leaders within the sectarian organization. However, given the dramatic events surrounding the Gohōjō, including the assassination of Kūkaku, one wonders if documents were destroyed by rival factions. Another possible explanation for the lack of records during this time period may be found a result of the 1872 law that allowed Buddhist priests to become Doctrinal Instructors 教導職 for the Meiji government's Daikyōin 大教院 for the first time. Though the Ōtani denomination's participation in the Daikyōin was short lived, it did create a temporary shift in priorities for young clerics from the survival of their own sect to building a case for Buddhism's place in service to the new Japanese state. As Ketelaar puts it, "The *gohō* ideology had been successfully linked to the conception of the preservation of the nation: *gokoku*."[24]

## Understanding the Gohōjō's impact

The brief history of the Gohōjō was in many ways a microcosm for the intellectual and spiritual debates occurring in many Buddhist circles in the early Meiji period. During this time a marketplace of ideas arose in response to the political, cultural, and economic changes that were taking place throughout

Japan. Conservatives in the Ōtani denomination wanted to reinforce traditional sectarian ideas and practices with a "back to [sectarian] basics" approach. This approach, as it related to Buddhist education, included a renewed emphasis on sectarian texts and ritual and an intentional exclusion of the study of Western subjects. For progressives in this marketplace, the way to survive all this change was not to return to tradition but to adapt with the times. Adapting with the times, however, meant different things to different reformers, and diverse movements arose that called for a variety of changes, including creating a unified Buddhism, trans-sectarian Buddhist education, unification with Shintō and Confucianism,[25] the integration of Western subjects into clerical curriculum, transnational intellectual exchange, and more. Though many of these movements failed to gain traction, educational reforms were adopted by most of the main sects in the Meiji period.[26]

Among the largest and most impactful of these reforms was the gradual shift from a traditional monastic academy to a modern university. Japan's major Buddhist sects had many reasons to adopt the university model, not least of which was a desire to showcase Buddhism's compatibility with modern institutions. But the new educational model created as many problems as it solved, and conservatives in all of the major sects worried that this new model and the inclusion of nonsectarian subjects threatened their sectarian worldview. The history of the rise and fall of the Gohōjō, Ōtani's proto-university, illustrates the complex set of questions and intra-sectarian conflict borne from the political, religious, and educational developments of the period.

## Political impact

The mission of the Gohōjō—to gain an understanding of the teachings of Buddhism's critics—did not just remain at the academy in Kyoto but also spread to other regions through former students and scholars. In some instances, the actions of Gohōjō alumni had significant political consequences. A famous example is that of two graduates of the Gohōjō, Ishikawa Tairei 石川台嶺 (1842–1871) and Hoshikawa Hōsawa 星川法沢 (1833–1873). Ishikawa and Hoshikawa were leaders in the Ohama Uprising (*Ōhama Sōdō* 大浜騒動) in Mikawa, an event chronicled in detail in Ketelaar's *Of Heretics and Martyrs in Meiji Japan*. Ishikawa and Hoshikawa, whose contribution has been succinctly summarized here, upon graduating from the Gohōjō founded a local group in Aichi Prefecture called the Mikawa Dharma Preservation

Society (*Mikawa Gohōkai* 三河護法会) in 1869. Responding to increasingly hostile actions of the Meiji government's *haibutsu kishaku* policy, the society quickly accumulated thousands of local followers. Tensions continued to escalate, and by 1871 a meeting between government officials and the Society's representatives ended with the brutal attack and killing of a young government official by an angry mob. All told, the government arrested and tried seventy-seven people, fifty-one of whom where priests. Hoshikawa was sentenced to ten years of banishment, but died in prison before his sentence was carried out; as the main leader of the uprising, Ishikawa was beheaded. Following this incident, the Gohōkai's initial demands were in fact met but at a steep price. In addition to the lives lost, new harsh regulations that limited members' ability to travel and hold public gatherings were placed on Jōdo Shinshū temples.[27] Ishikawa and Hoshikawa were among the first Ōtani priests to attempt to apply what they had learned at the Gohōjō in their local communities, and the severe consequences of their actions demonstrate just how much was at stake for everyone involved.

In addition to the spread of *gaigaku* and progressive reformers to the regions, the Gohōjō also dispatched academy leaders, Chiwaya 千巌 and Seki Shinso 関 信三 (1843 1880; priestly name 猶龍) to Nagasaki to learn more about Christianity. Seki apparently also worked as a spy for the government, reporting on Christian activities until 1872, though the Ōtani sources don't include this; instead they simply note that the Nagasaki trip made major contributions to the Gohōjō's Christian research.[28]

## From knowledge transmission to knowledge production

Despite repeated conflicts with the Gohōjō over the status of *gaigaku* within the monastic curriculum, the Honzan's actions during this period nevertheless indicated an acknowledgment of the importance of gaining a better understanding of *gaigaku*, even recruiting researchers from its branch temples. This and other developments, such as the creation of graduate education programs and the proliferation of scholarly journals can be understood as part of a larger systematic shift in Buddhist education—from knowledge *transmission* to knowledge *production*. In fact, this was a phenomena occurring in Western higher education as well, a result of a variety of sociocultural factors that converged on the valorization of the scientific method and inquiry.[29] John Roberts describes this phenomenon in the United States during the 1860s and

1870s as a time when religious colleges and universities moved the thrust of their efforts from "harmonizing science and revelation" to "altering biblical interpretations to comport with the findings of science."[30] In Japan, as in the United States, previous scholarship proved unable to adequately respond to the ideas posed by modern science, thus necessitating the production of new scholarship that adhered to these new standards and educational objectives.

The impact of this shift is compounded when we consider Hayashi's observation that the sectarian universities that preserved the most materials and produced the most scholarship in the Meiji period remain the most powerful into the present day.[31] Compared with smaller Buddhist groups, the Ōtani denomination's timely response to these new developments in higher education gave it an advantageous position from which to more readily engage in higher education networks nationally and internationally.

## Professionalization of the priesthood

A term that appears frequently throughout literature on the Gohōjō is 人材登用, "the promotion of talent[ed individuals]." Ketelaar pointed out that the notion of promoting *jinzai* was used by Meiji Buddhists as an alternative to the former model of inherited status (see Ketelaar 1991). In the wake of the upheaval of the centuries-long *danka* and *tera-uke* systems, Buddhist monks no longer assumed the same status within Japanese society. Furthermore, the early Meiji period signaled a massive overhaul in nationalized education, and as the average education level of the general populace rose, the priesthood had a harder time maintaining educational superiority over the laity. The university model exemplified by the Gohōjō provided a solution to both the status and educational problem, as priests became increasingly educated and encouraged by their sect to become educators themselves. Higher education ushered in the professionalization of the priesthood, and this professionalization became a way for Buddhist sects to reclaim their "usefulness" to the state: as the country's educators. Over half of all Doctrinal Instructors 教導職 for the Great Promulgation Campaign 大教宣布運動 were Buddhist. After the campaign ended and the Daikyōin closed (due in part to Jōdo Shinshū priests pulling out from the institute), Buddhists fought to maintain their status as educators, ultimately losing that battle with the outlawing of (non-State Shintō) religious education in schools. The Buddhists persisted, however, and Buddhist universities were eventually granted the ability to issue teacher's licenses to their graduates in the Taishō period.

## Considerations for future research

The case study of the Gohōjō raises an important fundamental question: What is the primary purpose of Buddhist universities? Is it to educate clergy, laity, or both? Is it to offer a broad-based education with a sectarian foundation, or conduct specialized research on important texts and figures within the sect? And if the latter, for whom is this research meant? These questions, brought on by the rapid changes in the Meiji period, continue to concern Buddhist universities and sect in the present day. As some Buddhist universities continue to grow and prosper, while others struggle to stay open, these questions hold enormous weight and relevance.

3

# Taking the Vajrayana to Sukhāvatī

Aaron P. Proffitt

## Introduction

In 2005 I graduated from college and moved to a small town in Japan, Tamana City 玉名市 in Kumamoto prefecture 熊本県, to work as an English teacher. The traditions I encountered in this small town, and the scholarship I read to make sense of what I was seeing, determined my future academic interests in Buddhist studies: heterogeneity, normativity, and sectarianism, and the historical development of the many connections between what scholars generally refer to as Pure Land Buddhism (Jōdokyō) and Esoteric Buddhism (Mikkyō). Rural Kumamoto appeared to be dominated by Jōdo Shinshū, the largest school of Buddhism in Japan. At that time, however, I knew almost nothing about Jōdo Shinshū or Pure Land Buddhism more broadly. I was surprised, or perhaps baffled, that as someone who had been reading about Buddhism for over a decade by that point, I had scarcely heard of the traditions and practices that likely constitute the dominant expression of East Asian Buddhism: chanting the *nenbutsu*, or the name of the Buddha Amitābha/Amitāyus (Amida Nyorai), "*Namu Amida Butsu*," and the aspiration for rebirth in his Pure Land. As a result, I became especially interested in learning about the complexities of this so-called "easy" path and began to investigate what factors had contributed to the neglect of Jōdo Shinshū Buddhist studies in particular, and Mahayana Buddhist Pure Land thought and practice in general. I spent that year learning from my friends, neighbors, and students, many of whom invited me to their family temples.

In addition, I was intrigued to find that in my town situated in a sea of Jōdo Shinshū Buddhist temples there was also one very active Shingon-risshū temple nearby, Renge-in Tanjōji 蓮華院誕生寺. The primary object of devotion at the temple is the Hieizan Tendai scholar-monk Kōen (d. 1169), author of the *Fusō ryakki* and one of the early teachers of Hōnen (1133–1212), the de facto founder of the Japanese Pure Land school. At the Renge-in, however, Kōen is worshiped as a *ryūjin daibosatsu*, a "great divine dragon bodhisattva," and is said to have been the person responsible for inspiring Hōnen to found the Pure Land school. The temple attempts to appeal to the local Shin Buddhist population using billboards, comic books, and elaborate tapestries to tie orthodox Pure Land patriarchs to their *honzon*. One sentence appears frequently: "Kōen was the teacher of Hōnen, who was the teacher of Shinran, who was the founder of Jōdo Shinshū." I became interested in how this temple employed, negated, and transgressed the boundaries (and basic history) that students of Japanese religion learn by heart. At this "Shingon" temple, they worshiped a "Tendai" monk, in the form of a "divine dragon bodhisattva," and explicitly proselytized to local "Pure Land Buddhists." Textbooks on Japanese religion scarcely prepare one for such boundary-transgressing experiences.[1]

While attending numerous popular festivals and holiday celebrations, I wondered if the people I saw at these events were all affiliated with this particular temple and the Shingon-risshū tradition, or, if like my friends who brought me to the temple, they technically belonged to one of the many Jōdo Shinshū temples nearby but felt a kind of simultaneous inclination to the apotropaic benefits promised by this temple. For example, one family I knew conducted the standard Shin Buddhist daily practice, including the recitation of the *Shōshinge* and so on, but also chanted a *dhāraṇī*, an Esoteric incantation or spell, at the end. According to textbooks and normative sectarian literature (and even the first page of the Jōdo Shinshū daily practice manual), Jōdo Shinshū Buddhists do not engage in such Esoteric practices. My friend who told me about this practice was almost apologetic about his family's unorthodox behavior. I assured him that my interests lay in what people actually do, not what textbooks or authorities of one kind or another say people should do.[2]

Years later while attending the *kechien kanjō* 結縁灌頂 for the Taizōkai Mandara 胎蔵界曼荼羅 on Kōyasan 高野山,[3] the mountain temple complex around the tomb of Kūkai, one pilgrim caught my eye. This pilgrim was wearing a Shingon school pilgrim jacket with *Namu daishi henjō kongō* (南無大師遍照金剛, a kind of Kūkai *nenbutsu*) written down the back, but she was also wearing the Nishi Honganji *wagesa* 輪袈裟 (surplus) around her neck. Here was someone who seemed to be proudly displaying her sense of "dual-belonging." A few years before this, also on Kōyasan, I asked a priest who I knew about how the Obon festival お盆 "worked" in Shingon. The Shingon tradition is often explained in reference to Kūkai's teaching that Shingon practice leads to the attainment of buddhahood "in this very body" (*sokushin jōbutsu* 即身成仏),

and in most normative sectarian literature, this is framed as an explicit rejection of other soteriological paths within Mahayana Buddhism, such as post-mortem Pure Land rebirth (*ōjō* 往生). Traditionally, Obon is regarded as a kind of "day of the dead" wherein Buddhists return to their ancestral homes to clean the *haka* 墓 (grave marker and repository for cremains) at their family temple, with some families setting out an elaborate altar at home to invite the spirits of their ancestors to dinner. While on Kōyasan I asked this priest where the ancestors "come from" for Shingon Buddhists. He said, "The Pure Land, of course!" As I began to reframe my questions around the *sokushin jōbutsu* doctrine (i.e., how could they attain buddhahood in this very body and also go to the Pure Land?), he just laughed, saying, "I think you read too many books."

In this chapter I wish to make connections between how we understand historical issues and how we make sense of contemporary Buddhist practices in Japan. Specifically, I will examine the re-visioning work done by Richard K. Payne and others revealing a pre-sectarian Kamakura Buddhism that featured what I call "Esoteric Pure Land" practice. Locating this history—once obscured by sectarian and essentialist assumptions made in scholarship—gives context to the complex identities and practices described above. Far from being a post-modern mishmash of disparate elements, this embodied practice has a history and a lineage revealed through recent historical studies. In other words, historical studies are important not just for historians, but for those working in ethnography and related fields that study living Buddhists.

## Re-visioning *Kenmitsu*-Pure Land Buddhism

Each of the encounters described above seemed to embody a kind of "duality," a dynamic engagement with the sectarian boundaries so often seen as representative of Buddhism in Japan today. Though there is clearly an "overlap" between Pure Land Buddhism and Esoteric Buddhism, the Anglophone scholarship has been both neglectful of Pure Land Buddhist studies as a significant dimension of Mahayana Buddhism more broadly and content to let modernist Jōdo Shinshū Buddhist discourse serve as the standard against which the diversity of Mahayana soteriological orientations are to be evaluated. In other words, there are multiple Pure Land Buddhisms, or, to put it another way, Pure Land thought and practice is simply part of what it means to be a Mahayana Buddhist. In addition, the history of Esoteric Buddhism in East Asia has been constructed around the normative sectarian history of the Shingon lineage and the doctrinal teachings of Kūkai. This occludes the complex web of Mahayana polemical strategies out of which "Esoteric" discourse emerged, and the fluid ritual context within which functioned the various lineages, practices, and material culture we now imagine as the property of something called Esoteric Buddhism.

The essentializing and ahistorical way that these two labels have been used, "Pure Land Buddhism" and "Esoteric Buddhism," has distorted our understanding of Mahayana Buddhist culture, especially in East Asia; it is much more complicated, and more interesting, than this taxonomic "founder-sect-doctrine" framework would have us believe. Aspiration for rebirth in the Pure Land of the Buddha Amitābha is ubiquitous throughout Mahayana literature, as are many of the rituals and practices now associated with Esoteric Buddhism, which were in many cases simply technologies developed within Mahayana ritual culture to accomplish this-worldly or otherworldly goals (including post-mortem Pure Land rebirth). That there would be areas of "overlap" seemed to me to be quite obvious. Yet scholarship that understands that this is an important, and unfairly neglected, area of academic inquiry, is somewhat scant.

Richard K. Payne is one scholar whose work offers a corrective to the essentializing and ahistorical tendencies described above. He writes of his somewhat accidental discovery of Max Walleser's translation and study of a Nepalese edition of the *Aparimitāyuḥ-sūtra*:

> Initially I was attracted to this text because it appeared to be simultaneously a Pure Land and a Vajrayana text, offering longevity and birth in Sukhāvatī through the recitation of a *dhāraṇī*. This struck me, those many years ago, as delightfully transgressive—it confounded the neat categories so familiar in the Buddhist studies of the 1970s, categories whose boundaries are overly-sharp, ahistorical, and either sectarian or ethnically defined. Since these boundaries continue to plague the field, the text continues to be a useful means of confounding these categories.[4]

He here notes a fundamental methodological problem within Buddhist studies: How are we to account for the diversity of Mahayana Buddhist traditions in practice when the very contours of the field are often so rigidly defined that they almost preclude the possibility of doing so?

Below I will sketch what I believe to be a new area of study in the field of Buddhist studies: Esoteric Pure Land Buddhist studies.[5] I regard Payne as the architect of this subfield both because of his own work on the topic and his work as a prolific editor who has pulled together many essays by other scholars, which, when taken together, may be seen as constituting a foundation or "scaffolding" for further study. This area of study shines light not only on the complex history of Buddhism in Japan, but helps us better understand contemporary Japanese Buddhists whose practices cut across essentialist and sectarian boundaries.

Kuroda Toshio's now famous *kenmitsu taisei* 顕密体制 theory provides a helpful balance to sectarian polemics in developing historical context for the early development of the Japanese Pure Land movement. Kuroda argues that Kamakura "New Buddhism"—Pure Land, Zen, and Nichiren—was actually quite marginal during the Kamakura period (1185–1333). Buddhist culture at the time was dominated by large temple-shrine complexes wherein the prevailing culture was premised on the interrelation of exoteric doctrine (*kengyō* 顕教) and esoteric ritual practice (*mikkyō* 密教), which together constituted what we think of as a pervasive *kenmitsu* 顕密 culture. That we now associate the early medieval period with Pure Land, Zen, and Nichiren is largely a function of contemporary sectarian polemics. These traditions dominate the institutional landscape of Japanese Buddhist studies scholarship, in Japan and abroad. One such polemical assertion is that Tendai and Shingon were decadent, elitist, and out of touch with the common person and were quickly replaced by the New Schools.

In order to understand the context within which Japanese Pure Land Buddhism developed, it's important to investigate how Pure Land thought functioned within, and not apart from, the dominant *kenmitsu* culture of early medieval Japan. George Tanabe provides a counterbalance to "Kamakura school" sectarian histories, disputing the assertion that the Esoteric schools, or so-called "Heian school," were in decline in the early medieval period.[6] He emphasizes the importance of Pure Land thought and practice for the revitalization of Kōyasan, detailing the ongoing activity in and around Kōyasan during the early medieval period. Other contributions, such as work by Mark Unno[7] and Richard K. Payne,[8] explore specific Esoteric Pure Land practices. Taken together, this scholarship sketches the contours of something like a pervasive Esoteric Pure Land culture in medieval Japan as perhaps one of the avenues by which the Esoteric traditions worked with elites and commoners alike.

Despite the wealth of scholarship on Shinran, Hōnen, and other Kamakura founders, there is surprisingly little scholarship on what we might call *kenmitsu*-Pure Land, in other words, the Pure Land traditions of the temples in and around Nara and Heian capitals. In most scholarship on the broader context for Pure Land Buddhism, Shinran or Hōnen is positioned as a *telos* whose teachings perfected what had come before. Scholarship on contemporaries of Hōnen and Shinran, other monks who might have wrestled with similar issues around the same time, is surprisingly lacking. In the immense Japanese language research on Buddhism, with its overabundance of material on just about everything, there is an intriguing lacuna. What did *kenmitsu*-Pure Land thought look like during the late twelfth to early thirteenth centuries, the formative years of the so-called Kamakura New Schools?

The problem is not that the primary source material is not out there. Rather, the problem is that almost no one has been reading the sources for *kenmitsu*-Pure Land (or, as I label it, "Esoteric Pure Land"). This is because in many cases scholarship and popular literature on Japanese and Chinese Buddhism has applied the sectarian rubric of early modern and modern Japan as a taxonomy for organizing the diversity of Buddhist thought and practice. Young scholars are often encouraged to choose a field (country, or "school," or "sect") such as Tibetan Tantra, Japanese Zen, Chinese Pure Land, etc. Scholars of Japanese *kenmitsu* culture (often assumed to be reducible to Esoteric Buddhism, at times uncritically conflated with the Shingon school) tend to ignore Pure Land, and scholars of Pure Land tend to ignore the broader *kenmitsu* culture of early medieval Japan. Pure Land Buddhism, we are told, constituted a rejection of Esoteric Buddhism, which was decadent and out of touch. Kuroda's scholarship and the scholarship of his interpreters and contemporaries demonstrate that this was not the case.[9] Pure Land developed within *kenmitsu* culture, not apart from it.

## Approaching Kakuban, Dōhan, and the "Multiple Logics" of early medieval Japanese Buddhism

Payne, as I note above, provided the scaffolding for a new kind of scholarship that recognizes the distorting effects of overreliance on national, linguistic, and sectarian boundaries as the guiding heuristics in the field of Buddhist studies. By focusing on something as ubiquitous as aspiration for rebirth in the Pure Land Sukhāvatī and devotion to the Buddha Amitābha, scholars may transcend such boundaries and thereby reveal the fluid nature of not only Kamakura-era Buddhism, but of contemporary Buddhism, as typified by the multi-sectarian practices I encountered among contemporary Japanese Buddhists.[10]

Sanford's study of Kakuban 覚鑁 (1095–1143)[11] is helpful in tracing a "lineage" of Esoteric Pure Land thinkers.[12] His essay on Kakuban challenges the received notion of Esoteric Buddhism to a degree by demonstrating that Amitābha Buddha did indeed serve as a significant object of devotion in the

Japanese Shingon tradition. Most modern scholarship approaches Kakuban from the perspective of the Shingon school, wherein he has often been labeled as the "second founder" after Kūkai. What is missing from Sanford's investigation into the Pure Land in Kakuban's thought is a critical reassessment of our received image of the Shingon school. It is important to keep in mind that Shingon in the late-Heian period was an area of study constituted by a fluid network of often overlapping and competing lineages spanning virtually all major temple-shrine complexes throughout Japan; it was quite different from the contemporary sectarian institution that today bears the title "Shingon school."[13] By approaching Kakuban as a "syncretizer" of Pure Land and Esoteric Buddhism, Sanford treats these as two necessarily exclusive and stable entities.

Kakuban received training in various Shingon lineages, including those of Kōyasan and Miidera (a temple commonly associated with the Tendai school). He also studied in the Hossō tradition of Kōfukuji. If we reduce Kakuban to being just a Shingon monk, though he was indeed an extremely important systematizer of the ritual and doctrinal works of Kūkai, we miss something important about the complexity of his identity and context. His Esoteric reading of the Buddha was but the tip of the iceberg of a much more pervasive Esoteric approach to Pure Land rebirth within the Mahayana tradition.

Kakuban's approach to Pure Land thought engaged and destabilized the polarities of samsara and nirvana via the *himitsu nenbutsu* (秘密念仏 Esoteric *nenbutsu*) in his major works.[14] But during Kakuban's time, there was not a "normative" view or tradition that we could call "Pure Land." In Kakuban's context, in the recently revitalized Kōyasan, Pure Land practice was a dominant mode of engagement with the legacy of Kūkai, by then regarded as a bodhisattva-like savior figure aiding beings in the attainment of Pure Land rebirth. Kakuban never had to "syncretize" Pure Land and Esoteric Buddhism. By the time he came on the scene, on Kōyasan and elsewhere, Pure Land was already very "Esoteric" in orientation, and Esoteric Buddhism was often employed to aid beings in the attainment of Pure Land rebirth. Before and after Kakuban's career, several of the most important Kūkai studies revivalists were also keenly interested in Pure Land practices.[15]

Traditions and lineages are always already in a state of flux and transformation, nodes in an interconnected net of different Buddhist traditions and practices blending, borrowing, and occasionally stealing from one another. Kakuban, his predecessors, his contemporaries, and those who followed should then be understood as participants in this complex intersectional dialogue and exchange, not as representatives of one tradition "syncretizing" with another.

Sanford also examines the thought of Dōhan 道範 (1179–1252), commonly regarded as the inheritor of Kakuban's Esoteric Pure Land thought. Dōhan was an early medieval scholar-monk on Kōyasan and a contemporary of Shinran. Like Kakuban, Dōhan was a specialist in the doctrinal works of Kūkai and wrote extensively on the major works of the East Asian Esoteric Buddhist tradition. Dōhan seems to have had some contact with monks who were associated with or responding to the growing movement we now associate with Hōnen and Shinran. As with Kakuban, Sanford suggests that Dōhan is another syncretizer of Pure Land and Esoteric Buddhism, but like Kakuban, I would argue that Dōhan is clearly participating in a broader Esoteric Pure Land culture.

Sanford examines Dōhan's understanding of the "breath of life," *myōsoku* 命息, which Dōhan argues is the very presence of the Buddha in/as the life force of infinite sentient beings (infinite beings = infinite life = Amitāyus), the compassionate activity of the Dharmakāya Mahāvairocana Buddha. Sanford suggests that Dōhan's innovation, however, is not a substitution but a conflation of Amida with Mahāvairocana Buddha, the all-inclusive Dharmakāya.[16] In Dōhan's understanding, the Pure Land is present within this embodied realm, not merely located far away. Beings and buddhas, this defiled realm and the pure lands, are but nodes in a broader net, all of which are but aspects of the *dharmakāya*. Therefore, everything is interconnected. Therefore, one does not have to wait until death to encounter the Buddha because it is happening each moment you are alive. This is called *sokushin ōjō* 即身往生, "in this very body, rebirth in the Pure Land."

Stone's work on deathbed practice, which reveals the dynamic way in which deathbed practices served as a site for the conflation of multiple modes of Buddhist thought and practice—which she describes as "multiple logics"[17]—is instructive here. She suggests that a closer reading of Dōhan's perspective on the Pure Land seems to ultimately allow a kind of tension to remain between samasara and nirvana, between this world and the Pure Land, between buddhas and beings. This unresolved tension appears to be a feature of Dōhan's thought shared with Kakuban to a degree.[18] It is possible that this perspective may draw upon the Tendai three-truths (三諦 *santai*) model wherein ultimate reality, provisional reality, and the "middle," the point of view that renders both ultimate and provisional reality one-yet-two, all stand together. That the "going" to the Pure Land is a "non-going" does not mean that nothing happens at the moment of death. For Dōhan, it would seem, awakening in this very body and the attainment of rebirth in the Pure Land are one event perceived from different vantage points.[19] In other words, the provisional reality of the Pure Land is still a kind of reality.

With Payne's critique of the distorting effects of normative sectarian prescriptivist historiography helping to guide our reading of this material, the apparent novelty of Dōhan and Kakuban's views are shown to be a byproduct of our contemporary founder-sect-doctrine lens (and their resultant blind spots). Dōhan's views were not novel for his time, nor were they unprecedented in the broader scope East Asian Mahayana tradition. Of the many ritual technologies available to the Mahayana Buddhist ritual master, the rituals associated with Esoteric Buddhism were widely regarded as a potent source of power to accomplish both this-worldly and otherworldly goals. Of the many goals a Buddhist might seek to achieve, Pure Land rebirth was certainly one of the most ubiquitous and sought after. While Sanford's approach begins from a position that essentializes both Esoteric Buddhism and Pure Land Buddhism as two inherently distinct paths that were "syncretized" by Esoteric Pure Land thinkers, Stone, by emphasizing praxis, is able to get at the very concrete ways in which those things typically labeled as "Esoteric Buddhism" and "Pure Land Buddhism" are able to occupy the very same space, functioning together as the warp and weft of a rich tapestry.

## Taking the Vajrayana to Sukhāvatī

One of Payne's contributions to this ongoing conversation includes his article on the Esoteric fire ritual dedicated to the Buddha Amitābha (*Amida keiai goma*).[20] He describes the fourfold ritual program known as the *shido kegyō*, which concludes with training in the performance of *goma* fire rituals. The first of the four phases of this training regime is the *jūhachidō* 十八道, wherein the trainee learns a series of *mudrās* and mantras and a kind of ritual template: entering into a ritual arena; establishing a sanctified space; inviting a buddha, bodhisattva, god, or some other deity into the space; communing with and in some sense becoming that deity; employing that deity's power in the world; and sending them back to their pure land.

This ritual template is used in many Esoteric rituals.[21] One of the texts used to design this portion of the training regime in the Shingon tradition is the *Wuliangshou rulai guanxing gongyang yigui* (無量壽如來觀行供養儀軌, T. 930), translated (or composed) by Amoghavajra 不空 (705–774).[22] Orzech argues that Amoghavajra seems to be drawing upon the *Contemplation Sūtra* (觀無量壽經, T. 365) in the composition of this text, for which he adapted a fairly common Esoteric deity yoga practice.[23] This is not to say, however, that "Pure Land" content is lacking in the East Asian Esoteric corpus; far from it. Texts such as the *Dhāraṇīsaṃgraha-sūtra* (陀羅尼集經, *T*. 901), for example, which is likely highly reflective of the medieval Indian context out of which later Esoteric systems developed, is notable for its significant Pure Land content.[24]

The second and third component of the *shido kegyō* includes an expansion of the *jūhachidō* template to include practices associated with the Kongōkai and Taizōkai mandalas, respectively.[25] Aside from Mahāvairocana himself, Amitābha/Amitāyus is the only other buddha to appear in both mandalas on the central dais, and historically, the Lord of Sukhāvatī has indeed been, and remains, one of the most popular central objects of devotion within Shingon temples.

The fourth component includes a similar expansion to include the performance of the fire ritual about which Payne has written extensively. Across Asia, from Iran to Japan, versions of this fire ritual are ubiquitous. Payne highlights how this Esoteric ritual could be deployed to engage with the Buddha Amitābha, which, he intuits, may be surprising to some readers:

> It would be easy to assume, as several scholars seem to have done, that the presence of Amida in the Shingon tradition is a reflex to the rise of Pure Land Buddhism in the Kamakura era—the presumption being that members of the Shingon tradition were attempting to take advantage of the popularity of Amida for their own purposes. Again, the situation is more complex. It is no doubt the case that there was a certain amount of competition with the increasingly popular Pure Land traditions—not only through the promotion of Amida, but also through the promotion of other, "simple" practices such as *ajikan* (visualization of the syllable *A*, written in the Siddham script). However, it is also the case that Amida was an important part of Shingon practice in Japan prior to the Kamakura era, and in the tantric tradition as a whole as well.[26]

Here again, by focusing on praxis, Payne directly addresses the methodological blind spots that have rendered invisible this important dimension of Esoteric Buddhism.

## Conclusion: How to think about Esoteric Pure Land Buddhism

As I have outlined above, Payne has had a significant impact on the field of Buddhist studies in many areas, as the other essays in this volume attest. In this chapter I have outlined briefly the ways in which his work as a scholar, editor, and

Buddhist thinker in his own right has also created space in the field for thinking about the "overlap" between Pure Land Buddhism and Esoteric Buddhism. There is still much to be done to better understand how Buddhists in East Asia and beyond "rode the Vajrayana to the Pure Land." What is Esoteric Pure Land Buddhism? Do we find it in a lost lineage of patriarchs: Atikūṭa, Amoghavajra, Kūkai, Kakuban, Dōhan, etc.? Do we find it in a lost textual corpus that scholars have neglected: *Dhāraṇīsamgraha*, *Wuliangshou rulai guanxing gongyang yigui*, *Amida hishaku*, *Himitsu nenbutsu shō*? I think not. Instead, I would argue that Esoteric-Pure Land Buddhism emerges as a distinct "kind" of Buddhism only if we forget the way that the taxonomic approach to the study of Buddhism precluded us from seeing this, and many other, dimensions of Mahayana Buddhist culture. As Payne notes,

> The terms and categories employed are in large part our own creation, and [we must] avoid reifying them by turning them into objects existing independently of our use. As such, we are responsible for the terms we use and for using them with adequate reflection on the presuppositions they bring—often covertly—into the field.[27]

Due to the distorting effect produced by taking contemporary sectarian rubrics too literally, we tend to assume a greater degree of coherence, an unchanging "essence" (Skt. *svabhāva*) that transcends time and space. As a scholar of Buddhism, however, I tend to emphasize the contingent nature of these labels, their "emptiness" (Skt. *śūnyatā*). In other words, the term "Esoteric-Pure Land Buddhism" is simply a heuristic device, a kind of fiction, an academic *upāya*, that allows us to better see certain aspects of Mahayana practice that have often gone unnoticed, while also pointing out the "emptiness" of all such labels as "Esoteric Buddhism" and "Pure Land Buddhism."

By pointing out the important areas of overlap between "Esoteric Buddhism" and "Pure Land Buddhism" the essentialist way of reading both may be called into question, perhaps inviting scholars to reevaluate their objects of inquiry not simply as "kinds" (or species) of Buddhism, but as discourses within Mahayana Buddhism that are articulated in different ways, in different times.

Part Two

# Textual Studies

Philology and textual studies continue to play a crucial role in Buddhist studies' methodological toolbox. More than merely the translation of texts or a concern for a text's origin or authenticity, textual studies shares with historical studies a concern for the past and thus reveals the complex development of Buddhist practices and interactions with broader cultural trends.

Part 2 opens with a translation and study by Charles Willemen, "A Scriptural Text about Impermanence." Willemen is concerned with the development of this text over time and how various ritual practices found their way into the text, practices that are part of multiple Buddhist traditions.

Takuya Hino presents a translation and study of the short text *Oni no Shikogusa*, popularized by Buddhist poets and monastics during the eleventh and twelfth centuries in Japan. Whereas the story features the familiar Confucian concern for filial piety, in the hands of esoteric Buddhists, it takes on new meaning in the development of rituals to placate disease-spreading spirits.

The final chapter in this section takes as its starting point a single practice rather than a single text. Charles Orzech concerns himself with the practice of seeing or visualizing the thirty-two major and eighty minor marks of a buddha, a practice referenced in multiple texts across different Buddhist traditions, languages, and times. Do these references point to a discrete practice rather than mere iconography?

Taken as a group, these examples of textual studies show this method's penchant for both focus and breadth, studies that dig deep into a single text or practice as well as those practices that overflow into non-Buddhist arenas or across traditions and time.

4

# Yijing's *Scriptural Text about Impermanence* (*T.* 801)

Charles Willemen

Yijing 义净 (635–713), who traveled to Sumatra and India from 671 to 695, is responsible for the Chinese text entitled *Wuchang jing* 无常经 (*Anitya-sūtra*, *T.* 801.17:745b7–746b8). The *Wuchang jing* includes a ritual supplement called "How to Bid Farewell in the End" (746b9–747a15). The Dunhuang 敦煌 text *T.* 2912, *Foshuo wuchang san qi jing* 佛说无常三启经 (*Buddhabhāṣita, Three Statements*), agrees well with *T.* 801. There is no original Sanskrit text extant. A 2010 translation of the *Anityatā-sūtra* by Bhikṣuṇī Vinītā[1] is quite different. The Chinese version, *T.* 158, *Foshuo zhuxing youwei jing* 佛说诸行有为经 ("all formations [*zhuxing*, *saṃskāras*] are formed [*youwei*, *saṃskṛta*]"), was done by Fatian 法天 (Dharmadeva) in 984. In the Song Translation Bureau the term *anitya* (impermanent) was regularly translated as *youwei* (*saṃskṛta*, "formed").) The *Fa ji yao song jing* 法集要颂 (*Udānavarga* 经, *T.* 213), chapter 1, *Youwei pin* 有为品, done in 985 by Śāntideva (Tian Xizai 天息灾), translating the *Udānavarga*, chapter 1, *Anityavarga*, does the same.[2] The title of *T.* 801, *Wuchang jing*, could well be the *Anitya-sūtra*.

Zhisheng's 智昇 catalogue dated 730, the *Kaiyuan lu* 开元录 (*T.* 2154.55:567c21), informs us that the Chinese translation also had the title *San qi jing* 三启经 (*Scriptural Text of Three Statements*) and that it dates from October 28, 701, the twenty-third day of the ninth month of Dazu 大足 1. It was made by Yijing at the Great Fuxian Monastery (Da Fuxian Si 大福先寺) in the Eastern Capital 东都, that is, Luoyang 洛阳.[3] The word *qi* 启, "to state, to inform," translates such words as *ākhyā*°, "to declare." *San qi* may thus be understood as "tripartite statement." A note inserted into chapter 12 of Yijing's *Nanhai jigui neifa zhuan* 南海寄归内法传 (*Record of the Inner Law Sent Home from the South Seas*, *T.* 2125.54:216c10), completed in Palembang, Sumatra no later than

691, informs us that the text was sent to China from Sumatra. Yijing himself may have inserted the note. The official publication of the complete Chinese text took place in 701 in Luoyang. Yijing had already written his travel account in Palembang, and he began translating the Mūlasarvāstivāda Vinaya.[4]

The text of the *Wuchang jing* is presented here.

## (745b7) *Scriptural Text about Impermanence* expounded by Buddha

Also called *Scriptural Text of Three Statements*

Translated by Yijing, Tripiṭaka Master of the Dharma of the Tang

I) I prostrate and take refuge in the Unsurpassed One.[5] He constantly raises his great vow, thoughts of great compassion, in order to save beings from the current of birth and death, so that they may obtain the safe[6] place of nirvana.

II) With great charity and guarding against what is wrong, with patient acceptance and without weariness, with application to undivided attention, and having the power of right wisdom,[7] he completely benefits himself and he benefits others. Therefore he is called Subduer, Teacher of Gods and Humans.[8]

III) I prostrate and take refuge in the treasury of the good Dharma. Its principle of three times four and of two times five is completely clear. The seven and the eight[9] can open the gate of the four truths. Its practitioners may all reach the shore of the unformed.[10]

IV) The cloud of the Dharma and the rain of the Dharma imbue all beings. They can do away with feverishness and eliminate any illness. They make those who are difficult to convert complaisant, giving guidance according to the circumstances, not by force.

V) I prostrate and take refuge in the congregation of true noble ones. The superior ones of the eight stages[11] may be free from taint. Their adamantine bolt of knowledge destroys the mountain of wrongness. They forever break their beginningless ties.

VI) From the Deer Park until the Twin Trees[12] they follow the entire life of Buddha, propagating the true teaching. Each in accordance with his former causality has practiced conversion. Their body of ashes and their knowledge of extinction[13] realize[14] the absence of rebirth.

VII) I prostrate and pay respect to all three precious and venerable things. They are called right causes, capable of universal salvation. When deluded about birth and death they guard against being submerged in them. They all allow one to escape to *bodhi.*

1. All who are born will die. Beauty will completely fade away. One's physical life-force is encroached upon by illness. No one can avoid this.
2. Even the Fine High Mountain[15] will completely crumble at the end of the eon. The great ocean, bottomlessly deep, will yet completely dry up.
3. The great earth, the sun and moon, all will turn to destruction when the time arrives. Never was there anything that was not swallowed by impermanence. (745c1)
4. Being born in the sphere without perception[16] on high, to a wheel-turning king[17] below, guarded by the seven precious things[18] on one's person, constantly surrounded by a thousand sons.
5. If one's life ends, in an instant and without stopping even for a while one will again drift in the sea of death, and [he or she] will experience every suffering in accordance with their causality.
6. One revolves in the three realms[19] just like when the wheel of a well is turned and draws up water, or just like when a silkworm, forming a cocoon, spins thread yet is itself bound up in it.
7. When even the unsurpassed World-honored Ones, *pratyekabuddhas*, and the multitude of disciples give up their impermanent bodies, how much more will the common people do so![20]
8. When one's parents and wife, siblings, and relatives observe the separation of birth and death, how could they not lament?
9. Therefore, all are urged to carefully listen to the true Dharma. Abandoning the place of impermanence, one should go to the deathless gate!
10. The Buddha's Dharma is like nectar. Doing away with heat, one obtains coolness. One should listen well [to the Dharma], with all one's heart! It can extinguish all afflictions.

Thus have I heard. At one time the Bhagavat was in the Jeta Grove in the city of Śrāvastī, in the Garden of Anāthapiṇḍada. The Buddha said to the *bhikṣus:*

> There are three kinds of factors that are undesirable, not lustrous, that are unpleasant and disagreeable in all worlds. What are the three? Namely, old age, illness, and death. O *bhikṣus*, old age, illness, and death in all worlds are really

undesirable, not lustrous, unpleasant, and disagreeable. If there were no old age, illness, or death in the world the Tathāgata, the Worthy One, the Completely Awakened One, would not appear in the world, expounding the Dharma he has realized for beings in order to subdue these [things]. Therefore, know that old age, illness, and death in every world are undesirable, not lustrous, unpleasant, and disagreeable. Because of these three things the Tathāgata, the Worthy One, the Completely Awakened One,[21] appears in the world, expounding to beings the Dharma he has realized and subduing them.

Then the World-honored One further spoke these verses:

1. The splendor[22] of external things will all turn to destruction, and one's own body will likewise perish. Only the excellent Dharma will not be extinguished. Wise ones should examine this well!
2. Old age, illness, and death are disliked by all. Their appearance is ugly and utterly disgusting. A youthful complexion remains only a short while and before long it will completely wither away.[23] (746a1)
3. Even if one were to live a full hundred years, in the end [he or she] will inevitably turn to and be compelled by impermanence. The suffering of old age, illness, and death always follows, constantly causing disadvantages for beings.

When the World-honored One had expounded this scripture the multitude of *bhikṣus*, gods (*devas*), dragons (*nāgas*), *yakṣas*, *gandharvas*, and *asuras* were all very glad then. They faithfully accepted and followed it.

1. Constantly wishing for the objects of desire, not practicing what is wholesome, how can one preserve one's corporeal life while not seeing the approaching encroachment of death!
2. When the vital force of the faculty of life[24] is about to end, the limbs and joints all separate. All suffering accompanies death. At that moment one can only sigh in grief.
3. Both eyes turn upward and the sword of death comes down, following one's actions. The mind is completely terrified. No one can save you!
4. One gasps deeply and the chest is agitated. One chokes[25] and their throat is dry. The king of death is on the lookout for your life. Relatives attend you in vain.
5. All consciousnesses[26] turn dark as one enters the dangerous fortress.[27] Your kinspeople all abandon you and let the rope drag you away.

6. You will reach King Yama and experience your retribution according to your actions. With excellent causes you will be born in a wholesome destination, but with evil actions you will fall into *niraya* (hell).
7. Among clear eyes none surpasses wisdom, and no darkness surpasses delusion. Illness is not overcome by any enemy, and among great fears none surpasses death.
8. All who are born will certainly die. The misdeeds one has done will cause the body to suffer. Be diligent tallying your three actions,[28] and always develop merit and knowledge![29]
9. All your relatives will abandon you and your riches will be taken by others. Just hold on to your wholesome faculties! The dangerous path has ample provisions.
10. Just as one rests for a while under a tree by the side of the road, not stopping long, one's carriages and horses, wife and children, will all soon be like that (i.e., fleeting).
11. Take, for instance, a flock of birds. At night they gather but at dawn they fly away. At death one goes away, departing from one's kinspeople. This separation is like that too.
12. Only the Buddha's *bodhi* is a true and reliable place of refuge. I[30] have given a brief explanation according to the scriptural texts. The wise should reflect on it well!

I) Gods, *asuras*, *yakṣas*, and others, those who come to listen to the Dharma should be utterly earnest! (746b1) They should uphold Buddha's Dharma so that it may last long! Everyone should diligently practice the teaching of the World-honored One!

II) All disciples who are listening, either on the ground or dwelling in the air, you should come to this! Always give rise to friendly thoughts for the human world! Personally abide in the Dharma, night and day!

III) May all worlds always be safe, and may endless merit and knowledge[31] benefit beings! May all evil actions be done away with! May you, free from any suffering, turn to perfect rest!

IV) Always anoint the bright body with the fragrance of morality, and constantly take the potion of concentration to sustain the body! Adorned all over with the fine flower of *bodhi*,[32] may you always be happy, wherever you stay!

According to the Vinaya.

The *San qi jing, Sutra of Three Statements,* is mentioned in fascicle 23 of Yijing's *Genbenshuoyiqieyou bu pinaiye* 根本说一切有部毗奈耶 (*Mūlasarvāstivāda Vinayavibhaṅga* [?], *T.* 1442.23:753c18, 753c25), translated in 703 at Ximing Temple 西明寺 in Chang'an 长安. The *Tripartite Statement* is also mentioned in fascicle 4 of Yijing's *Genbenshuoyiqieyou bu pinaiye zashi* 根本说一切有部毗奈耶杂事, dated 710 (*Mūlasarvāstivāda Vinaya Kṣudrakavastu, T.* 1451.24:223b21), and also in fascicle 18 (286c13, 287a2). The very long *Kṣudrakavastu* (*Zashi; Miscellaneous Elements*), which gives instruction for rituals, increased over time. We know that the non-Vaibhāṣikas were very diverse, so the *Kṣudrakavastu* may also show regional differences. Quite possibly the *Tripartite Statement* is a relatively recent addition to the *Kṣudrakavastu* Vinaya (*T.* 1442) and the first instance of *T.* 1451 mentions the text in the context of praise for the Buddha's qualities. The second instance of *T.* 1451 mentions the use of the text for cremations, just as *T.* 801 does. Chapter 12 of the *Nanhai zhuan* (*T.* 2125:216c10) also mentions the use of the text for cremation ceremonies. In the same text, Chapter 32, *Zanyong zhi li* 赞詠之礼 (227a7–227a24), explains the recitation of the sutra. *Zanyong* has the meaning of *kāvya, stotra*, "hymn of praise."

Yijing describes a ritual practiced in Tāmralipti (Danmolidi 耽摩立底), at the Bay of Bengal (227a4). In the passage Aśvaghoṣa (Maming 马鸣) is said to have "put together" (*jizhi* 集置) the *San qi jing* (227a14). Aśvaghoṣa and Mātṛceṭa are sometimes said to belong to a vehicle of those who praise the Buddha, *zanfo cheng* 赞佛乘 (*stotrayāna*?). It makes perfect sense that Aśvaghoṣa, a Sarvāstivādin influenced by (Bahuśrutīya?) Mahāsāṅghika views, is mentioned in the Mūlasarvāstivāda context here. He indeed may have composed—"put together"—the sutra. Yijing is also the translator of Mātṛceṭa's 150 hymns, the *Śatapañcāśatka* (*T.* 1680, *Yibai wushi zan fo song* 一百五十赞佛颂; *Buddhastotra*) at Nalantuo Si 那烂陀 (Nālandā Monastery).

So it is clear that there was a text, also known as the *San qi, Tripartite Statement*, used for ritual purposes. On the one hand, it was used to praise Buddha's qualities, and on the other, it was used for cremation ceremonies. Aśvaghoṣa is mentioned as the composer.

## Aśvaghoṣa's *Tripartite Sutra*

Fascicle 50 of the *Mahāvibhāṣā* (*T.* 1545.27:153c19) also mentions a *San qi* 三契. *Qi* means *qijing* 契经, *sūtra*; *San qi* thus means *Tripartite Sutra*. The

*Mahāvibhāṣā* was a new commentary on the new Sanskrit *Jñānaprasthāna* produced in Kaśmīra during the time of King Kaniṣka (155–179).[33] Kaniṣka was probably not a direct disciple of Aśvaghoṣa, as legend has it; Aśvaghoṣa probably lived ca. 100 C.E., or somewhat before that date.[34] This is also said to be a reason why Sanskrit was used for the new Sarvāstivāda "orthodoxy" in Kaśmīra. The *Mahāvibhāṣā* was completed after Kaniṣka's death. Aśvaghoṣa is also mentioned more than once in the first chapter, *Anityavarga,* of the *Chuyao* (*Udāna*) *jing* 出曜经 (*T*. 212), where he is said to be a Venerable One of previous times (*Xiri zunzhe Masheng* 昔日尊者马声, 613c21).

It is too great a coincidence that Aśvaghoṣa, who is said to have "put together" an *Anitya-sūtra*, is mentioned only in the *Anityavarga* of the Chinese *Udāna* 出曜经. An Aśvaghoṣa (Masheng 马声) is attributed as the author of some stanzas: 613c22–23 (Chinese Uv I 7) and 24–25; 616a16–17 (Chinese Uv I 14); and 626a2–3. A stanza at 614a5–6 is quite similar to the Chinese Uv I 9, but Aśvaghoṣa is not mentioned by name. The initial stanza 7 has a concordance with the Chinese Uv I 24. It is clear that the first chapter, *Anitya°*, of the *Udāna*[*varga*], and verses in Yijing's *Wuchang jing* are the work of Aśvaghoṣa.

The *Fu fazang yinyuan zhuan* 府法藏因缘传 (*T*. 2058), attributed to Ji Jiaye 吉迦夜 (Kekāya) from Xiyu 西域 (the Western Regions, Central Asia, perhaps the Bactrian region in the Gandhāran cultural area), and to Tanyao 昙曜, who initiated the construction of the cave temples at Yungang 云岗 at the end of the fifth century. Note 472, fascicle 5 of this text, which is most likely an apocryphal work of the sixth century, praises Aśvaghoṣa as a musician and a singer (315a28–b1). He is said to have introduced the practice of chanting, the musical recitation of hymns in praise of the Buddha.[35]

Li Rongxi translates Yijing's words in Chapter 32 of the *Nanhai zhuan:*

> The recitation mostly consists of three statements selected and arranged by Venerable Aśvaghoṣa. The first statement, containing about ten stanzas, is a hymn praising the three honored ones according to the contents of the scriptures. The second statement is the full text of the scripture recited, which consists of the words of the Buddha. After the conclusion of the hymn and the reading of the scripture, a resolution is made in more than ten stanzas for the transference of merits. As the recitation is divided into three sections, it is known as the three statements.[36]

In 1966 Kanaoka Enshō, drawing from Lin Liguang's 1949 research, said that the text as described by Yijing is indeed by Aśvaghoṣa.[37] He inspired more Japanese scholars to study the text; for example, in 1970–1971 Sasaki Kyōgo looked into the use of the titles *Wuchang jing* 无常经 and *San qi jing* 三启经 and placed the text in a Mūlasarvāstivāda context; Tokiya Yukinori/Kōki in 1985–1986 pointed out the difference between the Tibetan *Anityatā-sūtra* and Yijing's text and researched the use of the text in Chinese and Tibetan literature, distinguishing different kinds of burial; and in 1990–1991 Terasaki Keidō offered a synopsis of the religious uses of the sutra. But what is exactly Aśvaghoṣa's part? It is obvious that the text of the *Wuchang jing* (*T*. 801), as given in the English translation above, does not completely agree with Yijing's description. It contains VII (the triple refuge, VI + I) plus ten stanzas as Part I, followed by the brief sutra. Part III contains twelve + IV stanzas. Furthermore, why the change of title from *San qi* 三契 (*Tripartite Sutra*) to *San qi* 三启 (*Tripartite Statement*)?

## Composition of the text

Stanzas I–VII contain ideas that are not immediately linked with Aśvaghoṣa's Sarvāstivāda ideas. Stanza II, on the six perfections (*pāramitās*), is instead Mahāsāṅghika (Mahayana). Of course, the six perfections were known to Sarvāstivādins too. Stanza V, on the "adamantine bolt of knowledge" (*jingang zhi chu* 金刚智杵), reminds one of esoteric Buddhism as it may have been seen in Yijing's Tang times, and also in Sumatra. Vajrabodhi (Jingangzhi 金刚智, 671–741), a younger contemporary of Yijing, went to China after a stay in Sumatra (Śrī Vijaya), where he further studied the Mantrayāna. Even though the Mantrayāna is a Mūlasarvāstivāda development (taking in Hindu *yoga*), this kind of esoteric *yogācāra* did not exist in Aśvaghoṣa's non-Vaibhāṣika Sarvāstivāda times. The heptasyllabic verses of stanzas I–VII cannot be said to be Aśvaghoṣa's text. They were added later, when the text was being used for ritual purposes, adding a triple refuge. The first stanza VII actually suffices for the triple refuge. So it appears that parts I–VI were added later, even after VII. Keeping a balance with the initial part, sections I–IV were added at the end. The initial parts I–VI plus ten verses, and the final twelve verses plus parts I–IV add up to the same number.

The ten pentasyllabic stanzas 1–10 are the work of Aśvaghoṣa, as shown by the research of Lin Liguang and Kanakura Enshō. For example, stanza 2 can be found in the Chinese *Buddhacarita* (XX 31).[38]

The brief sutra itself is quite acceptable to all Sthaviravādins (i.e., non-Mahāsāṅghikas), as well as to Sarvāstivādins. Its three Chinese stanzas, in heptasyllabic format, may date from Tang times and are likely Yijing's translations.

The twelve pentasyllabic stanzas that follow the sutra are Aśvaghoṣa's work, as shown by Kanakura and Lin. For example, stanza 11 is found in the Chinese

*Buddhacarita* (VI 44).[39] In stanza 12c the "I" refers to Aśvaghoṣa. He ends this work in a very similar way to how the *Buddhacarita* ends, with a stanza (Chinese XXVIII 80)[40] rendered in the first person.

Stanzas I–IV at the very end do not show any trace of the idea of transference of merit, *pariṇāmaṇa*. Transference of merit may have occurred in a verse that was recited after the text proper. The sutra says only that the Buddha's doctrine, the Dharma, should be followed, and that *bodhi* is the only reliable place of happiness. These final stanzas make perfect sense in terms of offering solace to mourners and they were added for ritual purposes, such as a cremation ceremony, an especially appropriate occasion for the transference of merit. Li Rongxi, translating Yijing's words in Chapter 32 of the *Nanhai zhuan*, says:

> According to the teachings of the Buddha, when a *bhikṣu* is dead and his death has been ascertained, the corpse is carried to a crematorium, . . . A competent monk is asked to recite from the *Anitya-sūtra* . . . as little as half a page or one page.[41]

In Sengyou's 僧祐 catalogue *Chu san zang ji ji* 出三藏记集, dated 518, there is a *Wuchang jing* 无常经 of one fascicle (*T.* 2145:28b19). There is no mention of *san qi* 三契 or *san qi* 三启. Impermanence was a quite common subject in Buddhist literature, so this text may be unrelated to Yijing's text. On the other hand, however, it is not impossible that the *San qi* 三契 is meant here.

## Facts and insights

Aśvaghoṣa compiled a *Tripartite Sutra*, a *San qi* 三契, consisting of ten stanzas plus a brief sutra, followed by another twelve stanzas. Because this text offers the Buddha's teaching it could be called a sutra, as any traditional Sarvāstivādin would agree. Aśvaghoṣa was just such a traditional Sarvāstivādin, preceding the Vaibhāṣika "orthodoxy" that later, from ca. 200, can be called Sautrāntika, and Mūlasarvāstivāda from the end of the seventh century. The text was used for ritual purposes, to praise the Buddha's qualities, in line with Aśvaghoṣa's work. Because of its subject, impermanence, the *San qi* was also used for cremation ceremonies for monastics. A "triple refuge" was later added (first stanza VII), but it is difficult to say exactly when the first set of stanzas and the final stanzas were added.

The change of the title to, or with the addition of, *San qi* 三启, *Tripartite Statement*, seems also to be linked with the ritual use of the text. Is *San qi* 三启

Yijing's term? This term certainly predates the *Kaiyuan lu* of 730. This can be seen in Yijing's work and in manuscripts from Dunhuang. The initial stanza VI and the final stanza IV may have been added after Yijing had left Palembang, because in his description of the text in the *Nanhai zhuan*, recorded as he had heard it recited in Tāmralipti, these verses are not mentioned. The first stanza VII, on the triple refuge, may have been part of oral recitation. This stanza and Aśvaghoṣa's ten stanzas plus the sutra plus twelve stanzas may have been sent to China from Palembang by Yijing, who is certainly the translator of those stanzas as well as of the heptasyllabic verses in the short sutra. The addition "How to Bid Farewell in the End" may have happened after the first stanza VI and the final stanza IV were added. The addition of these stanzas may have been done by Yijing in Luoyang.

When did Aśvaghoṣa's text and its ritual use find its way into the *Kṣudrakavastu* of the traditional Sarvāstivādins (known as Mūlasarvāstivādins) at the end of the seventh century? We know that the Sarvāstivādins went through a period of Tripiṭaka formation in the second and early third centuries. The synod in Kaśmīra, where a new "orthodoxy" was created (consisting of a new *ṣaṭpāda* Abhidharma and an abbreviated Vinaya, the *Daśabhāṇavāra*) and the establishment of the *Udāna* as a member (*aṅga*) of the Buddha's twelve-part teaching (probably a Sarvāstivāda *Kṣudrakapiṭaka*),[42] reveal this fact. Aśvaghoṣa's *Tripartite Sutra* praising the Buddha's qualities, as mentioned in the *Mahāvibhāṣā*, may have been added at that time (*Kṣudrakavastu* fascicle 4). Later, due to its subject matter, the text was also used for cremations and added to the Vinaya (*Kṣudrakavastu* fascicle 18). In Luoyang, Yijing may have added stanzas (first VI and final IV) to the text, where it was used in cremation ceremonies for monastics.

5

# Dualistic and Bifunctional Spirits: A Translation of the *Oni no Shikogusa*

Takuya Hino

## *ONI NO SHIKOGUSA* (SPIRITS' WEEDS)[1]

[The origin and history of] the *Oni no shikogusa* (Spirits' Weeds) is [a story of "forgetting"] when long, long ago in a certain place, there was a man with two children. After their parents died, these children grieved at the death of their parents and never forgot [their parents' love] no matter how old they grew. Because in ancient times people buried corpses in piled-up mounds, the brothers went to visit the graves together as often as they yearned [and looked back fondly on the memories of their parents]. They cried over their parents' graves and discussed their pain and sadness, talking to their parents as if they were still alive. They did the same thing over and over.

After many years passed, the older brother, being a court official, spent all his time reminiscing about their parents [to such a degree that he] was hindered from doing his official duties by the reminiscences, and this increased his mental burden. He thought [about this] and said, "Even though I behave normally, I will never dispel this sorrow and suffering. 'Forgetting weeds' (*Hemerocallis fulva*) calm oneself." He planted the "forgetting weeds" close by the grave.

Subsequently, the younger brother often visited and asked his older brother, "Why don't you go visit the grave with me as usual?" His older brother took the initiative in engaging his work and did not go visit the grave. The younger brother sensed the unwillingness in his older brother's attitude and dedicated his time to filial affection night and day. He decided, "I will never forget [my parents' spirits]. 'Unforgetting weeds' (*Aster tataricus*) are for not forgetting what I think in my mind." He planted the "unforgetting weeds" close by the graves.

The younger brother became more and more determined to not forget and continued to visit the grave. One day, when he went to visit and looked at the graves, he heard a faint voice from the graves. It said, "I am a *preta* protecting your parents' corpses. Please don't be afraid. I am also thinking of protecting you." Though he was afraid, he continued to hear voices from the *preta*. The *preta* said, "You have a deep filial affection. It is as valuable as ever, even after this lapse of time. Your older brother felt sorrow and yearned for your parents as you had. Although he often went to visit the grave, he planted the "forgetting weeds" and attempted to cease remembering due to his official duties. It was successful. You planted the "unforgetting weeds"; your filial affection [toward your parents] is a sincere thing, and you are in the depths of sadness. My figure looks like a *preta*, but I have feelings of sympathy. In addition, I can foresee what will happen and will tell you in your dreams." He no longer heard the voice.

(After the incident, the younger brother always had dreams of what would happen the next day since the *preta* would tell him. When one hears this story, it is certain that the "unforgetting" weeds should be planted at one's house and always looked at for one who has cause for joy, not for one who has sadness.)

## Introduction

This chapter will examine a piece of medieval Japanese Confucian *waka* poetry called *Oni no shikogusa* 鬼のしこ草 (*Spirits' Weeds*), included in such medieval aristocrat manuscripts as the *Toshiyori zuinō* 俊頼髄脳 (*Secrets of [Minamoto no] Toshiyori*) and the *Konjaku monogatari* 今昔物語 (*Anthology of Tales from the Past*). The so-called "Tachikawaryū" 立川流 text, *Juhō yōjinshū* 受法用心集 (*Collection of Advice to Receive the Dharma*), which contains "heretical" doctrine of the Tachikawaryū (a religious movement focused on sexual rites and skull rituals), includes the narrative prose of the *Oni no shikogusa*. The story of the *Oni no shikogusa* appearing in the *Juhō yōjinshū* reveals a new facet of the Tachikawaryū and medieval Japanese esoteric Buddhist ideology: in the cult of making offerings to the dead, spirits come to be characterized as (1) honorific spirits and (2) vengeful spirits. These dualistic motifs underlie the twofold meaning of the *Oni no shikogusa*: spirits are perceived of as (1) the "unforgetting weeds" (*Aster tataricus*) and (2) the "forgetting weeds" (*Hemerocallis fulva*). In this chapter, which includes the first English translation of the *Oni no shikogusa*, I hope to engage in a new field of research in religious studies by investigating a philosophical or religious approach to medieval Japanese literature through the lens of botany.

Although the study of the *Toshiyori zuinō* and the *Oni no shikogusa* has done much for Japanese literature, little religious studies work has been done on these two literary manuscripts. In his study of the *Toshiyori zuinō*, Komine Kazuaki 小峯和明 takes as given that the *Oni no shikogusa* is based on the Chinese Confucian ideal of filial piety.[2] Moreover, he focuses heavily on Sensai 瞻西 ([?]–1127), a Tendai monk who was an expert sutra-preacher and *waka* poet, and asserts that Sensai began to preach and spread the *Oni no shikogusa* as a medieval Japanese Buddhist anecdote.[3] It is thought that Fujiwara no Nunetada 藤原宗忠 (1062–1141), a trusted vassal of Fujiwara no Tadazane, came to believe in the coming of Amida Buddha to welcome the spirits of the dead, and Komine argues that Minamoto no Toshiyori may have been a devout believer in Sensai's teachings. For this reason, it is believed that Sensai helped mold the *Oni no shikogusa* into a Buddhist anecdote. Takanose Keiko 高野瀬惠子 points out that though Minamoto no Toshiyori had much to do with Sensai, he and Fujiwara no Mototoshi 藤原基俊 (1060–1142) were rivals in *waka* poetry.[4] Akase Tomoko 赤瀬知子, building on previous scholarship, demonstrates that Toshiyori's approach to *waka* poetry had a significant impact on later poets, such as Kenshō 顕昭 (fl. twelfth century) and Fujiwara no Teika 藤原定家 (1162–1241).[5] Finally, Ikura Fumito 伊倉史人 points to the growing practice of pilgrimage around sacred places dedicated to Avalokiteśvara and demonstrates that the *Oni no shikogusa*, as a narrative describing spirits as guardian deities of graves, is related to Kannonji 観音寺, who is often referred to in Toshiyori's *waka* poems.[6] This scholarship reveals that there were many Buddhist poet-monks who played vital roles in popularizing *waka* poetry and spreading the ideas contained therein. The purpose of this article is to clarify the religious role of the *Oni no shikogusa* with attention to the concept of dualistic and bifunctional spirits as well as the intersection with Buddhist botany.

## Historical background

The *Oni no shikogusa*, compiled by Minamoto no Toshiyori 源俊頼 (1055–1129), first appears in a verse of the *Toshiyori zuinō*. It is unknown when exactly the *Toshiyori zuinō* was completed, but most scholars believe that it was written in the era between Ten-ei 天永 and Eikyū 永久 (1110–1117).[7] The *Toshiyori zuinō*, alternately called *Shunpishō* 俊秘鈔 (*Secret Notes of Toshiyori*), is a collection of treatises on *waka* poetry which is said to have been compiled for Fujiwara no Yasuko 藤原泰子 (1095–1156), a daughter of Fujiwara no Tadazane 藤原忠実 (1078–1162) and the wife of Emperor Toba 鳥羽天皇

(1103–1156; r. 1107–1123), by the direct order of Fujiwara no Tadazane.[8] Further investigation pertaining to when and for what reasons the *Toshiyori zuinō* was written is required. In its two volumes it defines new rules for composing *waka* poetry that attach importance to the history and tradition of *waka* poetry. By giving an example of *waka* poetry from the past, the *Toshiyori zuinō* uses tales to explain aristocratic rules of ceremony and etiquette in the society of court nobles. Subsequently, it became a medieval Japanese narrative of reminiscence, popularly known and repeated, that has since been handed down from generation to generation.

Scholars generally agree that the original manuscript of the *Toshiyori zuinō* no longer exists. It comes down to us in two versions, both based on manuscripts copied during the Kamakura period (1185–1333). One version of the *Toshiyori zuinō* is called *teikahon* (定家本) and the other *kenshōhon* (顕昭本).[9] The *Oni no shikogusa* appearing in the *Konjaku monogatari* is approximately the same length and is more concrete and detailed than the *Toshiyori zuinō* version.[10] Although the *Konjaku monogatari*, which was compiled around the same time as the *Toshiyori zuinō,* is said to have influenced the compilation of the *Toshiyori zuinō*, scholars are still debating which manuscript was completed first.[11] The *Oni no shikogusa* probably first appeared in the *Toshiyori zuinō* and later was formalized in the narrative literature of the *Konjaku monogatari.* The inherited beliefs and stories relating to the past that were commonly accepted as historical facts among medieval Japanese aristocrats became folk stories based on this popular literature. That the same story appears in various books indicates the pervasive popularity of oral literature in a society that had developed writing.

The *Oni no shikogusa* also appears in one version of the *Juhō yōjinshū.*[12] The *Juhō yōjinshū,* which was written by Jinjō 心定 (fl. thirteenth century) of Toyoharaji 豊原寺 in Echizen Province 越前 (modern-day Fukui Prefecture 福井), is a so-called "Tachikawaryū text," a text that contains the "sinister way" of the Tachikawaryū, such as skull rituals and sexual praxis. It comes down to us in two versions, both based on manuscripts written between the thirteenth and fourteenth centuries. One version is held at Kōzanji 高山寺 and the other at Zentsūji 善通寺.[13] The prose of the *Oni no shikogusa* appears only in Zentsūji version and is the same length and story as the *Toshiyori zuinō*. It is unknown exactly when and why the *Oni no shikogusa* was added.

It is possible that the *Toshiyori zuinō* was compiled in or around the first year of Eikyū (1113), when Ninkan 仁寛 (?–1114), the protector-monk (*gojisō* 護持僧) of

Prince Sukehito 輔仁親王 (1073–1119), put a curse on Emperor Toba 鳥羽天皇 (1103–1156; r. 1107–1123) in order to guarantee Prince Sukehito's succession to the throne; he was consequently exiled from the capital to a distant land, Izu Province 伊豆 (modern-day Shizuoka Prefecture 静岡). Perhaps in order to increase the legitimacy of the *Juhō yōjinshū* as a "Tachikawaryū text," the *Oni no shikogusa* was intentionally added. Another possibility is that the *Toshiyori zuinō* was written as an instruction manual for Empress Toba, Fujiwara no Taishi 藤原泰子 (1095–1156), for composing *waka* poetry. On Taishi's paternal side was Fujiwara no Tadazane 藤原忠実 (1078–1162), and on her maternal side was Minamoto no Akifusa 源顕房 (1037–1094), Ninkan's uncle. After the incident in which Ninkan put a curse on Emperor Toba, Murakami Genji 村上源氏, Ninkan's clan, is said to have fallen into extreme decadence. In addition, although Fujiwara no Tadazane was disfavored by Emperor Shirakawa, Emperor Toba called Fujiwara no Tadazane back to court and filled significant posts with his close aides by arranging for Tadazane's daughter, Fujiwara no Taishi, bridal entry into the court as an imperial consort. Though Tadazane restored the Fujiwara clan, the Fujiwara clan could not regain its former prosperity. After the Hōgen rebellion of 1156, Tadazane is believed to have become an angry spirit and to have cursed his descendants.[14] This story teaches that one should have tender affection for one's ancestors lest one's descendants perish and family be destroyed.

## Dualistic spirits

The bipartite Japanese religious view of dualistic spirits divides spirits into those who protect one's land and descendants (honorific spirits) and those who bring natural disasters and unnatural death (vengeful spirits). According to the *Nihon kiryaku* 日本紀略 (*Abbreviated Japanese Annuals*) entry for the twentieth day of the fifth month of the fifth year of Jōgan 貞観 (863), "honorific spirits" originally referred those who experienced political failure and died a miserable death.[15] One example of honorific spirits can be found in the *Honchō seiki* entry for the second day of the ninth month of the first year of Tengyō 天慶 (938), which reads as follows:

> Recently on the streets in the East and West capital, [people] carved wood, making [statues] of local deities, which they then enshrined. The body shape of these statues was completely robust, and crowns were put on [the statues' heads]. [The statues] had the hair on the temples hanging in pigtails down to the shoulders. The bodies of [the statues], painted with cinnabar, were the color

> of scarlet. In daily life, [the shape of the statues] were transformable. One after another, each statue had different forms. The shape of the female was carved so as to be robust, and stood upright. The image of the yin-yang was carved in the lower part of the waist, beneath the navel. Setting up a table in front of [the statue] and placing [the statue] on earthenware, [the statue] of a child was vulgar [in appearance]. Worshipping [the statue] was intimate, using a stick of silk strip [offered to the statue] or an offering of incense and flowers. [People] recited the guardian deities' names [*funado no kami* 岐神] and praised the honorific spirits [*goryō* 御霊].[16]

The guardian deity was seen as an honorific spirit who stood at the main and branch roads' crossings to prevent bad or suspicious activities that threaten body, soul, property, and honor from encroaching upon one's territory from another's territory. The honorific spirits must be prevented from invading one's territory and are identified as kind of fearful thing that nobody approaches.

Honorific spirits began to be linked to pestilence, which terrified people; thus, over time, the concept of spirits changed as they were integrated into a particular court ceremony passed from generation to generation. The ceremony consisted of three distinct but related rituals: the spirits' sign festival, the assembly for the honorific spirits, and the assembly of the recitation of the *Humane Kings Sutra*. The spirits' sign festival likely developed due to the tremendous extent of the smallpox epidemic. Descriptions of holding the spirits' sign festival appear in historical manuscripts and can be found in the *Nihon kiryaku* entry for the sixteenth day of the tenth month of the fifteenth year of Engi 延喜 (915).[17] This passage says that yin-yang masters carried out a service for purification at the gate of Kenrei 建禮門 due to the extent of the smallpox epidemic. Descriptions of holding the assembly for honorific spirits can be found in the *Nihon kiryaku* entry for the twenty-seventh day of the sixth month of the fifth year of Shōryaku (994).[18] The passage shows that this assembly was originally held for the dedication to a deity of plagues. The description of holding the assembly of the recitation of the *Humane Kings Sutra* can be found in the *Nihon kiryaku* entry for the eighteenth day of the intercalary fifth month of the fifth year of Kanpyō 寛平 (893).[19] This assembly was held because of the smallpox epidemic. The recitation of the *Humane Kings Sutra* was regarded as a prayer for averting celestial calamities, which were associated with pestilence.

The vengeful spirits (*kishin* 鬼神), alternately identified as the human mind, possess an invisible omnipotence and negatively influence humans and beasts.[20] A certain way of thinking was described as having "angry spirits," and this idea was eventually connected with the idea of honorific spirits.[21] The earliest mention of the "angry spirits" in Japanese historical manuscripts can be found in the *Nihon kiryaku* entries, where they are called the spirits of the dead (*mononoke* 物怪).[22] In medieval Japan, one example of the "angry spirits" paradigm is the vengeful spirits who were believed to wander from place to place and release pestilence upon the people. A clear definition of the vengeful spirits can be found in the *Honchō seiki*, an annalistic history divided into forty-seven imperial reigns that was compiled by Fujiwara no Michinori 藤原通憲 (1106–1159). It states that the spirits will bring misfortune not only to political opponents and enemies, but also to society, often in the form of epidemics.[23] More concretely, at least in Fujiwara no Michinori's view, the vengeful spirits were related to plagues; in our times the spirits can be described as "viruses" or "poisons" that cause disease in humans. According to the descriptions of the *Honchō seiki*, this idea of vengeful spirits originated when a great plague spread across Japan and killed many people during the regime of Emperor Ichijō 一条天皇 (980–1011; r. 986–1011), especially during the fifth year of Shōryaku 正暦 (995). Judging from the historical passages from the *Honchō seiki*, one can imagine that people in the capital at that time were thrown into confusion because the cause of the epidemic outbreaks was unknown.[24] For prevention of plagues, the court aristocrats held a special assembly for the recitation of the *Humane Kings Sutra*, which was considered the most effective religious text for ensuring the tranquility of the country.[25] Owing to the great epidemic outbreaks in the Shōryaku era, when a dramatic shuffle of court personnel, including top court officials, was carried out, Fujiwara no Michinaga 藤原道長 (966–1028) came to take leadership as the Minister of the Left, and the regency government reached its zenith.

People firmly believed that "demons" or "monsters" could deeply penetrate people's minds, and they began to fear getting close to the vengeful or wandering spirits in the capital. It was a belief among the people that proved to be popular in medieval Japan, particularly before the development of a distinct moral code among the samurai class. The *Honchō seiki* entry for the tenth day of the sixth month of the fifth year of Shōryaku states that people closed the gate due to being afraid of having strange dreams and that people took the day off to avoid getting close to the vengeful spirits.[26] Because the vengeful spirits stalked the streets in broad daylight, people closed the gate and waited patiently at home. These descriptions show that because the vengeful spirits (presently understood as disease-causing viruses) wandered from place to place, people were afraid of them entering their homes (which we now understand to be the prevention of spreading infection diseases).

## Bifunctional spirits

A mythological beneficent celestial spirit (the *preta*) appears in the story of the *Oni no shikogusa* and tells of the effects of the "unforgetting weeds" (*Aster tataricus*) and the "forgetting weeds" (*Hemerocallis fulva*) by giving a concrete example of filial piety to one's parents. This spirit is related to a sort of religious dualism. It is possible that the *Oni no shikogusa*, as *waka* poetry of Japanese proverbs, reveals the moral dualism of a theological framework that implies two opposite moral principles. One son is dedicated to his work; the other is dedicated to filial piety. Both were valued qualities in Heian society. Making distinctions between good and bad deeds is problematic because one's opinion is rooted in the contextual background of a historically particular culture and political climate, as well as one's personal circumstances. One may be prone to accepting arbitrary advice or acting on one's values by judging what is right or wrong or good or bad. But this judgment may be based on uncritically accepted knowledge or the authority of tradition. One's attitudes in ordinary daily life were believed to cause changes in one's twofold spirit; one spirit leaves the body after death and the other spirit remains with the corpse of the deceased. Confucian ideology itself includes bifunctional concepts: one should fulfill various virtues (such as loyalty, filial piety, contingency, honesty, etc.), while improving the five constants (benevolence, righteousness, proper rite, knowledge, and integrity).

The *Oni no shikogusa* describes filial affection using the language of *Aster tataricus*, which is also associated with two *waka* poems of the *Manyōshū* 万葉集 (*Collection of Ten Thousand Leaves*).[27] *Aster tataricus*, called *shion* 紫苑 in Japanese, was known among the Heian aristocrats.[28] The *waka* poetry shows that the *Oni no shikogusa* describes the "forgetting weeds" (*Hemerocallis fulva*) and the "unforgetting weeds" (*Aster tataricus*), both herbaceous perennials that wither in winter so that new shoots will grow the following spring. They are types of plants with flowers, which grow wild in fields and mountains. These two weeds have been valued and used as medical herbs and edible plants. The Heian aristocrats cultivated them as ornamental plants as well.

This example of Japanese *waka* poetry reveals that the plants were believed to contain spirits, which in turn created social customs. The two weeds can be seen to symbolize spiritual status, with different classes symbolized by plants of different kinds. Plants that produce good flowers have good roots. According to the *gātha* of the *Commentary on the Great Wisdom Sutra*, "If one seeds a field with grain, the seedlings, even though they are excellent, will not reach full growth because there are overgrown by weeds."[29] This reflects the idea that actions produce both seeds and roots. The blooming flowers that have good seeds and roots have a habit of doing good deeds. The weedy plants that take over a field represent the degree to which one has evil thoughts. Even if the leaves and stems become withered for some reason, the plants, if good roots still remain, will bear flowers.

Another way of framing the ideology pertaining to the bifunctional spirits is through the belief that plants possess spirits (or minds). This idea was put forth by Kūkai, who argued that plants have Buddha-nature.[30] This Buddhist view derives from the *Nirvana Sutra*, which claims that all sentient beings have Buddha-nature.[31] Because, like humans, plants have a limited lifespan, they must also have thoughts (or minds) clouded by delusion, and thus be sentient.[32] Deeper discussions of emotional qualities are apparent in Shingon esoteric Buddhism in discussions of Buddha-nature. If plants have Buddha-nature, are they are able to attain buddhahood through ascetic practices or do they even have the potential to attain buddhahood at all? In medieval Japanese esoteric Buddhism, plants do not possess intelligence per se but require air for respiration. Further, they are capable of nutrient intake and reproduction. Because the plants are living, they are always undergoing change according to environmental factors. This indicates that the plants are carrying out practice. They make up their minds to seek enlightenment by themselves; they never speak or move. In medieval Japanese esoteric Buddhist thought, true suchness, although tainted by the defilements to which human minds are attached, is equated with an original purity of the mind. Accordingly, defiled behavior, because it is ultimately the product of that originally pure mind, cannot be denied outright. The plants have the potential to be the Buddha as they really are. By planting seeds and growing plants, a human possibly realizes one's emotional possession (spirits) and sees oneself as having been kept alive by *nature*, which is itself the Buddha.

6

# A Note Concerning Contemplation of the Marks of the Buddha

Charles D. Orzech

## The marks that are no-marks

A passage in the *Vajracchedikā-prajñāpāramitā-sūtra* (*Diamond Sutra*) reads as follows:

> The Lord said, "What do you think, Subhūti? Can a Realized, Worthy, and Perfectly Awakened One be seen by virtue of the thirty-two Distinctive Features of a Great Man?" Subhūti said, "No indeed, Lord. Why is that? Whatever thirty-two Distinctive Features of a Great Man have been preached by the Realized One, Lord, have been preached by the Realized One as featureless. Therefore they are called 'the thirty-two Distinctive Features of a Great Man.'"[1]

There are other, similar passages in the scripture, and the logic is entirely in keeping with the agenda of undermining any substantive teaching contrary to the deconstructive doctrine of emptiness.[2] Thus, we also see the assertion that the Tathāgata espoused no teaching, and so on.[3] It should be noted that the passage implies more than mere seeing. Rather, what is being critiqued here is a kind of attentive fixing or apprehension. Indeed, the scripture begins with Subhūti's query about the proper way to meditate: "How, Lord, should one who has set out on the bodhisattva path take his stand, how should he proceed, how should he control the mind?"[4] In response to this query the scripture attacks any form of "fixing," "abiding," or "seizing" of objects or *dharmas* as proper meditative practice. For example:

> However, a bodhisattva should not give a gift while fixing on an object, Subhūti. He should not give a gift while fixing on anything. He should not give a gift while fixing on physical forms. He should not give a gift while fixing on sounds,

> smells, tastes, or objects of touch, or on *dharmas*. For this is the way, Subhūti, a bodhisattva should give a gift, so that he does not fix on the idea of the distinctive features (of any object). Why is that? Subhūti, it is not easy to take the measure of the quantity of merit, Subhūti, of the bodhisattva who gives a gift without fixation.[5]

And again:

> If the idea of a non-*dharma* should occur, for them that would constitute seizing upon a self, seizing upon a living being, seizing upon a soul [*ātmagrāho*], seizing upon a person.[6] Why is that? One should moreover not take up any *dharma*, Subhūti, or any non-*dharma*. It was therefore with this in mind that the Realized One said that those who understand the round of teachings of the Simile of the Raft should let go of the *dharmas* themselves, to say nothing of the non-*dharmas*.[7]

The target of this criticism (and it might almost be read sarcastically) appears to be specific devotional or meditational practices: "Can a Realized, Worthy, and Perfectly Awakened One be seen by virtue of the thirty-two Distinctive Features of a Great Man?" To what might the *Diamond Sutra* refer?

Passages on the thirty-two major and eighty minor "marks" are commonly taken to have an iconographic basis, and notions of these marks may have originated in oracular lore concerning physiognomy and childhood.[8] Recognizing these "arcane omens" involves a kind of spiritual acumen, yet scholars have seldom considered them to be linked to any meditative practice. However, there is considerable evidence that attention to the major and minor marks is linked to devotional and meditation practices.

James Egge examined passages concerning the Buddha's marks appearing in canonical texts from the Theravada traditions. According to Egge, the marks function in three overlapping but slightly dissimilar ways. In the first set of texts from the *Majjhima Nikāya*, the *Saṃyutta Nikāya*, and the *Theragāthā*, the brahmin Sela hears of the Buddha, visits him, and views his marks. Sela understands that the marks are significant but the Buddha has to inform him about their meaning, pointing out to Sela that he is not a *cakkavatin* but rather a king of the dhamma (*dhammarājā*). Sela and his entourage eventually take refuge.[9]

A second set of texts, including the *Lakkhaṇa-sutta*, assume that the import of such marks is unambiguous: they indicate the status of a buddha or a buddha-to-be, and in some cases viewing the marks elicits a display of devotion.[10] In a third set of passages found in the *Apadāna* the significance of the marks is self-evident and the sight of the marks precipitates immediate acts of devotion.[11]

None of the *Nikāya* texts present seeing the Buddha's marks as part of a formal meditative regime. Rather, they are linked to acts of devotion. But this does not mean the marks were not used as the focus of formal meditation.

The lore concerning the Buddha's marks is not confined to the canonical Theravada texts. Indeed, such lore is found throughout Buddhist works of all ideological stripes. Evidence from traditional meditation manuals and a range of Buddhist Mahayana and esoteric scriptures points to systematic meditative use.

Apprehending the body of the Buddha appears as a key element in certain visionary and meditation manuals examined by Nobumi Yamabe.[12] Thus, for instance, we see the following practice recommended in the *Scripture on Contemplation of the Buddha's Samādhi Ocean*:

> After the extinction of the Buddha there was a prince named Golden Banner (Jinchuang 金幢) who was haughty, held heterodox views (邪見), and did not believe in the Correct Dharma (正法). A wise monk named Samādhi Master (Dingzizai 定自在) told the prince: "There are Buddhist images decorated with various jewels and they are extremely lovely. You should go to a temple (塔) and observe (觀) the Buddha's image."[13] Then the prince, following the words of the good friend, entered the temple, observed the image, and saw the major and minor bodily marks. Then [the prince] told the monk: "Even an image of the Buddha [inspires] intense reverence. How much more so the real body of the Buddha!" When he said this the monk told him: "You have now seen the image. If you are unable to [go there and] worship it, you should chant: 'Homage to the Buddha.'" Then the prince held his hands in the *añjali* position and respectfully chanted: "Homage to the Buddha," and returning to the palace he held the image in the temple in mind (念念). Then, in the last watch of the night, in his dream, he saw the image of the Buddha. Because he saw the image of the Buddha, his heart was overjoyed and he abandoned his heterodox views and took refuge in the Three Jewels.[14]

The process depicted here of attentively viewing the marks, then being able to call them to mind in lieu of an external image, is a structured form of meditation that results in a visionary experience and, as we saw in the case of the brahmin Sela, also results in taking refuge in the Buddha. Other *chan* manuals found in Chinese translation and purporting to be translations of Indic texts, such as the *Scripture on Seated Meditation Samādhi* (坐禪三昧經, *T*. 614) and the *Scripture on the Secret Essential Methods of Meditation* (禪祕要法經, *T*. 613), prescribe observation of the Buddha and his marks, followed by withdrawal from the actual image in order to contemplate them mentally.[15]

> Thus should people be instructed in the single-minded recollection of the Buddha. There are three sorts of persons who can be instructed in the *samādhi*: those who are just beginning practice, those who have [commenced] practice already, and those who have practiced for a long time. If the person is just beginning, take him to an image of the Buddha or order him to go himself to attentively contemplate the major and minor marks of the buddha image. Each mark should be clearly recognized and held in mind (一心取持) while retiring to a quiet location. Contemplate the buddha image in the mind's eye, harnessing one's thought so as not to be distracted from recollection of the buddha image and do not allow other [kinds of] recollection.[16]

Yamabe points out that contemplation of the physical body of the Buddha and contemplation of his distinctive marks formed a part of practice both in the *śrāvakayāna* and in the bodhisattva path. Examining a variety of meditation manuals and "visualization" sutras, Yamabe notes that the visionary practices described in these works follow closely the structure of cemetery meditations found in the *Visuddhimagga* and in some Sanskrit works as well.[17] Indeed, when we examine the *Visuddhimagga*, we find not only meditations on the "foul" follow such structure, but many basic meditations connected with "mindfulness" (*satipaṭṭhāna*) also take this form.[18] For example, the meditation on the earth *kasiṇa* includes these instructions:

> The colour should not be reviewed. The characteristic should not be given attention. But rather, while not ignoring the colour, attention should be given by setting the mind on the [name] concept as the most outstanding mental datum. . . . When, while he is developing it in this way, it comes into focus as he adverts with his eyes shut exactly as it does with his eyes open, then the learning sign is said to have been produced. After its production he should no longer sit in that place; he should return to his own quarters and go on developing it sitting there . . . . Then if the new concentration vanishes through some unsuitable encounter, he can put his sandals on, take his walking stick, and go back to the place to re-apprehend the sign there. When he returns he should seat himself comfortably and develop it by reiterated reaction to it and by striking at it with thought and applied thought.[19]

The process prescribed here—attending to the object, seeing it clearly with eyes closed or open, retreating from the object while holding it in mind, and going back to the object if it cannot be recollected—corresponds to prescriptions found in the *Ocean Sutra* and other *chan* texts. The "calling to mind" of the Buddha is thus related to other applications of attentive recollection. Such practices of apprehending the body of the Buddha likely form the backstory to the passages in the *Diamond Sutra*.

## The Buddha's marks and the origins of "Deity Yoga"

It seems clear that a wide variety of Buddhists performed a kind of meditation that involved studying the bodily marks of the Buddha and then bringing them back into mind, and that this form of attentive awareness was structurally similar to other forms of contemplation, such as meditation on various *kasiṇa* and on the appearance of corpses.

Such forms of contemplation can be sharply distinguished from visionary experience detailed in esoteric and tantric texts of the eighth century and later. Esoteric and tantric texts are often structured by a visionary sequence involving the use of seed syllables (*bīja*). However, it is surprising that the so-called "tantric distinction," commonly defined as visualization of oneself in the body of a buddha or bodhisattva, predates the tantras and involves the Buddha's bodily marks.[20] Visionary programs in which one contemplates the Buddha's body and then imagines one's own body possessed of the marks can indeed be found in earlier texts. For instance, the fifth-century *Consecration Sutra* (灌頂經) includes instructions for imagining oneself as a buddha as a prophylaxis against evil spirits:

> You should first retain a recollection (存念) of your body in a likeness of my own image with the thirty-two marks and the eighty auspicious signs—a purple-golden body of sixteen feet with a radiant aura behind it like the sun. Having retained the thought (存想) of my body thus, next recollect the 1,250 disciples. Next recollect all the bodhisattvas and monks. Having completed the recollection of these three imaginings, moreover recollect the great spirits of the five directions. (*T.* 1331.21:515a25–29)

Here, in this well-known apocryphal text that predates what most scholars would consider tantra or esoteric Buddhism, we see contemplation of the Buddha's *lakṣaṇa* as a stage in imagining one's own body as possessed of the marks.[21] Perhaps an even more striking example can be found in the decidedly non-tantric *Guan jing*:

> Next one should imagine (想) buddha. How should one do this? All buddha-tathāgatas have a *dharmadhātu* body that enters (遍入) into all of the mental conceptions of the mass of living beings. Therefore, when a person mentally conceives of buddha, that [person's] mind is the thirty-two marks and the

> eighty auspicious signs. This mind that makes buddha is the mind that is buddha (是心作佛是心是佛). . . . Next, make a large lotus to the right of the buddha and imagine (想) the image of Avalokiteśvara Bodhisattva seated on the left side of the lotus throne emitting golden light rays, just like the previous [buddha].[22]

Not only is this a statement of mental apprehension, but the term "enter" used here (遍入) was also a standard Chinese translation for *āveśa* (阿尾捨, 扁入, etc.), indicating the process of entry in esoteric rites of possession as well as entry of the "wisdom being" in esoteric and tantric rites of consecration (*abhiṣeka* 灌頂).[23] This is not to say that the *Guan jing* is referring to a tantric *abhiṣeka*. Rather it is mistaken to categorically assert that imagining oneself in the body of the Buddha is distinctive of the Buddhist tantras. In turn, meditative contemplation of the Buddha's marks is found alongside deity yoga-type exercises in many tantric or esoteric manuals and is evidence of strong continuities in visual practices throughout Buddhist traditions.

## The marks in Esoteric manuals

The use of the marks as they appear in texts collected in volumes 18–21 of the Taishō canon can be classified into four types: those that are primarily iconographical, those with a philosophical agenda, those designed to procure a vision of the buddhas, and those that lead to obtaining the marks oneself. The iconographic use of the marks is straightforward and can be found in instructions for painting images and mandalas. Typical is this line from Yixing's *Commentary on the Mahāvairocana-sūtra*: "Next outward is the third court. Paint the sage-king of the Śakya clan wearing a *kāṣāya* robe and supplied with the thirty-two marks."[24] In contrast, and perhaps as an echo of the more abstruse concerns expressed in texts like the *Diamond Sutra*, we find some texts that take up more philosophical understandings of the Buddha's marks:

> Grasping (執取) the Tathāgata's marks refers to [recognizing] the Buddha's physical body of flesh and bones given birth by his father and mother. Bodhisattvas do not have these [marks]—why? The Tathāgata's body is like the mark of emptiness. Because it is marked by birthlessness they [the marks] do not clearly shine [forth]. But they are known everywhere on behalf of the mass of beings. In all the teachings they are manifestations of the Dharma body, but the Buddha's dharma-body has no place in the marks. Because [he is] completely

> lacking in marks [he] manifests the thirty-two marks. This is the profound meaning of the mark of birthlessness.[25]

Some manuals enjoin the worshiper to visualize the Buddha with all of his marks. The result of such practices is the appearance of *tathāgatas* before the worshiper:

> Imagine Amitāyus with his thirty-two marks and eighty auspicious characteristics each delineated. Then chant the mantra of the Buddha-Section *samaya*: chant it three times or seven times. Because of making this *mudrā* and chanting this mantra you will be awakened and perceive all of the buddhas of the Buddha Section who will assemble and empower, protect, and remember the practitioner of the mantra, and they will cause him to swiftly obtain purification of bodily karma, the elimination of crimes and obstructions, and an increase in blessings and wisdom.[26]

Yet other manuals recommend contemplation of the marks as part of a process deploying mantra and *mudrā* and extend this to one's own attainment of the marks: "Because of the empowerment from making this *mudrā* and chanting this mantra you will swiftly attain the thirty-two marks."[27] An odd twist on this is found in texts that coordinate calling to mind the thirty-two major marks with visualization of thirty-two armed deities: "If you seek the thirty-two marks you should contemplate [the image] with thirty-two arms. If one seeks the 84,000 dharma-gates one should contemplate with eighty-four arms."[28] Finally, a variety of tantric or esoteric texts enjoin the worshiper to visualize one's own body as possessed of the marks. For example, *Methods for the Worship of the Tathāgata Avalokiteśvara-rājā from the Scripture of Yoga of the Vajra Summit* 金剛頂經瑜伽觀自在王如來修行法 instructs the practitioner:

> Make this *mudrā* and use it to impress the characters on your body. Immediately your body is like that of the great compassionate Guanyin Tathāgata; a body shining pure golden in color and complete with the thirty-two major and eighty minor marks [confirming] the empowerment of the *tathāgatas*.[29]

The *Diamond Sutra*'s diatribe should alert us that visionary practices in which one sees one's own body bearing the marks of the Buddha were established long before the composition of the tantras, and that such practices continued to be advocated in esoteric texts.

## Part Three

# Ethnographic Studies

Whereas textual studies, especially those of ritual texts and tantras, remain an important tool for investigating Buddhist practices, sociology and anthropology are perhaps best suited for contemporary Buddhism as a lived religion. In Part 3, we turn to ethnography, a method that over the past few decades has increasingly found its way into normative Buddhist studies. This pair of chapters explores what ethnography can (and cannot) reveal about its subject.

Courtney Bruntz presents a brief case study of the Longquan monastic community in Beijing. In the context of popular discourses that discredit inauthentic Buddhism or criticize the commercialization of Buddhist sites, this monastery has embraced new technology specifically to spread the dharma to young Chinese millennials. Rather than viewing this work as a rupture from the past, Bruntz notes how community leaders situate their work within Buddhism's long history of using current technology to reach the people.

In "Describing the (Nonexistent?) Elephant," Chenxing Han reflects on the use of ethnography in the study of American Buddhisms. Whereas ethnographic studies have been used to create a picture of living Buddhist organizations, blind spots remain. In her study, Han uses a mixed-method approach to the study of young adult Asian American Buddhists, a population not easily contained in one tradition—let alone one temple. Her work explores creative approaches to studying populations that may prove elusive from the more common organizational approach to ethnography among scholars of US Buddhism.

These studies pick up the thread from historical studies that connects current practices with past tradition, practices that are also often preserved in texts.

7

# Buddhism, Consumerism, and the Chinese Millennial

Courtney Bruntz

## Introduction

This chapter presents a case study of the Chan (Zen) Longquan Temple, outside Beijing, and how its charismatic Master Xuecheng has been promoting Buddhism as an antidote to stress and unhappiness for disaffected Chinese millennials. The Longquan monastic community embraces the interconnectivity between Buddhism and modernity in order to affect their surrounding population. Their contention is that in a consumer-based society, you must meet the Chinese youth where they are (online), and you must transmit the dharma in manners that they enjoy (animation). This use of technological advancements to spread the Buddha's teachings is an interesting example of Buddhist entrenchment in socioeconomic contexts, and will enhance research on the ways in which Buddhist practices adapt to changing settings in the modern world.

In March of 2015, I arrived in Beijing to conduct research at monasteries that specifically missionize Buddhist teachings and practices to Chinese youth and young adults. Prior to beginning interviews, I shared dinner with a Chinese friend in his thirties who, upon me explaining my research, said that in comparison to China he much preferred Buddhism in Japan. "The temples are nicer, more peaceful, and not just about making money." Such an association between Buddhism and money, and a negative view regarding it, is not limited to my young friend. Even on my own campus where I teach in Nebraska I have heard our Chinese study-abroad students ask their American peers, "Are you truly Christian? Because in China people say they are Buddhist, but they are not actually Buddhist," and then go on to explain their opinion that some individuals who claim to be Buddhist are only interested in making money. It is my sense that such sentiments are a result of stories on Chinese social media of fake monks extorting practitioners as well as reports of China's wealthy Buddhists. In 2007, for instance, the *Xinhua News Agency* reported fake monks in the Southwest capital Guiyang, and warned Chinese to not buy amulets, peace symbols, books, or receive fortune-telling services from imposters.[1] Ten years later, individuals dressing up to act as monks are still present across Chinese temples. Recently I encountered such "fake monks" at the Famen Temple Cultural Scenic Area, and while visiting the Ten Thousand Buddhas Monastery in Hong Kong I noticed individuals posing as monks among signs warning visitors to be aware of them.

In addition to this press, some Buddhist teachers and temples have also been questioned for their interest in making money through religion. Commercializing Buddhism for the purposes of tourism has occurred by business corporations and monastic communities, drawing attention to the correlations between Buddhism and business. The most widespread case of a monk making money through Buddhism is the situation of Shi Yongxin—the abbot of Shaolin Temple in Henan Province. After taking leadership of the temple in 1999, Yongxin expanded the site's commercial operations in order to develop tourism. Shaolin grew to include not only a monastery but also an academy for kung fu, and Yongxin imagined the site to have a golf course, villas, and a four-star hotel.[2] Furthermore, in the 1990s he started the Henan Shaolin Temple Industrial Development Co. (now called the Shaolin Intangible Assets Management Co.) for the purposes of overseeing all trademarks and brands of Shaolin Temple (which exceed two hundred), and additionally created the Shaolin Kungfu Monk Corps—an internationally touring and performance troupe (Shaolin Temple). With of his involvement in business and politics, news agencies began calling Yongxin the "Shaolin CEO," and furthermore began reporting on the entanglements of commercialization and Buddhism—entanglements from relationships between Buddhists and companies that result in great annual revenues. In the case of Shaolin, this annual revenue is more than 100 million *yuan* (about $15 million).[3]

While my research in Beijing began with an interest in how Buddhism is spread to young Chinese, after conversations about Buddhism's entrenchment in business affairs I became interested in this additional layer. How are Buddhist communities responding to a reality of intersections between Buddhism and business? What challenges exist and what opportunities are available because of these relationships? In the following chapter, I discuss Buddhism's position in capitalist market economies and the changes that have taken place at temples and monasteries because of such realities. Drawing on ethnographic research,

I look at how Buddhist monastic communities are responding by embracing technology, new media, and digital opportunities to missionize the tradition for the purposes of reaching young Chinese online. I evaluate how one monastery—the Longquan 龙泉寺community—views recent growth of the tradition as a situation that requires protection from the state but also as an opportunity to legitimize the tradition as a modern religion. At the conclusion I contend that digitized Buddhism should not be viewed as a rupture from Buddhism's past but instead as simply the most recent way in which Buddhists creatively adapt the tradition to contemporary settings. Through technology, Buddhists are repositioning themselves in modern settings as an option for young Chinese, a religious tradition requiring official protection, and a global practice for foreigners and overseas Chinese.

## Restructuring China's economy and the commercialization of Buddhism

In 1979 Deng Xiaoping began restructuring China's economy, and to do so, incorporated foreign economic patterns and Western models and technology. "The modernization we are striving for," he said, "is modernization of a Chinese type. The socialism we are building is a socialism with Chinese characteristics."[4] Deng advocated for a policy of "selective experimentation," meaning that in the midst of economic reform, Confucian and feudal traditions of obedience and allegiance to the "group" remained.[5] At the same time, official policies rewarded individuals for their efforts and productivity. Deng did not believe that egalitarianism would work; instead he thought that it was fair for some individuals to become prosperous first, through their own hard work. Officials hoped that the prosperity of some would result in prosperity for all. This was China's version of the "trickle down theory of welfare."[6] Deng viewed egalitarianism as a road to poverty and socialism as a means to prosperity.

Accordingly, state-run enterprises began hiring workers on a competitive and contractual foundation,[7] and China's competitive economic market in this regard was viewed as "functional." In microeconomic sectors, capitalistic rules were allowed to regulate the markets. But China's macroeconomy was guided by socialist principles. Under Deng's reform, state-owned enterprises became quasi-independent economic units acting like private enterprises in a capitalist economy. They were not only able to make their own decisions regarding resources, supplies, costs, production targets, profits, but also assume responsibility for losses.[8] Furthermore, state-owned enterprises gained freedom to use profits as they wished, and not pay them to the state.

The effect this economic restructuring has had on Buddhist temple sites is great. Individual temple locations are part of China's microeconomy, where price and profit motives prevail. Following reform, revitalizations of Buddhist sacred mountains were legally guided by individualism and self-interest. Enterprises had freedom to develop locations, even going so far as to sell "stock" in Buddhist tourism corporations. Under this new economic structure, for example, the island Mount Putuo (the sacred *potalaka* of Guanyin Bodhisattva) established a Scenic Area Management Committee (an official administrative body), plus a state-owned tourism company. In 2008 the Mount Putuo Tourism Development Company began as a corporation committed to developing Mount Putuo's tourism activities. At present it has an annual profit of about 20 million *yuan*, and companies integrated into the corporation include the Mount Putuo Tourism Group 普陀山旅游集团, the Zhejiang Tourism Group 浙江省旅游集团, and the Zhoushan Islands Tourism Investment Development Company Limited 舟山群岛旅游投资开发有限公司. The Mount Putuo Tourism Group holds the most power, with 42 percent ownership,[9] and it includes the Putuo Passenger Ropeway Company, the Passenger Transport Company, the Mount Putuo Travel Service Company, the Gas Supply Company, and the Putuo Tianhua Souvenirs Company.[10] And in 2012, the Mount Putuo Tourism Development Company acquired the Passenger Service Company and the Mount Putuo Incense Factory. The tourism development company therefore became a collective enterprise, and during that same year (2012) representatives from the corporation announced plans to publicly sell shares through an initial public offering. With this, corporate commodities become stock. While the organization does not possess ownership over temples, by consolidating the abovementioned businesses under one corporation, the Mount Putuo Tourism Development Company has acquired a broad reach over Mount Putuo's economic field. This includes holding the key financial assets of travel and transportation (cableway, passenger buses, and ferries transporting travelers to and from the island), infrastructure (real estate development, hotel management, and shopping centers), retail and merchandise (statues, prayer beads, talismans, souvenirs, incense, etc.), and energy. This company, while officially state-owned, essentially functions like a private corporation.

It is this form of commercialization—the corporatization of Buddhism—that has been criticized in news reports and Master Xuecheng, the current president of the Buddhist Association of China, has responded to it; he calls this "passive" commercialized Buddhism.[11] In 2013, when he was vice president of the Buddhist Association, he said, "Due to the profit motive of commercial capital, all kinds of nonreligious bodies have used religion as disguise. This has significantly challenged peoples' belief in religion."[12] In 2016 he commented that the Buddhist Association does not advocate commercialization, nor does commercialization comply with fundamental doctrines of the religion:

> Circumstances may occur . . . that some of our temples . . . may have, or be surrounded by, business compounds . . . [because of this] people may . . . have the misunderstanding that Buddhism is encouraging commercialization.[13]

With a microeconomy of capitalism shaping economic contexts of temples, Xuecheng insists his monasteries do not charge admission, set up commercial shops, or perform commercialized Buddhist services.[14] Xuecheng does not, however, require his temples and monasteries to cease engaging in commercial activities. Instead, his goal is to increase Buddhism's presence and voice through manners that engage youth. And his temples do so by actively promoting the religion online and through new media. It is this engagement through technology that is the focus of this chapter. Through digital efforts, Xuecheng believes Chinese society can transform from being negatively affected by modern materialism, and that Buddhism will offer proper antidotes for stressed youth.

## Digitizing Buddhism for the millennial generation

When I ventured to Longquan Temple in the spring of 2015 I met lay volunteers plus the Venerable Xianqing—a student of Master Xuecheng. Located outside Beijing, Longquan dates back to the Liao dynasty in 957, but has gone through recent renovations, including the addition of an animation center that spreads Buddhist teachings through microblogs, WeChat (a Chinese mobile application), websites, and animated cartoons. Led by Master Xuecheng as head abbot, the community believes that no single doctrine of the dharma can be perfectly applied in any situation. Thus Longquan Temple monks and volunteers apply different high-tech methods to a number of Buddhist development projects.[15] As Xianqing explained, the intention of such efforts is to meet Chinese youth where they are—online. In 2015 Xuecheng was interviewed by CCTV, during which he advocated for monks not only studying Buddhist teachings and texts but also having a firm understanding of modern cultural tools so that Buddhism can more broadly, effectively, and quickly spread. Buddhism in modern times, he explained, requires monks to not only practice self-cultivation, but to also have a sense of urgency, to put forth aid in modern civilization: "Buddhists need to think big, promote Buddhism, and help others as a key part of practicing their faith."[16] To reach an audience beyond the physical space of the monastery, Xuecheng began blogging in 2006, and since then Longquan Monastery has gradually built a digital presence. Its temple space is thus not contained to a particular physical area, but instead, online, is spatially boundless.

## Writings and Dharma

After beginning to blog in 2006, Xuecheng in 2008, at 8:08:08 on August 8, began the *Voice of Longquan* website, a voice of the monastery that includes both Chinese and English versions. Through the site, users have access to the Venerable's writings and teachings on the dharma, animation videos, and blogs, and in addition to this website, Xuecheng writes on Weibo (a Chinese microblogging website similar to Twitter) and his writings are translated into eight different languages.

Online, Xuecheng's messages about Buddhism and society include translated writings and speeches delivered around the world. Xuecheng teaches:

> In the Buddha's enlightenment, he truly realized that, the nature of birth and death, suffering and joy, is pain. Happiness is just the temporary cease of suffering, and is impermanent. . . . The point is that we are all dragged by something in the endless ocean of mortality. This is the cause of suffering: self-attachment. This self-attachment is the root of all worries. Therefore, if we want to gain the real happiness, we should solve all from inside.[17]

His messages to the online community are aimed at improving one's life, and he is especially concerned with realities of modern life that include great pressures and high-paced lifestyles. These pressures include expectations for success, making money, gaining a well-respected education—all of which is part of modern competition in China. This makes individuals, he says, unsettled, restless, and sleepless. His antidote to difficulty is to change one's attitude—not dwelling on challenges, not presuming a negative outcome, but instead looking for paths to achieve goals and choosing to focus on the brightness in life.[18] Xuecheng's messages emphasize control over one's mind and emotions.

> Our inner mind is not under our control most of the time and is inclined to change as the outside world changes. All types of delusions and attachments prevent our mind from settling into peace, or from being set free.[19]

Modern settings result in people being extremely busy working and studying, he contends, and people care too little about others.

> Without our being aware of it, the psychological gaps between us and others are growing larger. . . . All these problems are actually caused by us. . . . The situation will improve if we start to feel others' emotions wholeheartedly.[20]

With more care and attention to others, plus less egoism, Xuecheng teaches that interpersonal relationships will improve.

When comparing messages of care, control, and positive thinking with the interviews I conducted while visiting Longquan, what is clear is that the Longquan community understands digital platforms as a mechanism for missionizing the tradition. While many people talk about living in a current age of darkness (*mofa*), one volunteer told me, Longquan volunteers believe they are living in the five hundred years in which Buddhism will spread rapidly before dying out. Their mission is to reach as many Chinese as possible, through whatever means necessary. Xuecheng believes it is "corrupt material culture" (*wu wenhua* 物文化) that is disrupting modern society. The problem, he argues, can be resolved through Buddhism's "mental culture" (*xin wenhua* 心文化).[21] As one of his students told me at the monastery, to help youth to not be so isolated, Buddhism is spread online. Xuecheng writes online,

> Happiness, if established on an outward basis, will not be stable. If we think we can obtain happiness by getting something from without, we set up the wrong goal. We, therefore, will not be able to gain neither happiness nor peace of mind.[22]

With modern technology, rather than having to venture to a temple or a monastery to hear such messages of inspiration, users can easily, and from any location, access such teachings. The Longquan community views new media as an advantageous way to spread the dharma and encourage "mental" over "material" culture.

## Robot Monk Xian'er

In addition to acting as a digital platform for spreading Master Xuecheng's teachings, the *Voice of Longquan* website is a mechanism for disseminating news and information about developments within Chinese Buddhism. One of the most important creations for the Longquan Monastery was the building of Xian'er 贤二, a two-foot robot who chants sutras and responds to verbal questions. Among all of Longquan's innovations, Xian'er has received the most international recognition. As Master Xuecheng writes in *A Roaming AI Xian'er, the Robot Monk*:

> Xian'er might contribute to [combining] Buddhism and Science. Or at least, it is an attempt, which is made by Buddhist practitioners and scientific researchers together, to seek for the truth of our lives. There is a new way other than duality. We have the ability to go beyond the duality, the conflicts and the contradictions between the spiritual and the physical world.[23]

In addition to making use of modern technology to spread Buddhism, it is clear that Xuecheng views Buddhism and science as well-suited for one another—that by embracing scientific achievements, Buddhists can better seek out truths of the world. The master who created Xian'er, Master Xianfan, contends that "science and Buddhism are not opposing nor contradicting, and can be combined and mutually compatible."[24] Working with a technology company and experts on artificial intelligence, Xian'er is the robotic version of Xianfan's 2013 cartoon. Since his creation, Xian'er—in both his cartoon and robotic forms—has become a marker of Longquan, and a symbol of a modern Buddhism that embraces scientific advancement. Furthermore, through animation, the stories of Xian'er teach Buddhism through quick entertainment. This portrays an additional example of Longquan making use of modern inventions plus relationships between Buddhists and businesses to develop new technology. Xian'er, as a pinnacle of technological and Buddhist achievement, serves as proxy, providing words of wisdom on behalf of the monastic community. This is especially evidenced in animation.

## Longquan animation

Beginning in 2011, the Longquan animation center began to design and create still cartoons and three-dimensional animation short films and clips to spread inspirational stories and messages. Short (less than one minute) flash clips are available online, and the longer *Story of Xian'er* series has online and television editions. According to Longquan monks:

> The purpose of producing animations is to spread Buddhist teachings in an easy and relaxing way. Masters are in charge of scripts and the characters. Volunteers are in charge of the production.[25]

In fall 2017, for example, Longquan videos aired on CCTV's new Animation Channel. The episode "Offering Incense" instructed one how to burn incense and avoid pollution. Within the video, Xian'er's companions ask him if it is the largest incense stick, or the number of incense sticks that matters for bringing about the most merit. Xian'er burns all of his friends' incense together, demonstrating the pollution caused. He then teaches that it is not the most nor the largest incense stick that is important, for all is equal before the Buddha. Also shown on CCTV was the video "Animal Liberation" that told the tragic tale of a young bird trying to prevent himself from being killed by a butcher. Each time the bird is caught, Xian'er steps in, paying the butcher to release the bird. This cycle of release and entrapment continues until Xian'er gathers his friends to create a vegetarian restaurant. And when the butcher dines there using coupons provided by Xian'er, he declares the vegetarian dishes are as delicious as ones with meat.

In addition to these videos, in cartoon form, Longquan animation publishes comic strips also distilling Buddhist teachings. In a cartoon regarding success, for example, the key takeaway is the message: "It is not necessary for one to completely understand themselves. If their behavior is good, persistence in character and direction is the real success."[26] Other topics within the cartoons include investigating the self, seeking peace of mind, improving one's mood, understanding the truth of emptiness, and how to deal with pressure. Regarding the last, one is taught that by exploring the heart, the individual finds that pressure is just a figment fabricated by delusion. In response, one should relax and simply do things well. And as another cartoon states, the real enemy is one's inner worry.

While at Longquan I was told that Buddhists are using entertainment media to teach a broader Chinese audience about the religion and how to apply its teachings in their daily lives. Furthermore, with translations of the cartoons and animations in multiple languages, Longquan's community spreads the wisdom of Xian'er and his companions to an international audience. Notably, the messages disseminated are about how to improve one's life and how to deal with the challenges one might face. In the cartoon "Anger Is Like Drinking Poison," Xian'er's companion asks why he feels so much pain in his heart. Xian'er responds that "his master says that being angry is like trying to drink poison and expecting others to suffer."[27] Through these sketches, short observations regarding how to improve one's perspective and thus one's life are delivered, and these cartoons are also sent through the mobile application WeChat.

## Mobile apps

Tales of Xian'er, his teacher, and his companions are not only published online but are also spread through the Chinese application WeChat. The little monk has his own WeChat account in Chinese, and, when one becomes friends with him through the app, the user is greeted with, "Although I am a robot monk, I am willing to be your good friend; if you have questions, I will seriously answer them; if you have trouble, I will listen to you!" As a friend of Xian'er on WeChat, one daily receives his words of advice. On December 5, 2017, for example, Xian'er addresses the issue of being mocked or made fun of by others. After listening to such a situation from his friend, Xian'er responds with the recommendation that when one is faced with the ridicule of others, the person should treat it as a chance of good fortune rather than letting their thoughts be preoccupied by it.

Another account associated with the Longquan community is the Longquan volunteer network. Followers of this account are sent daily posts of inspirational aphorisms. The message sent out on December 3, 2017 was, "Those who are able to overcome their afflictions are truly strong." Such quotations, all attributed to Xuecheng, are different than Xian'er's messages, for they do not include a story narration. However, they are similar in that they do not give concrete suggestions for how to implement the advice but rather are mere nuggets of information aimed at enticing the user to inquire more. And it is clear Longquan's online presence is attracting great attention. In 2016, for instance, on WeChat, Xian'er had over 200,000 followers, and when the robot monk gained the ability to communicate in English in 2017, over the course of a single day, Xian'er had received 42,000 questions.[28] These examples of Longquan's digital projects evidence skillful means utilized for the purpose of the Buddhist community gaining a presence with Chinese citizens online. But technology is also a method for altering public understandings about Buddhism, as well as a means for legitimizing the tradition to the state.

## Utilizing new technologies

Longquan monks and volunteers utilize new technologies as a way to spread Buddhism to the public from monastic communities themselves. With commercialization, some may, Xuecheng believes, misunderstand Buddhism and believe that it is entrenched in making money. Xuecheng's mission has been to alter this view, and thus transmit the *buddhadharma* especially to youth—many of whom may not yet know about Buddhism. Developing new media is thus skillful means to missionize the tradition to Chinese millennials who are already online. Xuecheng and the team of monks and volunteers at Longquan believe Buddhists should make use of the technological advancements available to them. Xuecheng writes,

> In terms of promoting the dharma, Buddhism should keep pace with the times. It is essential for Buddhism to exist in forms that are easy for people to access. Therefore, we should always promote new methods of communication, cultivating innovation.[29]

Such mechanisms allow the ancient to be contemporary, which is part of Xuecheng's vision—to educate citizens to implement Buddhist teachings into their daily lives. In its own introduction online, the Longquan community introduces the monastery as one dedicated to combining traditional Buddhist teachings with values in modern civilization. The community strives to integrate into, and serve, mainstream society, doing so by exploring new ways, methods, and forms for transmitting traditional Chinese culture. Along with frequent charitable activities, dharma assemblies, publications of books and DVDs, and the education of laity, animation and overall digitization is part of the monastery's strategy to missionize the tradition.[30]

Another reason the Buddhist community embraces new media and technology is that through science, Buddhists are able to legitimize themselves within contemporary Chinese Communist Party policies. As McMahan (2008) explains in *The Making of Buddhist Modernism,* fitting Buddhism into a frame of science is how Asian and Western advocators have legitimized the tradition. While Buddhism is one of China's legal traditions, one aspect of modernity that Chinese Buddhists battle is a lack of agency over temple spaces. Within modern settings, the commercialization of Buddhism has created the necessity to alter policies—to convince government officials to implement laws that protect Buddhist sites. Xuecheng's contention is that Buddhism's technological advancements have utility to the state, and Chinese Buddhism is in a unique position to spread Chinese culture online:

> Making full use of the Internet and other new media . . . [we] will actively promote the development of Buddhist culture's innovations, and will strengthen communication and development of Buddhism, modern science and technology. Buddhist culture's unique advantage reflects the contemporary value of

> Buddhism. . . . Fully using Buddhist cultural ties and Chinese Buddhism's "going out" (*zou chuqu*) [we will] spread wisdom of Chinese Buddhism to the world . . . promote Chinese culture, and promote China's religious freedom policy.[31]

Xuecheng believes Buddhism is an advantageous resource to the state because of its development of science and technology, and often suggests that Buddhism could function as a means to promote China's soft power. More recently, as a direct response to Xi Jinping's emphasis on enhancing the national soft power of culture that is part of Xi's vision to realize a "Chinese Dream," Xuecheng commented that moving forward, Chinese Buddhism will focus on three aspects in order to develop positive religious work:

> They will work to strengthen the role of the Chinese Buddhist Association in coordinating, supervising, and educating temple management to lead the Buddhist community and religious people in *loving the nation*, adhering to *socialism with Chinese characteristics*, and *contributing to the Chinese Dream*. They will also construct a Buddhist teaching style based on discipline, will supervise monasteries and schools around temples *to improve the quality of monks* . . . while at the same time *consciously resisting the chaos of Buddhism's "(passive) commercialization"* (被商业化) by actively cooperating with relevant state departments to remove non-Buddhist subjects from temples. Finally, they will actively carry forward socialist core values, deepen the development of Buddhist doctrine that is conducive to social harmony and progress, and emphasize Buddhist content that contributes to a healthy civilization.[32]

In an effort to obtain legal protection of sacred sites and to counteract accounts of fake monks at temples and commercialization, Xuecheng promotes Buddhism's utility to the state. And such efforts have produced the intended outcomes. On September 7, 2017, a newly revised "Religious Affairs Ordinance" was announced and was implemented February 1, 2018. Xuecheng's leadership helped produce a newly revised religious affairs ordinance that includes (1) the addition of protections against ownership of temples from those who give donations for a temple's construction; (2) the restriction against organizations and individuals other than religious groups in constructing outdoor statues; (3) the prohibition against commercial service outlets setting up vendors outside a religious site without consent of the religious group; and (4) the lawful ownership and use of buildings, structures, and facilities by religious groups and schools.[33] With these new jurisdictions, it is legally possible for Buddhists to prevent commercial operators from overrunning temple sites.

Finally, through technology, Chinese monks are able to spread Buddhism across the world and strengthen their international relationships. In addition to

Beijing's Longquan Monastery, in 2015 Longquan Great Compassion Monastery was founded in the Netherlands; and in 2016 Longquan Guanyin Monastery began in Los Angeles and Longquan Bohua Monastery was established in Botswana, Africa. More monasteries are planned, with the purpose of creating international places for overseas Chinese to gather. At a Theravada and Mahayana Symposium held this summer in Hong Kong, Xuecheng publicaly proposed that Xi Jinping's Belt and Road Initiative not only opens economic doors among nations but also activates deeper cultural connections for Buddhism. In the "Belt and Road Initiative," he said, "Buddhism itself can strengthen mutual understanding between different traditions, borrow and learn from each other . . . [to] help the birth and growth of a new civilization of the world."[34] In sum, in both digital spaces and international ones, Xuecheng puts forth a modern Buddhism that socializes the religion, blends religion with secular life to make Buddhist teachings relevant, aligns Buddhism's modernity with the state's global initiatives, and imagines domestic and international possibilities for the tradition.

## Conclusions

In his afterword in the volume *Buddhism beyond Borders*, Richard Payne argued that because chapters in that volume portrayed contemporary Buddhism as best understood as

> part of a continuity of ongoing adaptations and transgressions—adaptations to new environments and transgressions against expectations . . . it is necessary to critique a pervasive trope—the rhetoric of rupture.[35]

This rhetoric, Payne examines, is one that positions traditional versus modern with religion being "embedded" in premodern societies and "disembedded" in modern ones. It requires questioning, for current mobilities of Buddhism are not unique to modern settings (Payne 2015, 218; 220). This challenging of how Buddhism is categorized is a useful backdrop for understanding modern Chinese Buddhism, for in the digitization of Buddhism, monks like the Venerable Xuecheng are attempting to make the "ancient" contemporary. And Xuecheng does not view this as a breaking from the past, but rather, a utilization of modern technology to make Buddhist teachings germane to contemporary times. "I believe that if it were possible," he has said, "Venerable Master Xuanzang, Venerable Master Kumarajiva, and Venerable Master Jianzhen would have set up blogs in their times" (Shi 2016, 177). This view of creative adaptation fits Payne's contention that it is not that Buddhists in modern times are just now beginning to adapt teachings and practices to changing settings, but rather the entire history of Buddhism is one of movement and adaption. Xuecheng understands, and justifies, the use of modern technology and new media, as Buddhists making use of contemporary opportunities to disseminate the religion.

As Michael Walsh details regarding medieval Buddhist institutions and their surrounding economic contexts,

> Large Buddhist monasteries in China sought to produce and perpetuate monastic space by accumulating land to provide economic capital and secure their social position. As a commodified object, land was the key component in an exchange environment instituted by these powerful monasteries.[36]

In China today, digital space has arisen as a commodified object. While individuals may not have time to venture to a physical temple, they can easily, and quickly, access a digitized Buddhism. Viewed in this context of historical creative adaptation, Buddhist digital projects are modern techniques in which monasteries, as social institutions, continue acquiring and distributing cultural capital to missionize the tradition, legitimize it to the state, and counteract undesirable viewpoints.

# 8

# Describing the (Nonexistent?) Elephant: Ethnographic Methods in the Study of Asian American Buddhists

Chenxing Han

In his 2001 article "Describing the Elephant," Peter Gregory observes that "the phenomenon of American Buddhism is far too large for any one person to grasp in its totality."[1] He likens researchers in this emerging subfield to the blind men of Indian yore whose attempts to characterize an elephant are limited by their partial experience—one imagines a snake (having grasped the trunk), another a tree (the leg), another a wall (the flank), and so forth. Gregory invokes this famous parable to argue that "one of the central tasks facing researchers today is taxonomical: finding appropriate categories to describe the [American] Buddhist elephant."[2] Pointing to one of the lacunae in the field, Gregory highlights the need for "ethnographies that illuminate the religious experience of Asian American and Asian immigrant Buddhist communities *as it has been experienced by them*"[3] to supplement sociological studies on these groups.

Gregory recognizes the limitations to his pachydermic metaphor, which "presumes that there is an elephant, that this elephant is whole and unified, and that there is (in theory at least) a privileged position from which the elephant can be seen in its totality."[4] A 2009 book chapter by Joanna Cook, James Laidlaw, and Jonathan Mair question these very presumptions. "But what if there is no elephant?" they ask.[5] In urging fellow anthropologists of religion to interrogate the assumptions behind their choices of ethnographic field sites, the authors explore the possibilities of an "un-sited field" that "need not correspond to a spatial entity of any kind, and need not be a holistic entity 'out there' to be discovered."[6]

In this chapter I combine these authors' call for a critical assessment of ethnographic methods among scholars of religion with Gregory's call for greater attention to Asian American Buddhist experience through reflecting on the use, limitations, and possibilities of ethnographic methods in the study of Asian American Buddhists. I focus on Asian American Buddhists because, despite comprising more than two-thirds of American Buddhists, they remain underrepresented in both popular and academic literature.[7] In this sense, they are American Buddhism's invisible majority. I begin with an evaluation of five book-length ethnographic studies of Asian American Buddhists, with special attention to methods. I then go on to discuss the decentralized, "un-sited" approach of my own research on young adult Asian American Buddhists as an alternative to the congregation-based fieldwork of the previously discussed studies. Finally, I consider avenues for future research, highlighting the need to study ethnographic field sites outside of temples and to consider multiple axes of comparison.

## Five book-length ethnographies of Asian American Buddhists

In "Describing the Elephant," Gregory commends Paul Numrich's 1996 book *Old Wisdom in the New World: Americanization in Two Immigrant Theravada Buddhist Temples*[8] for bringing much-needed attention to the Buddhism of post-1965 Asian immigrants to the United States. A sociologist of religion, Numrich uses multiple methods in his study: participant observation at a Thai Theravada Buddhist temple in Chicago and a Sinhalese Theravada Buddhist temple in Los Angeles, structured and informal interviews in person and by phone, a review of primary documents such as temple newsletters, and a written survey completed by 221 respondents. Numrich characterizes his field research as "part-time ethnography" since he "never immersed [him]self totally in the day-to-day culture of the temple[s]."[9] Based on this research, he argues for the existence of "parallel congregations" of "American convert" and "Asian immigrant" Buddhists, who may practice under one roof but seldom interact. Emphasizing the difference between the two, he contrasts "the meditation-centered religion" of the former group with the "ritual-centered religion" of the latter.[10] He also places "American converts" in the category of new religious movements in America, and characterizes "Asian immigrants" as "more 'Asians-in-America' than 'Asian Americans.'"[11]

Numrich's "parallel congregations" theory bolsters the "two Buddhisms" taxonomy within American Buddhist studies, which posits "two distinct and mutually isolated brands of Buddhism practiced by groups composed largely of

Asian Americans, on the one hand, and Euro-Americans, on the other."[12] Much ink has been spilled over the implications and limitations of "two Buddhisms,"[13] a concept forwarded by Charles S. Prebish in 1979 to differentiate between "two completely distinct lines of development in American Buddhism" based on each line's level of organizational stability.[14] To Prebish's surprise, the schema has become strongly racialized. Interestingly, this racialization is used to both praise and critique the "two Buddhisms" model. Numrich believes it brings useful attention to racial inequalities in American Buddhism.[15] Critics of the "two Buddhisms" model, on the other hand, argue that it serves to perpetuate these very racial inequalities by obscuring the racism, Orientalism, and white privilege that underpin the model.[16]

In *Old Wisdom in the New World*, Numrich argues that "Americanization has begun at Wat Dhammaram of Chicago and Dharma Vijaya Buddhist Vihara of Los Angeles and, by extension, at the nearly 150 immigrant Theravada Buddhist temples across the United States."[17] He also claims that "we can expect to find parallel congregations at many of the immigrant Buddhist temples of America."[18] Such statements exemplify the holism within ethnographic studies that Cook, Laidlaw, and Mair challenge. The assumed generalizability of Numrich's findings requires conceptualizing these two temples as part of a greater, coherent whole.

As Scott A. Mitchell points out, subsequent scholarship complicates the picture of Theravada Buddhism in America.[19] In his review of Wendy Cadge's *Heartwood: The First Generation of Theravada Buddhism in America*,[20] Jeff Wilson praises this work as the first substantial, in-depth ethnography of Buddhist temples in America since Numrich's *Old Wisdom in the New World*. Cadge builds on Numrich's work by offering a systematic comparison of immigrant and convert Theravada Buddhists based on extensive ethnographic research at a first-generation Thai immigrant temple in Philadelphia (Wat Phila) and a first-generation convert Theravada Buddhist organization in Massachusetts (the Cambridge Insight Meditation Center, or CIMC).[21] Unlike Numrich, Cadge explains the rationale for choosing her field sites and examines how her own identities (white, female, not Buddhist) affected her research.

In an appendix, Cadge details her complete methods, which include participant observation over a period of two years in addition to twenty-five formal plus thirty informal interviews at Wat Phila, as well as more limited participant observation and thirty-seven formal interviews at CIMC. A close analysis of these "voices and stories of ordinary religious practitioners"[22] results in less dichotomous, more multifaceted interpretations of Buddhist practice, community, and identity than those presented by the "two Buddhisms" and "parallel congregations" schemata. However, while Cadge finds similarities between the "Asian" and "American-born" Buddhists at Wat Phila and CIMC respectively, the very act of conceiving these two groups as separate entities for comparison—as well as the terminology she uses to describe the two groups—in some ways reinforces a "two Buddhisms" divide. Like Numrich, Cadge does not employ race/racialization as a critical lens in her study. Neither scholar refers to their interviewees as "Asian Americans," possibly because they would reserve this term for the second generation, who were largely absent from their field sites. Indeed, some might take issue with Numrich's use of the terms "ethnic-Asians" to describe his interviewees of Asian descent and "non-ethnics" to describe their counterparts.[23]

Anthropologist Jiemin Bao foregrounds issues of race—as well as ethnicity, class, and gender—in her 2015 book *Creating a Buddhist Community: A Thai Temple in Silicon Valley*. Bao's fieldwork spanned nine years: during portions of summer or winter breaks she lived at Wat Thai (a pseudonym) in the Bay Area, California, where she engaged in participant observation and conducted interviews with a total of 112 Thai and non-Thai participants. She also interviewed people in Thailand connected to the Silicon Valley temple, making her fieldwork multi-sited. Like Cadge, Bao discusses her positionality at the temple; in particular, she cites her language abilities in Thai, Lao, and Mandarin Chinese as a boon to her research. Neither Cadge nor Bao (who is Chinese) are ethnically Thai, but they both enjoyed the support of the abbots at their respective Thai temples, who praised them as being "a Thai" and "[Thai] in a previous past life."[24] Unlike Cadge, Bao's self-reflexivity does not extend to her own religious identity, though her integration into temple activities suggests that she is very comfortable in Buddhist settings.

Bao's examination of the intertwined social, religious, economic, and educational spheres at Wat Thai highlights the inclusivity, interconnection, and interdependence she finds there. She differentiates her study by considering "a diverse assemblage of participants at a *single* Buddhist temple [that] crosses ethnic, racial, and religious boundaries."[25] It is debatable whether the boundary crossing she observes is a harbinger for the future of American Buddhism, or whether such diversity is unique to Wat Thai as a result of its geographic location. Wilson's regionalism theory of American Buddhism[26] would lean toward the latter interpretation, whereas Bao suggests that Wat Thai can be seen as an empirical case study whose results have wider applicability.[27]

Together, Numrich, Cadge, and Bao's books offer a valuable glimpse into the religious lives and organizations of Theravada Buddhists in America—but they are not without limitations. In her MA thesis, Mihiri Tillakaratne critiques *Old Wisdom in the New World* for its insufficient attention to the experience of 1.5- and second-generation Sri Lankan Americans Buddhists. Her connection to the project is "very personal . . . in the 1990s, when I was a child attending Dharma Vijaya, Paul Numrich did his research for his book on the temple."[28] *Heartwood*, which explicitly focuses on the first generation, also does not include the younger generation in its purview. *Creating a Buddhist Community* contains scattered references to Wat Thai's youth and young adults, but the bulk of the book centers the perspectives of older adults. One notable exception is the latter third of the penultimate chapter, "Shaping and Performing Thai Identities," which features the voices of several 1.5- and second-generation young adults who formerly attended the temple's Sunday school for kindergarten to high school-age children.[29] The chapter ends with the observation that "[these] young people have developed multiple, shifting, inconsistent, and fragmented identities," suggesting that they are a unique group whose perspectives merit deeper investigation.[30]

Two additional congregation-based studies featuring Asian American Buddhists also center on first-generation immigrants. Sharon Suh's 2004 book *Being Buddhist in a Christian World: Gender and Community in a Korean American Temple* and Carolyn Chen's 2008 book *Getting Saved in America: Taiwanese Immigration and Religious Experience* bring a welcome Mahayana Buddhist perspective to the three books discussed above.[31] Both studies argue that immigration is a catalyst for religious transformation among Asian American Buddhists.

Suh's study is based on fieldwork at a "primarily first-generation Korean American Buddhist temple"[32] in Los Angeles, where she spent most weekends for two years as both a teacher (for the temple's Buddhist youth group and its college for adult education) and observer. Suh conducted in-depth—often multiple—interviews with twenty-five laywomen and twenty-five men (two monks and twenty-three lay practitioners), either in Korean or a combination of Korean and English. Reading the data from these interactions "as ethnographic religious biographies wherein religious motivations are revealed and subjectivities enacted," Suh's stated aim is to illustrate the ways her participants use Buddhism to make meaning and construct a coherent sense of self, rather than to provide "a seamless ethnography of a Korean Buddhist temple."[33] As such, *Being Buddhist in a Christian World* is centered on individual narratives, in contrast to Numrich, Cadge, and Bao's books, which provide more information about the institutional structure and organizational history of their field sites.

Self-reflexivity is foundational to Suh's approach: she discusses how her gender made it easier to talk to women than men at the temple, and how her multiple roles as a researcher, participant, volunteer, teacher, student, second-generation Korean American, and daughterly figure impacted her research. Like Bao, Suh does not explicitly identify her own religious orientation, though her extensive involvement at the temple suggests that she is at least sympathetic to Buddhism. She notes that some temple members were surprised at her interest in Buddhism, as they are accustomed to second-generation Korean Americans converting to Christianity. As the book's title hints, Korean American Buddhists face challenges not just as ethnic minorities in America, but also religious minorities within their own ethnic group, for they are vastly outnumbered by Korean American Christians. Indeed, stories about the attrition of second-generation Buddhists—as one of her interviewees, a mother of two sons in their early twenties, laments, "Young people who go to temple don't exist!"[34]—are woven throughout the book, which ends on a note of ambiguity about the temple's sustainability due to the dearth of second-generation attendees. The appeal of Korean American Christian communities, language barriers at the temple (where little English is spoken), temple members' reluctance to proselytize, and members' belief that their children's religious affiliation is a personal choice mediated by their individual karma, all factor into the lack of second-generation members at the temple.

Unlike the four books discussed above, sociologist Carolyn Chen's *Getting Saved in America* offers a comparative look at Asian Americans of different religious backgrounds. Specifically, Chen conducted fieldwork in Southern California among middle-class Taiwanese immigrants at a Buddhist temple ("Dharma Light Temple") and an evangelical Christian church, including participant observation over two years and in-depth interviews (twenty-five at each site). Paying close attention to her respondents' conversion narratives, she analyzes various factors that caused these Taiwanese Americans to become more religious after immigrating to the United States in the late 1980s and early 1990s. Similar to Suh's interviewees, the Buddhists in Chen's sample face pressure from coethnic evangelical Christians to convert, a pressure that spurs them to "define, differentiate, and defend" themselves against "the oppositional foil of Taiwanese American Christianity."[35] They must also negotiate Buddhism's perceived foreignness and exoticism in the American context, as well as the denigration of Buddhism as a superstitious and backward religion of the uneducated in the Taiwanese context. These Buddhists exemplify Lisa Lowe's argument that Asian American culture is not a straightforward vertical transmission from one generation to another but is mediated by dominant representations that marginalize Asians and Asian Americans.[36]

Though Chen provides her interview schedule in an appendix, she does not detail what languages she used, leaving the reader to guess whether her interviewees spoke to her in Taiwanese, Mandarin, English, or a combination thereof. Such information would have been particularly clarifying when translating specific religious terminology. Given the centrality of ethnicity, religion, and gender in her analysis, it is a pity that we never learn how Chen's own positionalities affected her rapport with her research subjects. As for the generalizability of her findings, Chen cautions against taking Dharma Light Temple as representative of other immigrant Buddhist communities due to its large sangha and sizeable resources. Whether the dynamics she details extend beyond the middle-class first-generation Taiwanese American immigrant experience remains an open question. Dharma Light does share one feature in common with the immigrant Buddhist temples studied by Numrich, Cadge, Bao, and Suh, however: a dearth of religiously engaged second-generation youth.

All five studies discussed in this section take one or two Buddhist temples affiliated with a specific Asian American ethnic group as their locus of research. Though Bao emphasizes the diversity at her temple, where there are members from a range of ethnic (e.g., Lao, Chinese) and racial (e.g., black, Hispanic, white) backgrounds, the fact remains that her primary research site is still a *Thai* temple that self-consciously reinforces and reifies Thai identity, in part as a way to educate second-generation Thai Americans about their culture. Yet, as Lowe and Tillakaratne remind us, we cannot assume a vertical, unchanged transmission of culture (or religion) from parents to children. How, then, are we to study a younger generation of Asian American Buddhists if they are not to be found at temples?

## A decentralized approach to studying young adult Asian American Buddhists

As illustrated by the five studies discussed in the previous section, research on Asian American religions is dominated by a congregational analysis model.[37] In the case of ethnographies at Buddhist temples, this method privileges the perspectives of the older generation at the expense of understanding a younger generation of Asian American Buddhists on their own terms. A review of the literature on the religions of post-1965 American immigrants calls for more macro- and micro-level studies to address this tendency of using local religious organizations as a unit of analysis.[38] This opens up possibilities for studying Asian American Buddhists in social institutions (e.g., cities, families, schools, health-care organizations, workplaces) at the macro level, or in "more micro contexts focused on individuals' experiences *outside of religious gatherings*."[39] This section presents an example of the latter alternate method.[40]

As a 1.5-generation Chinese American immigrant raised in an atheist household, my college explorations of Buddhism led me to wonder about the lack of other young adult Asian Americans at the immigrant temples (Chinese, Cambodian, and Vietnamese American) and primarily white Buddhist meditation centers (Vipassana, Zen) that I visited. I was also struck by how the logic of "two Buddhisms" could be interpreted as promoting a conceptualization of Asian American Buddhists as a pan-ethnic, pan-Buddhist group—yet ethnographic, congregationally based studies of Asian American Buddhists usually focus on a specific ethnicity and its corresponding Buddhist tradition. I therefore considered a different approach to investigate the ethnic and religious diversity covered under the umbrella term "young adult Asian American Buddhist" (YAAAB).

I set out to interview YAAABs, though it became clear from the outset that this category would not be a tidily bounded one. Asian Americans hail from more than forty countries and speak more than 150 languages and dialects, forming a "community of contrasts"[41] that is characterized by difference as much as (if not more than) similarity. In a comparable vein, the presence of a mind-boggling variety of Buddhist groups leads many to speak of Buddhisms (in the plural) in America. Thus, the category of "Asian American Buddhist" encompasses people from a wide range of ethnic backgrounds and a large swath of Buddhist persuasions. Given that the categories "Asian American" and "Buddhist" contain enormous diversity and lend themselves to definitional ambiguity, combining the two creates an even more complicated construct. Is "Asian" a geographic or racial category? Do "sympathizers," to borrow Thomas Tweed's expression,[42] count as Buddhist? "Young adult" is also a slippery term with nebulous boundaries, making it all the more difficult to pinpoint precise parameters for the very category I set out to research.

Aware of the definitional ambiguities inherent in each of the identifiers of "young adult," "Asian American," and "Buddhist," I opted for considerable latitude when recruiting interviewees. I was open to interviewing people of full or partial Asian heritage, regardless of immigration/citizenship status. I did not require participants to be native English speakers, though the interviews were conducted almost entirely in English. Nor was self-identification as Buddhist a prerequisite; I wanted to include people who may not explicitly consider themselves "Buddhist" despite a personal engagement with Buddhist practices and/or teachings. As such, my research included perspectives from Tweed's category of Buddhist sympathizers and Anne Spencer and Scott Draper's category of "sort-of Buddhists."[43]

Taking a cue from the networked and decentralized approach Sumi Loundon used when seeking contributors for her anthologies, I set up a website with a call for participants. I used snowball sampling to find interviewees, asking for recommendations from respondents on whom else I might contact for the project at the end of each interview. I also introduced my project to potential interviewees at various Bay Area Buddhist conferences and events, including the TechnoBuddha conference for young adult (primarily Jōdo Shinshū and Japanese American) Buddhists in Berkeley, California.

I conducted the first set of one-on-one interviews in person, in cafes, college campuses, Buddhist temples, and homes in the San Francisco Bay Area (twenty-two interviews) and Southern California (four interviews). Many participants expressed gratitude for the opportunity to reflect on their religious lives, noting how rare it was to be able to talk about the sensitive and potentially polarizing subjects of race and religion on more than a superficial level. The semi-structured, open-ended nature of the interviews enabled participants to say as much or as little as they wanted. Most opted for in-depth discussion over cursory responses: the interviews ranged from one and a half to five hours, with an average length of approximately two and a half hours.

To accommodate requests from young adults I could not meet in person due to geographic distance or scheduling difficulties, I adapted the in-person interviews to an email format. In total, I conducted sixty-three email interviews. The email format enabled me to hear from young adults from a wider range of geographic locations, ethnicities, and Buddhist traditions, and had the added benefit of giving interviewees the flexibility and time to craft thoughtful written responses. Though the email interviews lacked the dialogical spontaneity of the in-person interviews, I was able to mitigate this limitation by asking follow-up questions via email. Outside of the asynchronous, one-time email interview and related email exchanges, I had real-time interactions with over half of the sixty-three email interviewees, either in person or through online video conference.

An obvious limitation of conducting in-person and email interviews is that I was not able to observe my interviewees' practices and communities in situ. Had I attempted this fieldwork component, however, I would have found myself traipsing from Southern California to Northern California to France to Uganda, going to dozens of temples and meditation centers, meeting Buddhist teachers and dharma friends of different ages and races/ethnicities—to follow just *one* of my interviewees! Or, for those whose Buddhist lives are less community-oriented, I would have had to peer over shoulders to watch dharma talks on computer screens or plant myself in bedrooms with makeshift meditation corners and personalized home altars. Though I did not locate my research at a temple, my YAAAB interviewees can hardly be said to practice a purely "privatized religion";[44] indeed, the number of Buddhist temples/centers to which my interview subjects were connected far exceeded the total number of interviewees. Still, it is clear that while I employed ethnographic methods through the in-depth interviews, my research was no substitute for a long-term ethnography that includes participant observation of YAAABs.

Because I was exploring the parameters of an ambiguous category, I included in my analysis interviews with people who tested the boundaries of the classification "young adult Asian American Buddhist." A few interviewees were in their forties, too old to be "young adults" by some standards. Several interviewees were less connected to the "American" aspect of "Asian American," not having grown up in the United States (these interviewees typically moved to America for high school, college, grad school, or work). A few were connected to *North* America, having grown up in Canada, though they now lived in the United States. Some felt less connected to the "Asian" aspect of Asian American (e.g., because they are multiracial and had limited exposure to their Asian heritage, or they are of South/Central/West Asian heritage and tended to associate "Asian American" with East and Southeast Asians). Still others did not self-identify as Buddhist, though their interview responses evinced a strong interest in Buddhism.

My participants ranged in age from eighteen to forty-six, with a median age of twenty-six and an average age of twenty-eight. They represent a younger generation of Asian American Buddhists than those studied in the five books mentioned in the previous section. Though I did not intentionally seek out gender parity, I ended up with a fairly gender-balanced group of forty-seven women and forty-two men. I did not notice a stark contrast between male and female respondents as did Bao, Cadge, Chen, and Suh, which raises the question of whether my methods were insufficiently attentive to the dimension of gender, or whether gender differences might be less pronounced among a younger, English-speaking generation of Asian American Buddhists.

I treated my eighty-nine interviewees less as a "sample" and more as "a set of cases with particular characteristics that . . . should be understood, developed, and incorporated into [our] understanding of the cases at hand."[45] The group's heterogeneity in terms of age, occupation, geographic location, ethnicity, generational status, and religious practice/belief attests to the limitations of viewing Asian American Buddhists as a coherent demographic category or, for that matter, as an "elephant" with easily identifiable parts and predictable behaviors.

Over the course of analyzing the perspectives of this remarkably diverse group of eighty-nine interviewees, I came to understand my research as a collective project of thinking into being young adult Asian American Buddhists. The double meaning of "thinking into being" is deliberate—there is "thinking into" in the sense of "thinking about," but also "thinking *into being*"—the process of thinking as an act of creation. In many ways, then, (young adult) Asian American Buddhists are an imagined community still in the making. My aim was to explore the themes and possibilities that arose from this act of imagination, rather than to present sociological descriptions of a specific group. To present my research as the latter would be quite misleading: Many of my interviewees admitted that our interview was the first time they had ever considered "Asian American" and "Buddhist" in combination as a single concept, though they identified with each of these labels separately. In introducing the very category of "Asian American Buddhist" for their consideration, I could be said to be influencing (or biasing) my research subjects by planting (or imposing) this hitherto unfamiliar notion in/on their consciousness. Fortunately, I had no pretensions of studying, zoologist-like, a group of people "out there" in their "natural habit." My research was enriched by the ways in which my interviewees responded to representations of Asian American Buddhists and grappled with their own relationship to the category. Ultimately, my research centered around an "un-sited field," since I engaged "young adult Asian American Buddhists" more as a malleable concept than an entity locatable in space. By using the very term "Asian American Buddhists," it may seem that I am presenting a bounded entity—yet the category's incoherence to many of my YAAAB interviewees suggests that there may be no "elephant" after all.

My own positionality as a young adult Asian American Buddhist seems to have helped build rapport with my interlocutors. One person visibly relaxed when they found out I was not Christian, in response to their questioning me about my religious background. I adopted an approach in the interviews with YAAABs that would later come into use in my work as a hospital chaplain resident: while I did not lead with an announcement of my religious affiliation or other identity markers such as ethnicity, I answered openly and honestly whenever asked, while keeping the focus of the conversation on the other person. In explaining her motivation to participate in the project, one interviewee, who grew up as an active member of a Sri Lankan-Sinhalese American Buddhist community in New York, wrote,

> While I wholeheartedly believe that Buddhism, as with all other forms of religion and philosophy, is something that everyone can be engaged in, on another level, I feel that acknowledging cultural roots is a critical part of that experience. As such, I was absolutely excited, curious, and quite frankly relieved that an Asian American-identified person was committed to bringing our stories to light.

In presenting these two examples, I do not mean to suggest that a non-Asian American, or a Christian/non-Buddhist, could not successfully interview YAAABs. However, I believe studies of Asian American Buddhism can only benefit from self-reflexivity on the part of researchers, especially since the sensitive topics of race and religion are not merely intellectual abstractions but very personal—and sometimes painful—for our research subjects.

## Thinking outside the temple: Possibilities for future research

Historically, the field of Buddhist studies has favored textual and philosophical approaches over ethnographic ones. A 2016 call for proposals for a conference on "Buddhism, Humanities and Ethnographic Methods" notes that ethnographic studies of contemporary Buddhism in Asia have become increasingly common over the past fifteen years, representing

> a disparate movement, growing out of different disciplines (Anthropology, Buddhist Studies, Sociology, Religious Studies, Area Studies, Political Science, Human Development), focused on different types of Buddhism (Theravada, Mahayana, Vajrayana), and different types of Buddhist populations (monastic, lay and ritual specialists).

These studies often center around monasteries, nunneries, and meditation centers,[46] not unlike the congregational approach common to studies of Asian American religions. Tweed observes a similar "ethnographic turn in the study of U.S. religious life."[47]

Given Richard Payne's characterization of Buddhism in the West as "Buddhist studies' unloved stepchild"[48] and Natalie Quli's observation of ethnographers' privileging of "traditional" Asia over the "modern" West as a field site,[49] it is unsurprising that ethnographic studies (a marginalized method) of Buddhism in America and other parts of the West (a marginalized subfield) are scant. This, along with the disproportionate focus on white converts within American Buddhist studies,[50] explains the urgent need for more studies of Asian American Buddhists, ethnographic and otherwise.

It does not help that the field of Asian American studies has tended to ignore religion due to Marxist and anti-Christian bias, as David Yoo, editor of *New Spiritual Homes*, one of the first books to address this lacuna, points out.[51] The sole chapter on Buddhism in the volume identifies a "paucity of studies on the Buddhism of Asian Americans."[52] Literature on Asian American Christianity is much more robust, bolstered in no small measure by Asian American theology, for which no appreciable Asian American Buddhist counterpart exists. The fact that Asian American Christians outnumber Asian American Buddhists three to one undoubtedly contributes to the disparity,[53] though the literature on—and, for that matter, by—Asian American Buddhists is still disproportionately thin. Christianity is a much stronger focus than Buddhism in a number of articles and edited volumes on Asian American religions.[54] As Rudy Busto notes, literature on "Asian 'New Immigrant' non-Christian traditions"—including the Buddhism of post-1965 immigrants—"is written predominantly by whites,"[55] whereas Asian Americans produce most of the scholarship on Asian American Christianity.

Limiting the study of Asian American Buddhists to first-generation post-1965 immigrants not only overlooks their 1.5- and second-generation children but also neglects Asian American Buddhists who have lived in the United States for multiple generations. Referred to as "old-line" Buddhists by some scholars,[56] this group includes Chinese American and Japanese American Buddhists. Within the latter group, Jōdo Shinshū (a.k.a. Shin) Buddhists are distinct for having the oldest Buddhist organizations in America,[57] including the Buddhist Churches of America (BCA). Existing studies of American Shin Buddhism and the BCA tend to be historically and/or institutionally oriented,[58] rather than focusing on the religious identities and narratives of contemporary individuals. Mitchell argues that a "narrative of decline" hangs like a pall over American Shin Buddhism, which the academic literature depicts as "traditional, conservative, and static."[59] As a result, Shin Buddhists are cast—and cast aside—as clannish foreigners. Their religious communities are too often relegated to "ethnic enclave" status, despite evidence to the contrary, including the involvement of non-Japanese American BCA members and high rates of intermarriage within the Japanese American community.

The marginalization and purported waning of the American Shin Buddhist community may explain why scholarship on the contemporary Jōdo Shinshū community in America is scant, and studies of its younger generation even more scarce. Patricia Usuki's survey research on female Jōdo Shinshū Buddhists includes responses from 161 BCA teenagers, a group of fourteen- to eighteen-year-olds who are primarily *yonsei* (fourth-generation Japanese American), though she does not analyze this age group's responses in-depth.[60] Anne Spencer's analysis of survey data on 407 Shin Buddhists is also skewed toward her older informants due to the small sample size of respondents below the age of thirty.[61] While sociological, survey-driven approaches are helpful for garnering information about large groups of people, anthropological studies that incorporate participant observation and in-depth interviews can offer rich descriptions and nuanced insights into a phenomenon that is difficult to quantify: Asian American Buddhist religiosity.

With its majority-Buddhist countries, geographically bound Buddhist villages, and plethora of Buddhist temples, monasteries, and nunneries, it is tempting to view Asia as an optimal site for Buddhist ethnographies.[62] Yet the absence of these characteristics in the West should hardly disqualify field sites outside of Asia as subjects of ethnographic inquiry. Indeed, the unique situation of Buddhism as a minority religion in the West, with practitioners and sympathizers who are not always easily locatable in Buddhist enclaves and temples, lends itself to creative new possibilities in the ethnographic study of Buddhism. To generate these possibilities, scholars of Buddhism in the West might look to the growing body of ethnographies of Buddhism in Asia (as well as ethnographies in the United States of non-Buddhist religions) for inspiration. The innovative approaches they employ can, in turn, contribute to methodological conversations in Buddhist studies that have heretofore been dominated by Asia-based research (or, in the case of US religious studies, dominated by studies of Christianity).

Even if we only consider the specific category of Asian American Buddhist youth, unexplored research paths abound. Youth groups and summer camps where YAAABs congregate are an underexplored site for ethnographic studies that can offer a different vantage point than temple-based ethnographies focused on first-generation immigrant Buddhists. Such research might look at youth groups in a specific organization across multiple field sites—the YBAs

(Young Buddhist Associations) of the BCA immediately come to mind. For second-generation Asian American Buddhists, groups such as the Vietnamese Buddhists Youth Association (also known as Gia đình phật tử Việt Nam) and the Buddha's Light International Association Young Adult Division connected with Fo Guang Shan have parallels in Asia, opening the possibility for transnational ethnographies akin to C. Julia Huang's study of Tzu Chi.[63] Several of the second-generation YAAABs I interviewed spoke of the formative role that Buddhist summer camps (e.g., at Chuang Yen Monastery in New York) played in their religious lives. In addition to these Mahayana groups, there are also similar programs at Theravada Buddhist temples for Thai, Sri Lankan, and Burmese American youth;[64] analogous offerings for Cambodian and Laotian Americans[65] may be more limited, due in no small part to socioeconomic challenges that these communities face.

Beyond these youth groups and summer camps, which are still largely hosted at temples, Buddhist gatherings on college campuses, such as Tzu Chi's Tzu Ching groups and SGI-USA's campus clubs, constitute another possible field site, one where YAAABs may or may not be a racial majority. Asian American Christian campus groups make for an interesting point of comparison in this regard. Yet another possibility is to explore the perspectives of YAAABs who attend people of color meditation groups and retreats (e.g., at the East Bay Meditation Center in Oakland, CA, the Insight Meditation Society in Barre, MA, or the Spirit Rock Meditation Center in Woodacre, CA) or who are part of international sanghas such as Wake Up, which describes itself as "an active global community of young mindfulness practitioners, aged 18–35, inspired by the teachings of Zen Master and peace activist Thich Nhat Hanh."[66] Apropos of a generation marked by rapid advances in digital technology, the "Find a Group" page on the Wake Up website lists no physical addresses or phone numbers, only email addresses and Facebook pages.

Virtual ethnography offers yet another avenue for studying YAAABs. In his contribution to the edited volume *Buddhism, the Internet, and Digital Media*, Gregory Grieve reflects on using this method to study a Buddhist community in the virtual world of Second Life.[67] My email interviews with YAAABs also fall under the purview of digital ethnography; Dhiraj Murthy comments on the ways online questionnaires and email interviews can expand one's cohort of respondents and even lead to physical ethnography when respondents subsequently agree to be interviewed in person.[68] Social networking sites could serve as another site for ethnographic research. Even blogs, which might seem better suited to textual than ethnographic analysis, can be an important locus for what Rashmi Sadana calls an "ethnography of literature" involving "the places, people, and the institutions that produce literature."[69] While an interesting study could be made of interviewing Buddhist writers and publishers in person, blogs conveniently centralize writers, publishers, and even readers (whose views we can glean from their comments on the blogs, and whose print-book-perusing counterparts are much more difficult to pinpoint) in one digital place.

In a paper given at the 2010 "Buddhism Without Borders" conference at the Institute of Buddhist Studies in Berkeley, California, Mindy McAdams argues that blogs by younger American lay Buddhists give us access to "voices [that] might not be evident in the established Buddhist press controlled by older convert Buddhists, or in the temples controlled by older immigrant Buddhists."[70] Tweed also calls for more attention to online media in studies of American Buddhism.[71] Given the dearth of publications by and about YAAABs, it behooves us to pay attention to online writing by people like the late Aaron Lee, who founded the *Angry Asian Buddhist* blog. YAAAB voices are often overlooked or dismissed—even by scholars who acknowledge the importance of studying the Buddhist blogosphere.[72] Blog posts by various young adult Asian American Buddhists, as well as a twenty-eight-minute ethnographic documentary film by Wanwan Lu[73] about youth group members at a Chinese American Buddhist temple in Southern California, proved invaluable for my research on YAAABs.

As Cook, Laidlaw, and Mair reassure us, "Unlike the blind men in the Buddhist parable, who were required by their king to try to identify something they could not perceive with the data available to them, anthropologists are free to choose for themselves analytical objectives that can actually be achieved."[74] The same can be said for scholars of (Asian) American Buddhism, anthropologists and otherwise, who choose to use ethnographic methods in achieving their analytical aims. The importance of "foster[ing] multiple axes of comparison"[75] cannot be overstated here. As we have seen with the case of Asian American Buddhists, many such axes are possible. We can compare within an ethnic group across religions (Korean/Taiwanese American Buddhists vs. Christians, South Asian Buddhists vs. Hindus), across ethnic and/or racial groups within a tradition (Sri Lankan vs. Thai American Buddhists) or lineage (Asian American vs. white Zen Buddhists), across generations (third- vs. fourth-generation American Shin Buddhists, first- vs. second-generation Cambodian American Buddhists), across groups of different ethnic/racial and Buddhist sectarian backgrounds at a single temple[76] or in a specific city,[77] and across other variables such as gender, class, geography (local, state, national, hemispheric, or global levels), sexuality, employment, and so forth.

Thinking about these possible projects raises the question of whether Asian American Buddhists should be situated among American Buddhists generally or people of color Buddhists specifically, among coethnics of various religious groups (e.g., Chinese American Buddhists vs. Christians vs. non-religious), among Americans of various ethnic/racial backgrounds of a comparable immigrant generation (say, *yonsei* Buddhists vs. fourth-generation Jews in America), as diasporas of their respective ethnic/cultural/religious groups in Asia—here again, the possibilities proliferate. There is little research on people whose mixed ethnic/racial/religious belongings include Asian American and Buddhist components, as well as Asian Americans who have left Buddhism (for another religion or no religion)—what methods must we create to account for these largely neglected viewpoints? And what about American Buddhist institutes of higher education, or Buddhist chaplaincy in America? Ultimately, it may be best to replace the word "should" in the first sentence of this paragraph with the word "can," in recognition that the multiple ways in which Asian American Buddhists may be positioned is not a problem but an opportunity that opens up exciting new research vistas beyond the temple. These studies may show us that American Buddhism is more chimera than elephant—or they may suggest new metaphors that have yet to be imagined.

## Part Four

# Theoretical Concerns

In her contribution in Part 1 of this volume, Montrose reflects on the ways in which modern critical scholarship affected Buddhism's development. Indeed, scholarship does not stand outside the tradition. It is not in a separate realm from Buddhism, but interacts, shapes, and is shaped by the tradition. Thus, critical self-reflection on the task of scholarship is necessary and brings us to Part 4.

Critical self-reflection may take the form of examining and reexamining the terms scholars use in their studies as Charles Jones does in his "Is a *Dazang jing* a Canon?" Jones notes that the word "canon"—deployed frequently and unproblematically in Buddhist studies—has a particular set of meanings derived from Christian scholarship. Do these meanings translate into Buddhism? Does our work in translating and constructing canons affect the development and practice of Buddhism?

This relationship between scholarly activity and Buddhist practice is the focus of Franz Metcalf's contribution, "Our *Buddhadharma*, Our Buddhist Dharma." Metcalf is specifically interested in the ethical responsibility scholars have toward Buddhism and Buddhists, challenging us to abandon the assumption that non-Buddhists are objective observers of the tradition.

This ethical responsibility is taken up by Natalie Quli in the concluding chapter, wherein she examines the Orientalist origins of Buddhist studies scholarship, its intersection with discourses of white authority and authenticity, and the effects these discourses have on Buddhist communities of practice. Quli's work skillfully weaves together historical studies and ethnography, tracing the intersection of Buddhist practice and Buddhist scholarship.

9

# Is a *Dazang jing* a Canon? On the Nature of Chinese Buddhist Textual Anthologies

Charles B. Jones

## Introduction

This chapter focuses on scholarly categories in religious studies, specifically those in Buddhist studies. In particular, it is about the problems that arise when scholars from one cultural/linguistic group form the categories by which they study and analyze the religious traditions of other cultural/linguistic groups. I want to examine the use of the Western term "canon" as a designation for collections of Chinese Buddhist religious literature.

Scholars of East Asian Buddhism habitually refer to the published anthologies of Buddhist texts that have appeared over the centuries as "the Buddhist canon." Our understanding is that the texts contained in such anthologies are, in some unspecified sense, scriptural. However, when one examines their contents, one finds that they contain a wide variety of texts in many disparate genres. There are sutras to be sure, but one will also find histories, dictionaries, learned treatises, poems of praise, ritual texts, instruction manuals, monastic regulations, and others besides.

This leads the present author to wonder if "canon" is a useful designation for such anthologies. In order to explore this problem, the author introduces the etymology and history of the word "canon" in Western religion and scholarship. Beginning in the Roman Empire as a way of designating books deemed essential for a proper education, the word came to mean a set of texts that provided a "rule" or a standard for a religious tradition.

This survey complete, the chapter then probes the Chinese Buddhist anthologies in order to see in what ways they do or do not fit the category. This means looking at the Chinese term for such anthologies, *dazing jing* or "great treasury of classic texts," to see to what extent its semantic range coincides with that of the English word "canon." In conclusion, the author presents suggestions for a different mode of analysis and a better, more accurate terminology in the hope that better categories will yield more clarity in scholarly communication. While I do not anticipate that the field will abandon the word "canon" as a result of this exercise, I hope at least to make scholars aware of the connotations that the term brings with it, and to stimulate discussion on the things that make Chinese Buddhist anthologies distinct from Western canons.

## What is a "canon"?

The word "canon" goes far back in Western linguistic history. Scholars speculate that it derives from a Sumerian word for a particular kind of reed plant that was used for measuring, and made its way into Greek via various Semitic languages. In Greek, the word came to mean both "rule" (something normative) and "list" (something purely descriptive and synonymous with *katalogos*). This second meaning as "list" appears later in history and is rarer.[1] While these two meanings may not always apply to all phenomena known as "canons," Einar Thomassen points out that in the case of lists of canonical books, they do; such lists are both normative and descriptive.

However, a closer look at the usage of the word "canon" in all its contexts reveals a much broader semantic range. For instance, as Jonathan Z. Smith points out, we may use the word "canon" to indicate the list of an author's authenticated texts (as in "the Shakespearean canon").[2] The word has been used to describe a more informal list of works deemed desirable for basic cultural literacy. Tomas Hägg notes that the Greeks first used the word in this sense to indicate works of drama, philosophy, and oratory that they considered essential for education.[3] In fact, the related word "classic" originally meant works to be read in class for the training of students.[4] In both of these cases, the word "canon" points only to a catalogue, not a published collection.

The use of "canon" to indicate a normative set of texts arose strictly within Western religious traditions. Judaism, Christianity, Islam, and various Iranian religions acted on the increasingly perceived need to create a closed set of privileged texts, a process Wilfred Cantwell Smith called "scripturalization."[5] These texts functioned in specific contexts, sometimes liturgical (what books may be read during a religious service?) and sometimes juridical (what books may serve as ultimate authorities for regulating the life of a community?). In this regard, it is interesting to note that not all sets of authoritative or normative texts receive the designation "canon": no one refers to the US Constitution and Bill of Rights as canonical, despite their privileged role in law and politics.

Scholars of religious studies have contested the concept of "canon," in part because the category of "canon" is inadequate to the evidence when applied globally. Gregory Schopen has already shown convincingly that the Western academic study of Buddhism was initially conducted within a Protestant framework, in which written scriptures reigned supreme over all else (*sola scriptura*).[6] However, I would extend that claim and say that an essentially Protestant view of scripture has informed not just the study of Buddhism but also the overall approach of religious studies to canons in general. For example, scholars regularly assert that works deemed "scripture" within religious communities achieve canonical status because of a putative connection with "the sacred," an idea that reflects the Western monotheistic idea of scriptures as the word of God.

This idea can lead to confusion when applied to other religions, however. Kendall Folkert, in his brief study of the concept of canon, pointed to a particular puzzle in the academic study of Jain scriptures. On the one hand, Jains officially recognized a certain body of scriptural texts as a formal canon. On the other hand, there were texts outside of this canon that clearly enjoyed high status and a prominent place within the ritual life of the Jain community. Folkert resolved this problem by proposing a twofold typology of canon, "Canon I" and "Canon II." Canon I comprised texts that gained their authoritative status through their employment by the community; in this case, he meant liturgical texts that gained their privileged place through their long-standing use within ritual. Canon II, by contrast, comprises texts that are authoritative in the way that Protestant theology conceives of the Bible; they are inherently authoritative due to their divinely revealed source and content. Folkert contended that confusion arose when scholars were mistakenly trying to understand "Canon I" texts (privileged by long-standing use) as if they were "Canon II" (privileged because divinely revealed), applying a strictly Protestant notion to a non-Christian phenomenon.[7]

In a similar vein, Einar Thomassen notes that texts may become authoritative for a community through either revelation or tradition. If it comes to the community through revelation, then it is the status of the source that grants the text its authority. If tradition is the mechanism, then long usage becomes the basis for a text's privileged status. While this vocabulary is different, one may detect some overlap with Folkert's categories. Tradition and usage would correspond to Canon I, while revelation would align with Canon II. However,

Thomassen goes on to say that the two categories may converge in a single text when a community attributes a text long in circulation to revelation. At this point, the text exhibits features belonging to both categories of Canons I and II. Thomassen claims that a text becomes sacred scripture when this convergence occurs.[8]

I wish to propose here that we also need to look at canons from two perspectives. Following Folkert's dual model with Thommassen's modifications, I will suggest that canon formation takes place in two stages. The first, corresponding to Folkert's Canon II, takes place prior to canonization and involves the setting of criteria for the acceptance of texts as canonical, and that under this heading, few of the texts of the various Chinese Buddhist canons would qualify. The second takes place after the establishment of a set of texts within a catalogue and corresponds to the kind of ritual usage that Folkert describes as leading to Canon I, and under this rubric I believe that the Chinese anthologies do qualify as canonical. In other words, I will describe the process that flows into the assembling of a set of privileged texts in terms of Folkert's Canon II, and the continuing evolution of that assemblage's privileging in terms of his Canon I.

## The formation of the Chinese Buddhist canon

Tanya Storch has ably described the earliest phases of the process of canon-formation in Chinese Buddhism in her book *The History of Chinese Buddhist Bibliography*. At the outset, there were no unified collections of Buddhist texts, only a set of manuscripts that grew as texts entered China and were translated. The earliest products of this effort were what Jonathan Z. Smith would call simple "lists" of texts with no criteria of inclusion. In the next phase, critical lists of Buddhist texts produced by a series of monk-scholars beginning with Daoan 道安 (312–385) over several centuries correspond to what Smith has called "catalogues," that is, ordered lists with stated criteria of inclusion having internal organization.

As Jiang Wu notes, these were entirely Chinese creations; there was no Indian model of a canon for catalogers to emulate.[9] Thus, it is not surprising that the only texts included in the earliest Buddhist bibliographies were those attributed to the Buddha and the small set of Indian thinkers who composed the Abhidharma texts. Cataloguers authenticated texts by verifying that they had been put into Chinese by a known and trusted translator.[10] It is also not surprising that these early cataloguers classified indigenous Chinese texts as "spurious" or omitted them altogether.[11] Such native productions lacked both the claim of revelation and validation by tradition. Such catalogues, however, lacked two things: authority and closure. (1) It is not at all certain that any Chinese Buddhist individual or institution had any obligation to use these catalogues to regulate their own collection and use of manuscripts. (2) New texts and translations continued to appear, precluding any catalogue from achieving finality at this early phase. The catalogers themselves were aware of this problem. As Stefano Zacchetti explains, the story of Ānanda reciting the entirety of the Buddha's teaching at the First Council planted the idea of a defined corpus of texts within the imagination of the early catalogers. This idea impelled them to seek out more texts in order to complete this imagined canon.[12]

The first of these two limitations changed when the imperial court involved itself in the process. Emperor Wu of the Liang dynasty (Liang Wudi 梁武帝, 464–549) was the first to commission catalogues, and for a time both officially sanctioned catalogues serving imperial interests and independent catalogues serving the needs of the sangha coexisted.[13] Eventually, the imperial court began assembling its own collection of manuscripts that served to provide official versions of Buddhist texts against which to check other manuscripts for accuracy, and catalogues changed their names accordingly from *The Multitude of Sutras* (*Zhongjing* 眾經) to *Inner Canon* (*Neidian* 內殿), implying that the true canon resided within the palace, with the emperor as guardian.[14]

The final evolution took place during the Tang dynasty (618–907). It was at this time that the court moved from sponsoring catalogues and accumulating manuscripts to publishing the collection of scriptures as a unified set. They determined the contents of the project based on the *Da tang kaiyuan shijiao mulu* 大唐開元釋教目錄 by Zhisheng 智昇 published in 730. This bibliography formed the basis for all subsequent printed editions of the canon.[15] The Tang dynasty also saw the first use of the title *Dazang jing* 大藏經,[16] printed texts rather than manuscripts, the adoption of a call number system, and a precise system of classification. The advent of printed collections replaced the manuscript practice that had made catalogues necessary in the first place.[17]

From the Tang dynasty forward, the imperial court generally ordered, supervised, and underwrote the publication of printed *Dazang jing*. The *Jiaxing Canon* broke that pattern, though, with interesting consequences. As Lianbin Dai explains, the *Jiaxing Canon* was planned by Zibo Zhenke 紫柏眞可 (1543–1603) with the help of lay patrons, and they produced a rationale for its contents. However, when the project was taken over by the monk Xingcong 性琮 (1576–1669), accusations of profit-seeking came forward and editorial control over the contents loosened considerably. Works originally excluded were now incorporated into the project, and contemporary works were selected for inclusion, possibly to gain subventions from the authors.[18] One example is the inclusion of the *Xifang helun* 西方合論 by Yuan Hongdao 袁宏道 (1568–1610), a work completed in 1599, when the publication of the *Jiaxing Canon* was already well underway. The consequence of this has been the expansion of subsequent Buddhist compendia such as the Taishō to include many more texts of less obviously canonical status than had been the case previously.

To review, so far we have seen that in the earliest phase of this process Buddhist scriptures entered China as Indian and Central Asian monks came in and, with the aid of teams of native literati, translated scriptures. Next, as the manuscripts began to accumulate and circulate, a few monks began putting together lists so as to create a kind of inventory of literature. Beginning with Daoan in the fourth century, monks and literati moved from making lists to making catalogues that both provided criteria for authenticating reliable literature and exposing spurious texts, and began organizing the literature by genre. By the sixth century, beginning with Emperor Wu of the Liang, the royal court began taking over the function of creating catalogues, and later courts began accumulating collections of manuscripts in order not only to establish catalogues of reliable texts, but also to maintain authoritative editions. By the end of the Tang, the court moved into actual production of printed editions of authenticated Buddhist literature.

By this time, nearly a thousand years had passed since Buddhism arrived in China, giving ample time for a tradition to develop. With this, the conditions were right for books to become canonical simply by communal acceptance and/or ritual usage over a long span of time. What had been a Canon II/revelation process of establishing texts by the authority of the source (the Buddha) and validity of transmission into China (identification of reliable translators) now had room for a Canon I/tradition process to work as well. At this juncture, the collection of Chinese Buddhist literature does not yet fit the conditions for the genesis of a canon as outlined by most scholars. There is as yet no convergence of revelation and tradition (Thomassen). There is no closure, since new literature continually appeared, necessitating new bibliographies.[19] Only some of the texts within the catalogues were normative in the sense that they could serve as courts of appeal for settling disputed questions. The process has moved from lists to catalogues, but no farther.

In the next section, however, I will argue that the publication of printed anthologies under the title *Dazang jing* 大藏經 created the conditions for a true canon to appear.

## Print canons

What I described in the previous section may be regarded as the processes that flow *into* the creation of a canon; none of the products of these processes is a canon yet, but provide the conditions for canon-creation. Now I will turn to the phenomena that flow *out of* the formation of a canon. I choose the appearance of printed anthologies in the tenth century as the pivot point between the flow in and the flow out because a printed anthology of texts, regardless of the motives that brought it into being, produces unintended consequences, consequences that contribute to the canonization of its constituent texts.

Once all the texts within the collection have been set in a uniform font on pages of uniform size and format and have been bound in uniform covers with uniform binding, the simple visual impression that the set conveys as a whole is one of uniformity of content and status. As Jonathan Z. Smith observed, canonization and canon are as much products of technology as theology; the invention of the codex matters. The codex and printing can turn a miscellaneous library into a single work.[20] The title *Dazang jing* gives the aura of "canonical text" (*jing* 經) to *all* the works included, even if individual texts lack this designation and status on their own. The use of a standard call number system for retrieving individual texts also contributes to the impression of unity.

In the case of the Chinese Buddhist *Dazang jing*, this homogenizing process gives rise to concrete effects. To understand what it did and did not do, we may turn to Miriam Levering's contribution to the 1989 book *Rethinking Scripture*.[21] In her discussion of scripture in Chinese Buddhism, she identified four different modes of reception and use: the informational, the transactional, the transformative, and the symbolic. In the first two of these modes, the creation of an anthology with uniform production features does not seem to have made all the texts equal, while in the last two, it seems to have had just that effect.

(1) Reception may be described as *informational* when members of the community read texts for their ostensive meaning in order to inform themselves. Clearly, only a handful of Chinese Buddhists have ever read through an entire printed collection for this purpose. The modern monk Yinshun 印順 (1906–2005) did so,[22] but I know of no others. The vast majority select from a few sutras that have achieved high status; Raoul Birnbaum notes that by the early twentieth century, the *Lotus Sutra*, the *Huayan Sutra*, and the *Śūraṅgama Sutra* were preeminent,[23] while my survey of late Ming dynasty literati conversation literature has revealed a few more. If one were to regard the entire *Dazang jing* as canonical, then we might consider these texts as a "canon within the canon."

It is within the informational mode of reception that individual texts within the Chinese Buddhist canons function to provide authoritative support in settling matters of doctrine. For example, as I have written elsewhere, Chan practitioners often disparaged Pure Land practice in late imperial China. The Pure Land side responded by saying that their beliefs and practices were supported by sutras, which were by definition the word of the Buddha. The Chan side, in contrast, relied on treatises and the "recorded sayings" (*yulu* 語錄) of past Chinese masters. In this case, the Pure Land side claimed that texts of higher status and authority supported their practice. The Chan side, relying on texts of lower status, were in no position to criticize.[24]

(2) By *transactional* Levering refers to texts used primarily in rituals in order to do things such as create merit, obtain the empowerment (*jiachi* 加持) of a buddha or bodhisattva, or produce a magical effect such as making rain. As with the first category, it would be rare for a practitioner to use the entire *Dazang jing* for this; in general, one uses a particular sutra or *dhāraṇī* text for this purpose. One exception to this is the practice of leafing through the entire *Dazang jing* with a glance at each page as a way of gaining merit. Otherwise, transactional practices such as recitation (without regard to whether or not the reciter understands), writing out scriptures in blood, and so on utilize only the sutra literature, and focus primarily on the same small set of scriptures mentioned above.

Over the years, scholars have noted many kinds of practices that fall under this rubric. Robert Campany documented many cases during the early period in which simple ownership of a Buddhist sutra benefited a family, regardless of whether anyone could read it for its meaning or not.[25] Many scholars have documented the practice of hand-copying a sutra, sometimes using gold or silver ink on fine paper, sometimes mixing one's blood with the ink. For example, Beverly Foulks McGuire included the late Ming dynasty monk Ouyi Zhixu's (藕益智旭, 1599–1656) practice of blood-writing in her survey of his religious practices.[26] Ouyi himself explains the rationale for selecting the text for this practice in an epilogue (*ba* 跋) to a lay devotee's blood-copied *Lotus Sutra*. Comparing the search for wisdom with the drilling of a well, he states that one must first get through the dirt of the Āgamas, then the damp soil of the Vaipulya sutras, then the mud of the Prajñāpāramitā sutras before one arrives at the spring water of the *Lotus Sutra*.[27] Even though all the works Ouyi mentions are in the *Dazang jing*, and indeed all are sutras, he states clearly that the *Lotus Sutra* is of greater transactional value than the other named works. Clearly the texts of the *Dazang jing* are not of equal status.

(3) In the *transformative* mode, one engages with texts neither to gain information nor to transact exchanges of merit, but for personal transformation. Reception of scriptures in this mode pulls away from particular texts and can potentially extend to the entire collection since understanding of the words is not strictly necessary. Levering reports on elderly female devotees that came to sutra lectures but appeared not to be paying attention to the lecturer as they sat quietly and recited Amitābha's name or engaged in another practice.[28] For them, the selection of the text did not matter, though within the lecture context it was certain to be a sutra. However, Levering reports another case in which a man, after having experienced enlightenment, took up the life of a hermit and developed the practice of reading through the entire collection over and over. He said that he did not always understand what he was reading, but that after his initial enlightenment he still drew inspiration from the practice. Significantly, he said he learned this practice from his teacher, who also read all fifty-five volumes of the *Dazang jing*.[29]

(4) When we come to the *symbolic* approach, we encounter the mode of reception most likely to encompass the entirety of the published collection. According to Levering, this derives naturally from the early Mahayana "cult of the book," in which written texts symbolized the ongoing presence of the Buddha and his dharma. In later Chinese Buddhism, a monastery or convent sought to acquire a complete set; from the dynastic period monasteries besought the court to bestow the imperially sponsored published anthology, and Holmes Welch tells how the abbot of the Guanzong Temple 觀宗寺 in Ningbo traveled to Beijing in order to raise the money necessary to purchase a set.[30] This mode of reception most strikingly exhibits the tendency of published collections to take on a symbolic value by their mere existence as repositories of the entire Buddhist tradition. Their comprehensiveness and uniformity of appearance, and their enshrinement in a central part of the monastery, announces the centrality of the *buddhadharma* to all residents and visitors, whether or not anyone ever takes a volume out from behind the sliding glass doors to read.

While the symbolic mode of reception requires only the presence of the collection in a prominent place, it can intersect with the transactional or transformative modes when the site of display functions also as a locus of ritual performance. A good example of this is the practice of some monasteries of displaying the entire canon in a "revolving repository" (*lunzang* 輪藏). This was a specially made cabinet in which the monastery would display the entire print canon. The cabinet might sit on a pivot so that the entire structure would turn, or it would be stationary but have room for devotees to circumambulate it. The presence of this display satisfied the requirements of the symbolic mode, and in the transactional mode, individuals could vow to turn the cabinet or circle it a certain number of times in order to fulfill a vow or gain merit. In some cases, witnesses reported that the cabinet turned spontaneously in response to the fervor of the devotee's wish.[31]

## Analysis: Privilege and experience

We turn now to the question that forms the title of this presentation: Is a *Dazang jing* a canon? If so, in what sense(s)?

The answer is complicated. For one thing, the very process of identifying privileged texts within Chinese Buddhist history changed several times. Once a mass of texts in manuscript form began circulating, lists appeared, and after a while, the lists became catalogues. The catalogues were compiled according to stated standards, and the pre-Tang bibliographies, confining their contents to Indian and Central Asian Buddhist literature in translation, excluding Chinese productions, and presenting judgments on the reliability of this or that text, could be said to constitute a canon since they included texts taken as authentic and normative. They correspond to Folkert's Canon II insofar as the source of the text (the Buddha and a qualified translator) give the texts an inherent canonicity.

After some time, however, the imperial court took over the task of commissioning bibliographies, and once the catalogues served court interests rather than religious purposes, one might say the status of the texts became mixed. The advent of printed collections continued this trend, with textual normativity deriving from imperial sanction and the association of less normative texts with highly valued ones simply by virtue of a common imprint and standardized format. The *Jiaxing Canon*, in which editorial control was seemingly lost in a haze of commercial interest, could hardly be said to constitute a canon.

If we were to accept the definition of "canon" put forward by other Western scholars, we would be hard pressed to accept later published *Dazang jing* as canons. From the *Jiaxing Canon* to the Taishō, we have now to do with quite a large and motley collection of sutras and sophisticated Indic *śāstras* (often in multiple translations) mixed with Chinese commentaries, dictionaries, epistolary exchanges, Chan "recorded sayings" literature, ritual texts, non-Buddhist texts, and even the bibliographies themselves. This hardly comports with a collection of texts that is (depending on the scholar putting forth the definition of "canon") normative in its entirety, a resource for resolving disputed questions, a closed set, or an anthology sanctioned by its origin in revelation or long-standing tradition.

However, as I have tried to show, there is some room for regarding the various *Dazang jing* as canons. They contain texts that are unquestionably canonical such as the *Lotus Sutra* or the three Pure Land sutras. The publication of *Dazang jing* with identical design and publishing specifications gives, as Smith noted, an *appearance* of uniform canonicity, which comes to expression in such practices as reading through the entire set (whether in earnest or by simple leafing through) and acquiring the entire set and putting it in a centralized display as a symbol of the Buddha's presence. The very same set of texts, if purchased from difference sources with different cover designs, sizes, and fonts, would not give this same appearance or inspire the same practices.

Let us see if we can make some sense of this complexity. As a start, let us tentatively set aside words such as "canon" and "scripture" and focus on a term I have already used a few times herein: "Privileged texts." The advantage of this term is that it includes a verb, "privilege." While "canon" and "scripture" as nouns focus our attention on the objects and move us to try to understand them in an essentialist way, the inclusion of the verb "privilege" reminds us that the identification of texts as canonical is a human activity and invites us to examine the workings of human agency in all its intricacy. It also frees us from the need to see if Buddhist literature meets the criteria for inclusion in Western categories, allowing us to consider its function from a purely emic perspective.

Human beings may privilege texts in many ways and for many purposes. For instance, we have already seen that sutras, as word of the Buddha, formed the initial core of the canon and were subsequently deemed the sine qua non without which a collection of Buddhist literature could not be a canon. However, lest we are tempted simplistically to identify the sutra literature as a "canon within the canon," let us remember that even within the sutras themselves we can see variations in privileging. Ouyi identified the *Lotus Sutra* as preeminently suitable for the ritual of blood-copying, while other sutras were of lesser status. The idea of a "canon within the canon" allows only for a single subset within the larger whole. In reality, levels of privileging form a continuum. In cases where the devotional practice involves placing the entire canon in a central space in order to symbolize the presence of the Buddha and his teaching, then all of the texts of the canon can serve regardless of their individual levels of privilege. The symbolic function requires the sense of completeness. At the other extreme, a practice such as blood-copying utilizes only a single text privileged over all the others. Therefore, we must be prepared to identify many different levels of privileging even within a single canon.

The idea of "privileged texts" also allows for a more phenomenological account of canon. Attention to the human element when discussing canonization reminds us that the way human beings *experience* such texts is a part of the phenomenon. In order to describe this experience, I will borrow terms from the sociologist Peter Berger. For him, the social creation of a world-of-meaning takes place in three stages: externalization, objectivation, and internalization.[32] I will utilize the first two of these: externalization as the process whereby human beings create understandings and project them out into the world, and objectivation, whereby the projected ideas come to acquire the status of ineluctable objective reality and people forget that they were originally human products.

Several of the analytical moves made already in this chapter have pointed to this process. Folkert's Canon II, Thomassen's revelation, and my own exposition of processes that flow into canon formation represent the stage of externalization. These are processes by which texts appear and readers make judgments on whether and how much to privilege them. Every step from Ānanda's reputed recitation of all the Buddha's sermons to a Chinese cataloger declaring a text "authentic" or "spurious" to court scholars settling the contents of a printed canon represents this externalization, this production of a reality. Folkert's Canon I, Thomassen's "long usage," and my own description of processes that flow out from canonization demonstrate the second step of objectivation. Texts that human beings at first simply *deemed* canonical are now experienced as *really* canonical. Later generations were not present during the phase of externalization but inherited the products of this process, and so the collection of texts confronts them as objectively privileged. From this point, the ritualization of textual practice reinforces the texts' objective canonical status. While one rotates a "revolving repository" because it contains the canon, the ritual act itself ongoingly constitutes the collection of texts as canon. While one makes a blood-copy of the *Lotus Sutra* because it is preeminent among sutras, the ritual act of blood-copying ongoingly constitutes the text as preeminent. The experience validates the rituals, and the rituals sustain the experience.

The socialization of individuals into the Buddhist community, ritualized textual practices, and any number of other factors may help maintain the privileged status of a text or collection of texts, but Berger reminds us that all such social constructions are fragile. Thus, we could ask how changes in the transmission and format of the canon might alter its status. Several authors, such as Fang Guangchang, have pointed out that the current work of digitizing the Buddhist *Dazang jing* will inevitably change the nature of the canon.[33] One could ask what is to become of the ritualized practices that center on the canon and maintain its canonicity. Can one circumambulate a DVD-ROM or place it on a high seat and reverence it? What kinds of practices may one direct at texts that appear on websites? When the whole collection resides only on the internet and one may open only one page at a time, how will it perform its function of symbolizing the totality of the Buddha's teaching? It is still too early to say what effect digitization will have on the community's experience of the canon in the future.

Of more consequence, I believe, is modern critical scholarship itself. Here is an anecdote: While pursuing my doctoral research on Buddhism in Taiwan many years ago, I came across a copy of *Sangha Magazine*, a publication for monks and nuns. Inside the front cover was an editorial by a monk then attending a Buddhist seminary. He expressed great confusion over the fact that every day he recited the *Amitābha Sutra* (*Fo shuo amituo jing* 佛說阿彌陀經, *T.* 366) as part of the morning liturgy, then went to classes in which he learned that this sutra was probably not really the word of the Buddha. While the ritualized practice reinforces this text's status as canon, his academic work undermined it and made it appear an ordinary human production. As Berger says, reminding members of a religious community that the contents of their reality were externalized by human beings lessens their ability to regard such reality as objective. Individuals under these circumstances may experience a text as privileged less and less. The ultimate impact that critical scholarship will have on the ability of Buddhists to continue regarding their *Dazang jing* as canon will bear monitoring as time goes on.

## Conclusion

The complication of this analysis was inevitable. Canonization of a text or a set of texts is, in the end, a human process of privileging some texts over others. The act of privileging has been done, as we have seen, by catalogers, exegetes, and the imperial household. After the religious community has accepted that privileging and it becomes part of the worldview with which members of the community are raised, the texts then take on the aura of sacrality and the community responds by engaging in acts of exegesis and devotion, and by experiencing the accepted moods when in their presence. "Privileging," however, is not a single act that applies uniformly across all texts. It is done differently in different contexts and for different purposes. Ouyi thus identifies the *Lotus Sutra* as supremely privileged for purposes of a transactional practice such as blood-copying, while an entire printed canon of many heterogeneous texts may be privileged in order to symbolize the Buddha's presence or as a focus of merit-making practice when it is enshrined in a revolving repository. The multiplicity of modes, contexts, and purposes for privileging texts will make the identification and study of canons perpetually complex.

Shifting from the essentialist language of "canon" to the dynamic language of "privileging" allows for analysis of textual practice along multiple dimensions:

1. The dimension of *rationale*: Why has a text or set of texts been privileged? For example, is it because the text is purportedly the word of the Buddha, or because an editorial board decided for its own reasons to include it in a collection?
2. The dimension of *intensity*: To what extent is a text or collection privileged, and are all texts within the collection equally privileged or are there variations? If there are variations, are they random or arranged within a hierarchy, as in various Chinese Buddhist *panjiao* 判教 (scriptural classification) schemes?
3. The dimension of *context*: Is a text privileged within all contexts or only within specific ones? For instance, do various schools or individual practitioners privilege individual texts from the same collection differently? Is one text privileged most highly within a ritual tradition while in another context it is used for purposes of lecture and study?
4. The dimension of *acceptance*: Do all members of a community accept the privileging of a text or a collection to an equal degree? Does one segment of the community prize one text most highly while other segments revere a different text?

Concomitant with the language of privileging is the language of *de*-privileging. The study of canons and canonization must also attend to developments such as Chan's rhetorical deprecation of scriptures and modern academic critical studies of Buddhist literature. These trends may erode the very bases upon which the privileging of texts rests, and canonical studies must pay attention to this as well as to the processes of canonization.

Finally, should we continue to translate *Dazang jing* as "canon"? Scholars will have to answer this question based not only on the academic criteria they establish for their own use, but also by observing the way the Buddhist community experiences and interacts with its "canonical" collections of texts. In some cases, it may be appropriate to use a different term. Levering, noting the problems with the term "canon," for the most part simply transliterates *Dazang jing* without translation. I suggest that the word *zang* could be translated as "treasury," which in English denotes a curated collection of texts, among other meanings. However, the term "canon" has become so entrenched that even in this chapter I could not refrain from applying it for productions such as the *Jiaxing Canon*! If this discussion has at least raised some reflection on the implications of the term, I will be satisfied.

10

# Our *Buddhadharma*, Our Buddhist Dharma

Franz Metcalf

What you are now reading is a revision of the 2012 commencement address for the Institute of Buddhist Studies (henceforth "IBS") that Richard Payne, then dean, invited me to deliver. As such, it is more intimate and less polished than the usual academic chapter, but perhaps it makes up in gratitude and candor what it lacks in intellectuality. I state this up front because I feel there is no understanding of the point and possible use of this text without an awareness of its original context of time, place, and audience. I do, now, include bibliographic references and quotations not present in the original address. More importantly, I extend the argument to be more relevant to scholars of Buddhism, as well as "mere" Buddhists, and I update my argument in response to recent work in the—I am deeply happy to say—increasingly sophisticated study of contemporary global Buddhist practices and cultures. All that said, I still invite the reader to engage this chapter as did its original audience of sincere scholars and practitioners of Buddhism, assembled under Richard's eye to honor and encourage the achievement and promise of a new generation. Scholar, practitioner, or both, please ask yourself: What is *my* dharma toward the *buddhadharma*?

* * *

I propose to ask and answer two questions—just two, and they are exceedingly simple. First, who *is* (a) Buddhist? Second, what should be a Buddhist's *relation* to Buddhism? These questions intend to explore the matter of the chapter title: just what is the *buddhadharma* and what (if you will pardon a rather Hindu usage) is our Buddhist dharma, or duty, toward it?

Who is Buddhist? A common-sense answer might be "someone who participates in Buddhism." Trouble is, in this matter, we do not *find* clarity. If we want clarity, we shall have to *create* it, and that creative activity entails an ethical relationship with Buddhism and with Buddhists.

The last two decades of scholarship have unmasked the Orientalist project of defining Buddhism, revealing an unflattering reflection of Western colonialism. I am aware that my entry into this process of definition cannot but perpetuate some of those dynamics. Yet, I see denying my role (and yours) as an abdication of my ethical responsibility. In their introduction to *Defining Buddhism(s)*, Karen Derris and Natalie Gummer powerfully articulate this situation:

> To characterize defining Buddhism(s) as an ethical process is thus quite distinct from a simplistic or self-righteous moral condemnation of Orientalist scholars from previous generations; instead, it necessitates that scholars recognize both their responsibility for their representations of Buddhist traditions and the dynamics of power operative in the production of knowledge about Buddhism(s).[1]
>
> Those of us engaged in the study of Buddhism(s) are inevitably engaged in defining Buddhism(s), even if we refuse a positivist definitional project; such is the power inherent in representation. Reconceiving of definition as an endless dialogical process does not eradicate that power, but rather places it in service of the (necessarily imperfect and ongoing) ethical project of reciprocal elucidation.[2]

So, why would I want to blunder into a colonialist and positivist definitional project? I do this to remind us how alluring that project remains and how likely we are to engage in it despite our conscious efforts not to. As the Buddha taught us,

> People love their place . . . : they delight and revel in their place. It is hard for people who love, delight, and revel in their place to see this ground . . . , "because-of-this" conditionality. . . . And also hard to see this ground: the stilling of inclinations, the relinquishing of bases, the fading away of reactivity, desirelessness, ceasing, nirvana.[3]

Admitting, then, that I am such a person and that you are also such, at least at times, let us indulge ourselves in a brief and at least partially self-aware excursion into our primitive Buddhological past: the quest for clarity on what Buddhism is. I shall start that quest with a provocative article in which Hillary Rodrigues provisionally granted Buddhist status, indeed, *buddhavacana* (word of the Buddha) status, to the teachings of Jiddu Krishnamurti, the great twentieth-century anti-guru. She asked "where we as scholars should cast the perimeter around our subject matter, about what is properly Buddhism, and what constitutes dharma, and what should or should not be regarded as *buddhavacana.*"[4] Her answer, rooted in Śāntideva's *Śikṣāsamuccaya* and, even earlier, in *Aṅguttara Nikāya* 7.79, the *Satthusasana Sutta*, is that words that lead toward nirvana are *buddhavacana*, whoever says them. After an overview of Krishnamurti's life and (anti-)teachings, Rodrigues concludes that his words do indeed lead toward nirvana and thus qualify as *buddhavacana*. I suggest that *buddhavacana* must by definition form part of Buddhism. Following this logic, is a person—in this case, Krishnamurti—who speaks or heeds those words Buddhist?

Not to take anything away from Rodrigues, but I found myself unwilling to follow her in labeling a man who for sixty years pioneered a pathless path, denying religion's very usefulness, a Buddhist. Krishnamurti infamously asserted, "I maintain that Truth is a pathless land, and you cannot approach it by any path whatsoever, by any religion, by any sect."[5] It seems to me this pronouncement is simply not in harmony with a religion calling itself the middle path. Nor did I wish to label "*buddhavacana*" the words of a man who said,

> For centuries we have been spoon-fed by our teachers, by our authorities, by our books, our saints. We say, "Tell me all about it—what lies beyond the hills and the mountains and the earth?" and we are satisfied with their descriptions, which means that we live on words and our life is shallow and empty. We are second-hand people.[6]

If Krishnamurti's words are *buddhavacana*, then those who participate in the choiceless awareness he advocated must be Buddhists. These conclusions feel false to me.

Our escape from this predicament is abetted by the work of Jonathan Silk, who attempted to find a definition for the elusive term "Mahayana."[7] He wisely turned to the experts in definition: semanticists, linguists, and philosophers. What did they teach him? They speak of two types of definitions for things: stipulative and lexical. Stipulative definitions define things exactly, as in legal contracts. Unfortunately, we must, at the very beginning of trying to define Buddhism (or any other religion), give up the quest for a stipulative definition. The work of scholars over at least the last two centuries has shown us that we could spend our whole lives pursuing such a definition in vain. My seventh cousin, Lewis Carroll,[8] imagined a civilization that "made a map of the country, on the scale of *a mile to the mile!*" When asked if it got used much, one of Carroll's character's answered, "It has never been spread out, yet . . . the farmers objected: they said it would cover the whole country, and shut out the sunlight! So we now use the country itself, as its own map, and I assure you it does nearly as well."[9]

We do not want to darken Buddhism with an artificial cover, no matter how exact it may be, if using Buddhism itself does nearly as well.[10] So, giving up the stipulative map/definition of Buddhism as large as the territory, we turn to the lexical definition, a few words that *refer* us to Buddhism, allowing us, as Mr Carroll says, to "use the country itself, as its own map." But we find this task, though diminished, still daunting and even possibly unending.

It turns out that Rodrigues, Śāntideva, and the *Aṅguttara Nikāya* were all defining Buddhism using what biologists call a phenetic definition. A phenetic definition is one that depends not on history, not on a diachronic development of a phenomenon over time, but rather on a similarity of characteristics without regard to history. A lexical and phenetic definition is how most of us define, for example, religion in general. I might assert that religion is a set of symbols, behaviors, institutions, and material objects that work together to give potentially ultimate meaning and certainly social cohesion to groups of persons. Various things may all be religions, even though they have no historical connection to each other. Thus, using a phenetic definition, Krishnamurti's teachings can be Buddhist simply because they sound that way. If we read *Aṅguttara Nikāya* 7.79 as saying that words in harmony with the Buddha's words and leading to nirvana are *buddhavacana*, then we are employing a phenetic definition of *buddhavacana*. And, if we do *that*, then we might do the same with Buddhism itself. Our definition might be: "Buddhism is that which is consonant with what has been accepted as Buddhism and which leads to nirvana." The task, then, would be to put criteria to the phrase "what has been accepted as Buddhism," as well as to define what, precisely, "nirvana" is.

But, as I say, I am not comfortable with this definition, so let us return to our project. If we do not wish to accept Rodrigues's phenetic definition of Buddhism (which results in our being almost comically inclusive), we must turn to something more historically rooted. As I expressed above, most of us feel intuitively drawn in this direction. We feel that what we call Buddhism or who we call a Buddhist must not simply *look* like Buddhism or Buddhists (e.g., Krishnamurti). We feel that what is Buddhist and what are Buddhisms must be in historically demonstrable continuity with established streams of Buddhist tradition. They must, to use the evolutionary term, *derive* from them. Thanks to Jonathan Silk, we know this sort of definition is called "phyletic" or "cladistic." We can now say Buddhists are people following streams of practice and their supporting texts and institutions that are derived from what we can trace back to recognized practices within the monastic sangha and, finally, to Gotama Siddhattha.

But what if we find something—the example of Aum Shinrikyō comes to mind—that is clearly phyletically Buddhist, but we would like to read out of the tradition? There is no question it is rooted in Buddhism, but we abhor it. What to do? Here is where I think a phenetic definition comes to the rescue. Did Aum Shinrikyō's teaching and practice lead to nirvana? If not, using the canonically supported phenetic definition, Aum Shinrikyō did not teach *buddhavacana* and it cannot be Buddhist. Our working definition of Buddhism is now complex, including both phenetic and phyletic dimensions. The latter is already problematic, since it entails tracing back forms of Buddhism to the founder. The former dimension, though, is even more challenging.

What exactly *are* the qualities we find exhibited in "Buddhism" and by "Buddhists"? Ideally, we wish to exclude everything that does not belong to the category, while including everything that does. We start with what we have already: things in harmony with Buddhism and which lead toward nirvana. But, as we have seen, this is too inclusive in one way and too exclusive in another. Krishnamurti's teaching is in (because his words are in harmony with *buddhavacana*), but, say, Bon Odori dancing is out (because it doesn't lead to nirvana). The problem here is we are using a monothetic approach: what is Buddhism must contain all of the qualities of Buddhism, and who is Buddhist must exhibit all these same qualities. Unless we want to restrict "Buddhists" to members of the *ariyasangha* and the *ariyapuggala* (those who have attained at least the first level of awakening, stream-entry), we need to scale back a bit. What we need is a polythetic approach: Buddhists and Buddhisms must have some good number of the qualities we find in a diffuse cloud that would then constitute the tradition. This approach is, serendipitously, a good sight more Buddhist, as well, as it does not posit an unchanging essence to the tradition. Rather than defining Buddhism by one criterion, it defines Buddhism as a loose and changing group of things that share family resemblances (to appropriate Wittgenstein), none of which are necessarily exclusive to Buddhism, and not all of which are necessary for something to be categorized as Buddhist. Rather than any posited essence, Buddhism, by this working definition, is defined by a set of qualities shared to greater and lesser degrees by institutions calling themselves "Buddhist," throughout space and time. We define Buddhism itself, as we ought to, as integrally part of *paticca-samuppāda*. Just as Gotama Siddhattha likely claimed to be recovering an already old and forgotten teaching, we continue to lose and find the face of Buddhism through its fleeting arisings. And, further, our acceptance of these familiar features is a constitutive part of that process.[11]

We seem to be getting closer to defining Buddhism. The devil is in the details, though, and it becomes our job as scholars—and perhaps even more so as practitioners (if we are such)—to get in there and do the devil's work. So, is being self-consciously "Buddhist" one of the familiar qualities of Buddhism? I think so, and both Krishnamurti and his teaching lack that quality. One strike against him. Do we need three to strike him out? Should we add "participates in ritual"? Or "values the Three Treasures"? Or "promotes the Eightfold Path"? Or "believes in *anatta*"? (A lot of would-be Buddhists would whiff on that pitch.) I believe we may need three of the latter to strike out a batter, but we need only the first to induce an out. A person can only be Buddhist who sees their self that way. This is true because, at least in my evolving view, persons can only be Buddhist if they are both phenetically and cladistically so. And what could constitute the personal embodiment of cladistic Buddhism? Buddhists must have histories, affinities, allegiances, or interactions actively connected to Buddhism in their individual experience. They are only Buddhist if their practices derive from Buddhism and they are conscious and accepting of this derivation, otherwise we do violence to their view and intention by labeling them Buddhist against their will. *Things* (in this case, what we call Buddhisms) may not have the necessity of this last criterion, but those "things" are fundamentally composed of persons with intentions and performing actions, and thus those things might also, at one remove, require a kind of self-consciousness to their Buddhism to be considered genuinely Buddhist. Things aside, certainly persons, because they have consciousness and intentions, are only Buddhist when they resemble Buddhists *and* consider themselves so *and* have experienced contact with Buddhism.

Tellingly, it is possible to consider Krishnamurti's words *buddhavacana* without them being Buddhist. This because we can define *buddhavacana* as words expressing awakened truth and then admit this truth is not cladistically "Buddhist." That is, as the canon has the Buddha himself say (for example, in the *Nagara Sutta*, *Saṃyutta Nikāya* 12.65), he was merely rediscovering an ancient understanding of things as they are. No tradition could coherently claim such understanding as its property, solely. We might accept that Krishnamurti's words express one specific formulation of how things are, that *buddhavacana* also expresses a formulation of how things are, and that these formulations overlap substantially. They exhibit strong phenetic similarity. Yet Krishnamurti's words need not be Buddhist; for that, they would need cladistic connection to Buddhism. I acknowledge that it is jarring to call something as far from

Buddhism as Krishnamurti's pathless land "*buddhavacana*," but at least I am here preserving us from having to call it "Buddhist." I would, in fear and trembling, assert that the tradition's use of *buddhavacana* is highly misleading, and that the term ought to be *bodhivacana* or even *dhammavacana*; the meaning lies in the message, not the messenger. Indeed, this raises profound questions about what really matters in "Buddhism." Ought it not, perhaps, be called "Bodhism" or "Dhammism," and ought we not perhaps let go of the Buddha? Essentially, Buddhadasa Bhikkhu and Stephen Batchelor, to give just two examples, have infamously and influentially answered, "Yes, let him go." Alternatively, one might let go of the aspiration to change Buddhism and just go to life with the religion you have, not the religion you might want or wish to have at a later time.[12] In any case, I am sorry to tell you—well, honestly, I am relieved to tell you—it is time for me to stop this train of thought and to leave the job to you. See, there is cladistics in *action*: I hand *you* the Three Treasures to define (and perhaps take refuge in). "Buddhism" is your responsibility now.

Wait! Is this right or fair? I believe so: scholars must define what "Buddhism" is. And this is simply because "Buddhism" is a scholarly category. But, as Jonathan Z. Smith famously wrote, "Map is not territory."[13] "Buddhism" will always and only be a map—something quite useful and over which its cartographers (in this case, scholars of religion) have rightful dominion. But there will also and always remain the territory of symbols, beliefs, rituals, groups, objects, and experiences our label "Buddhism" only maps, only signifies. In that realm, that *reality*, practitioners have dominion (though you will soon see that I also believe scholars have legitimate voice).

This brings us, as promised, to the question of our roles vis-à-vis this vague and vital thing we call—because our lives are too short to pronounce its full and ever-lengthening name—"Buddhism." What dharma, what duty, do we owe this *reality*? Are we really supposed to continually juggle these bowling balls—I am sorry, Treasures? In answer, I am going to invoke a currently highly influential authority, Thomas Tweed. Tweed recently wrote, in the virtual pages of the *Journal of Global Buddhism*:

> There is no pure substratum, no static and independent core called "Buddhism"—in the founder's day or in later generations. What we have come to call "Buddhism" was always becoming, being made and remade over and over again in contact and exchange, as it was carried along in the flow of things. Buddhist leaders have the right—even the role-specific obligation—to determine what constitutes "authentic" Buddhism, but scholars—and Buddhist practitioners when they contribute to academic conversations—have another duty, I suggest:

> to follow the flows wherever they lead. To study the historical or contemporary expressions of Buddhism is to trace the flow of people, rituals, artifacts, beliefs, and institutions across spatial and temporal boundaries.[14]

I admire the work of Professor Tweed and I am relieved that he lets us scholars off the hook. We need not—even *should* not—define what constitutes real Buddhism. That is for "Buddhist leaders." There is just one problem with Tweed's advice here: it is absolutely wrong. I say this with trepidation for stepping on his powerful toes, and, more importantly, for contradicting a vastly greater scholar than I shall ever be. Still, Tweed, as many (most?) others, presents what I find to be a disingenuously narrow view of "scholars" and "academic conversations." It is as if his definition of religion as translocative flowing and dwelling applies only to the vague and liquid sea of *religion* and stops at the firm and dry coast of *scholarship*, as if we could stand aside from the flow of contemporary Buddhism even as we study it. Of course Tweed himself knows we cannot. But he concludes his article with a strangely passive admonition:

> So recognizing the transfluence of fact and value and the mutual intercausality of all things—including our own scholarship—perhaps we should just lay back, point our toes, look skyward, and let the swirl of the cultural currents we study toss us this way and that. Let the fullness of the Buddhist tradition, in all its meanderings, wash over us, as we examine methodological assumptions and moral commitments, as we follow the flows that carry all of us along.[15]

Tweed seems here to see scholarship as W. H. Auden did poetry: it "makes nothing happen."[16] Auden might have been right about poetry, but I feel Tweed is wrong about scholarship, at least good scholarship. And when I say "good," I mean solid, useful, and effective. In fact, I dare to utter the word "prophetic." I suppose I should add something like Luther's "*Hier stehe ich, ich kann nicht anders, Gott helfe mir, Amen*" ("Here I stand; I can do no other. God help me, amen").

Tweed once asked, "But is it appropriate for religious studies scholars, as specialists in the comparative study of religion, to enter the public conversation about how they—and others—ought to act in the civic arena, at the PTA, the mall, or City Hall?"[17] For me the question is absurd on its face. I am reminded of Hillel the Elder's own powerful questions: "If I am not my self, who is? But if I am only my self, what am I? And if not now, when?"[18] It *is* for scholars to define Buddhism. It is for us to do *now*. And this now is *always*. The way we shall define Buddhism is by learning its views, values, practices, and institutions; critically holding all these up to Buddhism's own standards; clarifying where it succeeds and fails; and putting all this in the larger contexts of psychology, culture, history, and our own dialogue with Buddhists. Note that I am not speaking only of Buddhist scholars of Buddhism, I am speaking of *all* scholars of Buddhism, indeed, of all scholars of *religion*. Scholarship on matters of culture cannot divorce itself from values, cannot be value-neutral. I lack the space to adequately argue this position here; let us just say my view has roots stretching from Max Weber ("Objectivity in Social Science and Social Policy"), through George Devereux (*From Anxiety to Method in the Behavioral Sciences*), to Jürgen Habermas (*The Theory of Communicative Action*), and, closer to home, to Courtney Bender (*The New Metaphysicals*) and to Derris and Gummer, quoted earlier.

With regard to religion, again in my view, our work must examine traditions not only to inform the larger public, but also to guide those traditions, illuminating them for and with their practitioners. If our work is not revelatory, we have failed and our failure further erodes any chance that future work will be revelatory or even relevant. This is precisely Tweed's "transfluence of fact and value and the mutual intercausality of all things—including our own scholarship." Bender was surprised in her fieldwork by how deeply scholars and practitioners are caught in webs of relationships and appropriations that they themselves are often unaware or even in denial of. Religious landscapes (particularly in more educated and translocative contexts) exist fully enmeshed in their surrounding cultures, including scholarly ones. Indeed, they cocreate each other. Bender was surprised, but neither Buddhists nor scholars of Buddhism should be. I would add that *Buddhist* scholars of Buddhism need to be even more self-aware, as they need to embody Buddhism during the performance of their efforts, beginning with right speech, the first duty of scholars (not only Buddhist ones), but expanding, at least ideally, through the rest of *sīla* to *samādhi* and then to *pañña*.[19]

I might—well, okay, I have always planned to—go on to ask the question: If all this is so, then can a genuine scholar of Buddhism be *only* a scholar? Can you do this well and yet distort the *buddhadharma*? Can you do so and yet intentionally practice *himsa* or wrong speech? And, if not, then are you not also practicing Buddhism? Are you not displaying a good few of those family resemblances I spoke of? You may argue that you are not really a practitioner, you are really a scholar; that is your essence. But Buddhists smile condescendingly at the notion of essences, don't we?

This makes Buddhist scholar-practitioners contemporary versions of the *gantha-dhura bhikkhu*, the scholar-monk, a position that traditionally afforded considerable freedom of critique of the tradition. The position, first attributed to contemporary scholars by Charles Prebish,[20] might even partially apply, for reasons I barely mentioned, above, to committed and responsible scholars of Buddhism who do not consider themselves Buddhist. Natalie Quli (and, no doubt, others) may well object that this might be stretching the scholar-monk term too far. Further, she extends the anti-Orientalist warning against our scholarly tendency "to silence the native, the old colonialist strategy of controlling the native through controlling her history, ensuring that only elite, academic experts have the knowledge necessary to 'speak' for Buddhism."[21] Historically, she is certainly right, and I have to ask whether not just the Orientalist project of defining Buddhism for naive Buddhists, but also my larger call for the involvement of scholars in the shaping of the religious institutions they study, reinscribe old privileges. Perhaps my voice, despite my own preference for it to be merely one in a chorus, silences those of others. But who is to say? I mean that non-rhetorically. Who really is to say who can—who *must*—speak for and against Buddhism? And whose voice will be heard? What of you all, sitting there and being feted today? Who among you deserves the honor, or must face the duty, of critique? To echo Rabbi Hillel: If not you, who? If not now, when? I am afraid that, in my view, it is all of you, all of us, very much including myself.

So, it is not for me to withhold from any of you the privilege and the responsibility of flowing on with Buddhism into the future. As if you could exist separately from the dharma! As if I could withhold it from you! You are not merely following those flows: you are part of them. You may lay back and point your toes, as Tweed advises, but your every breath impedes and impels the smallest of those flows. More: I hope and trust that some of you will rechannel those flows, even the deepest and greatest of them. This is your dharma in all its senses: your teaching, your responsibility, what you uphold and what upholds you. You have been dharma students; now you will be dharma teachers, whether you chase PhDs or *anuttarā-samyak-saṃbodhi*. May all living beings benefit from your work.

11

# On Authenticity: Scholarship, the Insight Movement, and White Authority

Natalie Fisk Quli

## Introduction

When I was a young undergraduate student some years ago, I went on a class field trip to a Buddhist monastery in California. It was my first taste of Buddhism in a non-convert Buddhist setting: a temple complex largely maintained and attended by Asian American heritage Buddhists.[1] Raised in a non-religious, post-Christian, atheist family, I had always imagined Buddhism as an ancient, rational philosophical system that could offer the medicine of belonging to alleviate my alienation, a religious path focused on spiritual experience rather than rote ritual, one that didn't fall prey to the hierarchy and "superstitions" I saw in the other religions around me.[2] The field trip lasted a weekend, and during that time I encountered something other than what I had hoped to find. I discovered that Buddhism was a thoroughly human religion, lived by humans who were sometimes patriarchal, hierarchical, and so many of the things I wanted Buddhism *not* to be. I cried a lot that weekend. The Buddhism I wished for did not exist.

I think of this experience sometimes when I read about "real" Buddhism, particularly the Buddhism that has been formulated from the desires of sympathizers and converts. What I longed for was an ancient, authentic Buddhism, what I believed the Buddha must have taught. Instead, I was disappointed that living Buddhist traditions did not accord with my expectations or desires, which cannot be separated from my life experience and the cultural values I inherited as a white middle-class woman raised by moderately liberal atheist parents in predominantly white US suburbs.

The idea of authenticity via an ancient origin of the tradition (a "metaphysics of origins"[3]) operates not only on an individual level (e.g., outlined above) but in the drama of power, prestige, and influence in Buddhist social worlds. Authenticity in this respect functions as an authorizing narrative, a discourse of power through which a certain ideal is valorized and held up as proper by citing its ancient origins. Used as an authorizing discourse, authenticity narratives in Buddhist communities and in Buddhist studies scholarship function simultaneously as a means to empower one school, sect, or ideal of Buddhism as *the* true or real or original or proper "Dharma," as well as to disempower other Buddhisms as false, degraded, superstitious, childish, spurious, or otherwise unsuitable or improper.[4] Religious authenticity is a discourse of power: the power to authorize one's own views, teachings, practices, and even caste, race, etc., while cloaking any questionable motivations under a veil of religious purity.[5]

Thomas Tweed has urged scholars to "follow the flows" of Buddhist traditions wherever they lead.[6] In this chapter, I follow a flow—white authority—that has fed both certain streams of American Buddhism and strands of Anglo Western scholarship of Buddhism. The former derives part of its authority from the latter, as I try to demonstrate below. This particular cultural flow begins with Orientalist scholarship and its assumption of natural white authority. Expressed in a discourse of science and detachment, the researcher distanced him- (and her-) self from native "informants," who did not apprehend history and therefore were out of touch with the "real" origins of their religion. Their superstitions revealed as much, for the Buddhism narrated by early scholars was a textual, rational, scientifically measurable *thing* to which scholars had access by means of their superior historical methods.

Controlling Theravada's history in this manner dovetailed with an authorizing discourse, a metaphysics of origins, that exists in both Pali Buddhist and Western positivist traditions. This shared discourse, an instance of what Hallisey calls "intercultural mimesis," lent legitimacy to Orientalist scholarship, giving the scholar authority to speak for "tradition."[7] Once established as authorities on "real" Buddhism, scholars could compare living Buddhists with Buddhist texts, with the latter acting as a simple measure of the former's authenticity. Endowed with the power to speak for Buddhist authenticity coupled with racist assumptions of white supremacy that fueled the colonial project led to new developments in Buddhist traditions among white converts, who brought in their own cultural values and beliefs while cloaking them with an aura of tradition. This authority to speak for Buddhism's history and authenticity in convert circles is yoked to the assumption of white authority.

In this chapter I discuss authenticity discourses that join a metaphysics of origins with white authority, discourses of power that flowed from Orientalist scholarship through white convert discourse. Here I trace its movement from academic Buddhist studies through Col. Henry Steel Olcott to one of the offshoots of the Theravada tradition, the American Insight community. In all three cases—colonial scholarship, Olcott, and the Insight community—the use of Orientalist assumptions about living Asian Buddhist traditions form the foundation of claims for purity and authenticity, allowing for the exclusion of Asians and, in the case of American Insight, Asian Americans, as authorities. Being "real" Buddhists imbues convert discourse with power. Noting the persistence of this flow, I suggest scholars might look at the field of Buddhist studies itself to find evidence of this persistent stream of white supremacy expressed in authenticity claims.[8]

Drawing on Metcalf's call for ethics in scholarship in the previous chapter, I focus on the San Francisco Bay Area Insight community as a case study for naming harm—in this case, harm toward Asian Americans in the form of Orientalist stereotypes and exclusion based on racial bias—without need of evaluating Insight's authenticity. I hope to demonstrate that evaluating a group's relationship to "authentic" *buddhavacana* is not an important dimension of ethically grounded scholarship. In other words, we can criticize particular manifestations and discourses of Buddhism in the contemporary world without need of cloaking our critique in the faith language of authenticity, which is itself an expression of power.

Further, I note the manner in which a metaphysics of origins as a discourse of authenticity and therefore power (authority) plays out in sectarian identities, with the Bay Area Insight community developing an exclusivist sectarian identity based on racial stereotypes that disempower contemporary Asian and rival Asian American Theravada groups in the San Francisco Bay Area. Rather than taking part in this sectarian power battle myself by labeling Insight as discontinuous with Asian traditions (and therefore outside the field of Buddhist studies), I seek to demonstrate that this convert group's basis for claims of authenticity is in fact consistent with the Mahāvihāra lineage they seek to embody. Noting the manner in which Insight groups have made use of authenticity claims informed by implicit assumptions of white supremacy in the lineage of Orientalism, in a fashion quite similar to that of Col. Olcott, I intend to demonstrate how authenticity claims, white authority, and power via sectarianism are joined.

Finally, I question the scholarly use of authenticity discourses, both overt and covert, in describing contemporary Buddhists. Scholars, too, are rivals in the use of Buddhism as a means of obtaining and maintaining power, prestige, and influence. If we wish to both understand Buddhists and maintain an ethical presence in the field, I suggest following Tweed's approach in naming as "Buddhist" anyone who lays claim to this identity.[9] This does not prevent us from identifying areas of concern; rather, an honest appraisal of the constructed and contingent nature of the category of "Buddhism" frees scholars to engage ethics more directly through confronting harm, rather than obscuring it with authenticity claims and taking part in sectarian squabbles. We as scholars are ourselves embedded in systems of power, and as such we are in part responsible for the continuance of existing systems of racial, gender, and socioeconomic hierarchies in which we actively or passively participate. If we recognize our complicity in maintaining such hierarchical structures, then we may see our use of authenticity claims to exclude certain groups from the label "Buddhist" as what they are: a means to conceal our scholarly self-interest in maintaining or expanding privilege and authority.

## White authority and early American Buddhist converts

In *The American Encounter with Buddhism, 1844–1912*, Tweed created a typology of white converts, dividing them into esoterics, rationalists, and Romantics.[10] Popular among American converts and sympathizers was the idea that the Pali canon as preserved in Ceylon (Sri Lanka) was the earliest and therefore most authentic representation of the Buddha's teachings. This idea was formed in large part based on reading Anglophone scholarship.[11] Rationalists, in particular, who tended to be left-leaning professionals with an inclination to view Buddhism in terms of science, positivism, and logic, cited Theravada and Pali scriptures as the most authoritative representation of Buddhism. Tweed notes,

> Theravada Buddhism had been presented by Western scholars and Asian adherents as a rational tradition that emphasizes self-reliance, tolerance, psychology, and ethics. The tradition, the story went, rejects the unscientific and superstitious doctrines of Christianity such as the notion of a substantial self and a personal deity.[12]

The American Col. Henry Steel Olcott (and his associate Madame Blavatsky)[13] made headlines by publicly converting to Buddhism, taking the five precepts in

Ceylon in 1880. Riding the wave of a Buddhist revival that had already seized Ceylon,[14] Olcott assumed the responsibility of "cleansing" Ceylonese Buddhism by returning it to its pristine Pali roots, even going so far as to compose a *Buddhist Catechism* in 1881 to be used to educate Sinhalese Buddhists on their own religion. Olcott's hubris is somewhat astonishing, given that this man came from a non-Buddhist background and had studied Buddhism for only a few years at most, at a time when very little was known about Buddhism in white American circles. Yet he believed he was in the position to educate born-and-raised Buddhists on what their religion "really" was, in a country with more than two millennia of Buddhist history. Following the attitudes of many Western Orientalists in the academy, Olcott believed that original Buddhism had degraded under the Ceylonese,[15] and to this end he produced the Buddhist catechism in order to teach them what their religion *really* was.[16]

By what authority did Olcott presume to know more about what the Buddha taught, given his limited exposure to Buddhism and heritage Buddhists with deep family histories of Buddhist practice? By what rhetoric did he establish himself as the authority on authentic Buddhism? I recognize at least three types of authority at work: the traditional authority of the Sinhalese sangha, which he harnessed through the blessings of Ven. Hikkaḍuvē Sumaṅgala in the form of a certificate of approval printed at the front of *Buddhist Catechism;* his own charismatic authority; and the authority of whiteness legitimated through Orientalism. Olcott's assumption of natural (white) authority dovetailed with his very real access to channels of power granted only to white men. These two factors in concert granted him real authority on the ground.

Pali Text Society leader Thomas Rhys-Davids transformed the native's own story into the *world's* story through the alchemy of the Western (white) scholar's alignment with objective, universal science. The colonial-era Asian Buddhist was there to guide in the correct selection of texts to subject to careful study, allowing the scholar to uncover Buddhism's origins using historical techniques. Col. Olcott was heir to this "universal" Buddhism as a white man who understood Western science more than Sinhala Buddhists. Olcott presented his version of Buddhism—deeply flavored by esoteric, rationalist, and Protestant norms and modes of discourse—as the most authentic and valid version.

Scholars have applied the postcolonial critique of Edward Said to Western conceptions of Buddhism both during the colonial period and among contemporary converts,[17] noting the ways that early Western scholars of Buddhism, working in the period of European colonial domination in Asia, reproduced assumptions of Western imperialism in their scholarship on Buddhism. For example, early scholarship is rife with the idea that a philosophically advanced Buddhism had once flourished in ancient India but decayed among the ignorant masses. The Asian Buddhism that Western colonial-era scholars saw around them was decadent, superstitious, childish, and far removed from the pure, original, rational Buddhism that scholars (and converts like Olcott) believed had once existed. In this sense, colonial governmental control of Asian societies was seen (by those very colonial powers) as an act of charity: because Asians were by nature emotional and prone to barbarism they were unable to establish just societies or protect their own cultural heritage. The colonial administrator, rather than serving as an agent of colonial greed for domination, was instead cast as a benevolent ruler over childlike Asians. The colonial scholar curated the cultural treasures of authentic, original Buddhism, which had degraded under Asian mismanagement. In other words, both colonial administrators and colonial scholars shared the assumption that Asians could not be trusted to care for themselves; in order to save Asians and their cultural heritage, the benevolent West must take control.

For their part, early Orientalists saw in contemporary manifestations of Buddhism a degradation of their wished-for Buddha, who they imagined had been a great rationalist and not at all like the superhuman heroic Buddha represented in Asian Theravada circles.[18] Orientalists, working from the presumption that "real" religion is found in texts rather than practice,[19] worked on the Pali canon instead of studying and interacting with living Buddhists, who they saw as having limited authority when it came to understanding their own religion's history. Because scholars knew the texts better than Asians, they therefore knew "real" Buddhism better than the Asian people who actually engaged in the practice of the tradition. Using descriptors like "original Buddhism" or "pure Buddhism," scholars were set on rescuing Buddhism from superstition.

Given that early Western scholars and converts alike were inclined to use their white authority to power claims of authenticity, I suggest that rather than judging Olcott's Buddhism as inauthentic due to its hybridity with Western cultural flows,[20] we view it as one among many visions of Buddhism that brought together multiple streams of history, culture, philosophy, and so on.[21] Taking Olcott at his word that he's Buddhist, we're free to turn our attention toward other issues, such as those suggested by Peter Moran: "Through what discourses, and under what conditions, claims can be made to apprehend authentic Buddhism . . . [and] what subject positions are thereby valorized or rendered marginal in this process."[22]

## Defining authentic Buddhism

How can we see the project of scholarship *about* Buddhism as separate from issues of defining authentic Buddhism? Here I think Richard Payne's comments are instructive; he notes,

> As a concept, "Buddhism" is a nineteenth century invention. . . . It arises out of the imperialist expansion of Euro-American societies, which encountered a variety of differing local traditions and thereby created the intellectual horizon upon which these could be constellated as part of the "same" religious tradition.[23]

I see Buddhism not as a real thing "out there" that we can define, but rather as a set of constantly shifting discourses with no center.[24] Buddhist studies is, by way of this definition, about the discursive practices of human beings who call themselves Buddhist; it is not about Buddhism. This field includes human beings who call themselves Buddhists and all the activities therein: philosophy by humans who call themselves Buddhists; writings by people who call themselves Buddhists; group rituals by people who call themselves Buddhists, etc.

Buddhist studies, at least Anglophone scholarship from the United Kingdom and its former colonies, rests on a bedrock of Orientalist scholarship that defines Buddhism in ways that lend authority to colonial and contemporary Anglophone scholars. How we define "real" Buddhism has effects in terms of which projects are funded, what types of expertise are rewarded, and who is granted access to various channels of power. Given that the very definition of an "authentic" Buddhist (as opposed to a self-identified Buddhist) is intertwined with structures of power in academia—both in terms of *who* is doing the defining and *why*—I am skeptical of attempts to determine authenticity by means other than simple self-identification.

Still, I appreciate Franz Metcalf's attempts to work on such a definition in that it presses us into seeing our own roles as scholars in producing authorizing discourses that are, in turn, picked up and used by Buddhists. In his contribution to this volume,[25] Metcalf proposes that there is a "tradition" that makes up authentic Buddhism. That tradition, he proposes, is expressed in *buddhavacana*, "the word of the Buddha," and thus *buddhavacana* should form at least part of our definition of real Buddhism and real Buddhists. Instead of simply taking Buddhists at their word that they're Buddhist, we should evaluate their authenticity.

How do we define *buddhavacana*? Which Buddhists should we ask? Which texts (if any) should we consult, and why those and not others?[26] Peter Skilling, in his essay "Scriptural Authenticity and the Śrāvaka Schools,"[27] notes that despite efforts to locate truly authoritative texts that reflect the authentic teachings of the Buddha (*buddhavacana*), we remain at an impasse. Scholarship reveals that many of the texts that found their way into various canons are spurious or at least later writings, and many others simply either now exist only in translation or never had original Indic versions. Setting these aside for the moment (and admitting that doing so undermines the practice of a great many Buddhists, as Charles B. Jones notes in his contribution to this volume[28]), what of the Indic language texts we possess? Should they not be considered *buddhavacana* or "authentic Buddhism"? Certainly such texts were written or preserved by people who considered themselves Buddhists, but do they reflect the Buddha's real, historical teachings? Skilling notes that many among these texts are decidedly partisan. While some devout Buddhists may claim, for example, that the entire Pali canon dates to the very first *saṃgīti*, this claim is weakened by the inclusion of materials of later composition (e.g., the *Katthāvatthu* of the *Abhidhamma-piṭaka*). The multiplicity of Buddhist languages also introduces the complication of translation in conveying an author's "original" meaning, which may have long since been obscured.

We might try to locate authentic *buddhavacana,* for the purpose of comparing living "Buddhists" with texts to determine the former's authenticity, by assembling all the various sutra literature from all sources and declaring as likely authentic the ones that are found in all canonical collections. As Skilling points out, however, we have sutra literature from only three of the purported eighteen schools of early Buddhism. This is hardly a robust sample. He notes in his evaluation of Bhāviveka's excerpts from no-longer-extant texts:

> One thing is certain: most of the texts, titles, and even genres are unknown to us today. His [Bhāviveka's] brief citations of lost texts offer a glimpse of another side of the iceberg: they are not mere variant versions of known texts, but are texts about which we know absolutely nothing. This fact, combined with the recent revelations arising from the study of Gandhārī manuscripts, the Schøyen manuscripts, and new manuscript finds from Xinjiang and Tibet, leads us to the conclusion that there is much we do not know about the Buddhist literature of the early period.[29]

How are we to assume that something is *not buddhavacana* if our record is so utterly incomplete? If we intend to use texts to lay the foundation of what is Buddhism and who is an authentic Buddhist, the knowledge that we're missing considerably more than half of the early schools' canons should give us pause.

As Robert Sharf writes,

> The term "Buddhism" turns out to be a site of unremitting contestation as a cacophony of voices—each averring privileged access to the essence of the tradition—lays claim to its authority. Our own attempts to identify or stipulate the fundamental tenets, core practices, or even "family resemblances" that characterize Buddhism do little more than to add to this unremitting din, while at the same time distracting us from the obvious: the power of the term is sustained in part by its very indeterminacy, its function as a placeholder. The authority of the word "Buddhism" lies not in its normative signification(s) so much as in its rhetorical deployments.[30]

While I admit that it may throw the doors open wide, allowing some people we don't like to be included in the category of "Buddhism," a less sectarian and less exclusionary approach allows us to inquire into groups that may be harmful in various ways. Our ability to critique is not diminished; our call to ethics does not evaporate; our responsibility to the good remains. Metcalf is correct in noting that scholars are inevitably part of the streams of contemporary Buddhisms, whether we want to be or not. Realizing this leads me to question deeply my own responsibilities and motivations.

It seems to me that while determining authenticity may be a perfectly reasonable activity for Buddhists acting within their various traditions, a sectarian approach is ill-suited for producing knowledge about humans who call themselves Buddhist. The project of separating real Buddhism from false Buddhism is an act of faith, built on too many assumptions about what the Buddha may have been like, or might have taught, to be of value to scholars. Again, I do not mean to suggest that such acts of faith are unimportant for Buddhists; indeed, they are. It simply does very little to further our understanding of Buddhists when we scholars do it. To me, the more interesting questions are why someone would choose to identify as Buddhist; by what standards, criteria, and motivations are arguments over authenticity forwarded; and who benefits from the assignment of authenticity and its authorizing power.

In the following section I take up these questions by looking into a Buddhist group that has largely been ignored by Buddhist studies[31] scholarship for some time; at the same time it has been characterized by American religion scholars as a "new religious movement," suggesting that it does not have any historical continuity with Buddhist traditions in Asia (a not-so-subtle dig at its authenticity). Setting aside questions of authenticity (i.e., how continuous or discontinuous with Asian cultural flows it is, and therefore how much it reflects what the Buddha "really" taught), I consider: How has white authority, couched in a language of authenticity, undergirded sectarian motivations? What can we learn from this group about the operation of white authority in the construction of Buddhist authenticity? The last question has implications for scholarly practice.

## Case study: Bay Area Insight and white sectarianism

The mostly convert community that formed around the teachings of American Buddhists Jack Kornfield, Joseph Goldstein, and Sharon Salzberg, all of whom studied Thai Forest and Burmese *vipassanā* Theravada traditions in Southeast Asia in the late twentieth century, has a strong presence in the San Francisco Bay Area. The sectarian boundaries around the Insight community are porous in many ways; individualism is strongly valued in the acceptance of teachings and practices from a host of Buddhist and non-Buddhist traditions, notably convert American forms of Tibetan Tantra and Zen. It is a question whether or not these groups should be described as Theravada or if another label might be more appropriate; I have opted to simply collectively call these groups Insight communities (from the English translation of the Pali *vipassanā*), which has the added benefit of being an emic term.

As previous studies have noted, Insight communities have historically been mostly white and middle class, and their members are more highly educated than the average American.[32] Most community members who attend Bay Area Insight events or who are sangha members are largely first-generation white converts; there is a minority component of non-whites (Asian American, African American, LatinX, and others), many of whom are first-generation converts from various faiths.[33] Additionally, a small contingent of heritage Buddhists from Asian American backgrounds, as well as second-generation white Buddhists, are active in Bay Area Insight organizations.[34]

A number of studies of American alternative religions have identified such groups as new religious movements (NRMs), with roots in 1960s counterculture.[35] Of course, Buddhism is not a "new" religion at all, so placing these groups in the category of NRMs highlights their discontinuity with established religious traditions, and this too carries with it claims regarding authenticity. For example, the apologetic scholar Jacob Needleman notes, in his 1970 monograph *The New Religions*, that regarding Buddhism in [white]

America, "from where we stand, there is still the possibility that nothing at all will grow, or that what does grow will be twisted and barren." His concern with authenticity flows throughout this work, evidenced by comments such as the following: "If someone were to predict that in ten or fifty years, twenty million Americans would be Buddhists, it would by itself mean nothing. If twenty million Americans became *real* Buddhists, that of course would be extraordinary."[36] This sort of anxiety in the scholarship on the growth of white convert Buddhism in the 1970s and 1980s is frequently weighted by judgments of shallowness, faddishess, and so on. The framework of NRMs seeks to highlight the *newness* of these groups and their *discontinuities*, rather than continuities, with established Asian Buddhist traditions. American religion scholar Paul Numrich suggests that this is appropriate, in that (non-Asian) converts "come to their new faith from completely different experiences and perspectives than do the immigrant Asians who were born and raised Buddhist."[37]

Much of early NRMs scholarship came out of my own alma mater, the Graduate Theological Union (GTU) in Berkeley, California, one of the first US educational institutions to study and document the growth of non-Abrahamic religions in the United States through its Center for the Study of New Religious Movements. The center's 1983 report to the Rockefeller Foundation describes its intentions to document NRMs as a "response to changes in the basic values" of Americans that was "linked conceptually with the notion of a crisis in values" fomented by the Vietnam War and the Watergate scandal. One of the projects undertaken by the center was collecting original source materials related to NRMs (pamphlets, books, flyers, etc.); this material is now archived in the Center for the Study of New Religious Movements Collection at the Flora Lamson Hewlett Library. A substantial number of Buddhist materials were collected, overwhelmingly of Tibetan and Zen convert groups, with some Insight and Nichiren materials as well. Nothing whatsoever was collected from heritage Buddhist groups, such as the Buddhist Churches of America (BCA).

The materials included in the files (e.g., new age Christian groups, convert Buddhist groups), coupled with the groups that were excluded (African American, Asian American, fundamentalist Christian movements, etc.), suggest that whether implicitly or unconsciously, the center focused its research efforts on groups that were perceived as threats to mainstream or conservative white Christianity. This helps contextualize the ways in which these groups, including Buddhist ones, were constantly scrutinized for their authenticity by early (and later) scholars, many of whom were in fact Christian apologists. As stated previously, authenticity is a discourse of power, and those in power saw white convert Buddhism as a threat to white Christian authority.[38] Emphasizing convert Buddhism as a break from tradition, as a "new religion," obscures its connections to Asian Buddhist traditions and erodes its legitimacy and authority.

What if we focused on Insight's continuities with tradition rather than its discontinuities ("newness")? The roots of the American Insight community do, of course, lead back to Southeast Asia, where many of its founding members trained as monastics or laypeople in the Thai Forest and Burmese *vipassanā* movements in the late twentieth century. The Mahāvihāra-derived Pali Tipiṭaka forms the authoritative textual tradition for the Insight movement, which is also consonant with Asian Theravada traditions. Instead of a "new" religious movement, Insight can be seen as a sectarian movement within the greater Theravadin tradition.[39]

The Pali canon holds a special place of authority in Southeast Asian Theravada traditions, yet it has always been used in tandem with other forms of authority, particularly the authority of the commentaries and of the monastic sangha itself. Only when sectarianism and the elimination of rivals became important was the Pali canon trotted out to wield its metaphysics of origins in order to authorize one group's special claim to purity.[40] This tactic seems to go all the way back to the very inception of the canon:

> Rather than pre-existing the Theravāda school, as the textual basis from which it arose and which it sought to preserve, the Pali Canon—by which I mean the closed list of scriptures with a special and specific authority as the avowed historical record of the Buddha's teaching—should be seen as a *product* of that school, as part of a strategy of legitimation by the monks of the Mahāvihāra lineage in Ceylon in the early centuries of the first millennium A.D.[41]

Steven Collins argues that the production of the Pali canon coincides with sectarian rivalry in the Sri Lankan court, and that the Mahāvihāra, whose attitudes toward the legitimacy of other groups was, by Buddhist standards, highly critical, sectarian, and exclusionary, sought to *close* the canon in an effort to disempower groups using materials outside of the Mahāvihāra's scope of approved oral or written literature. This is important: there is ample evidence suggesting that Indian Buddhists who made use of Mahayana teachings and those who didn't often practiced side by side in groups that followed the same *vinaya*, and there was a measure of tolerance regarding doctrine.[42] The situation of the Northern schools of India was one of "textual pluralism," in which all of the various eighteen schools contained elements of *buddhavacana*. The attitude of the Mahāvihāra, the group responsible for assembling the Pali canon and declaring it closed rather than open (i.e., certain texts and no others are deemed authentic), however, is decidedly exclusionary and overtly sectarian. In contrast to the sixth-century Buddhist Bhāviveka, who saw fit to quote passages from all eighteen schools' literature to support various doctrinal positions,[43] the Mahāvihārins, in the Sri Lankan chronicle the *Dīpavaṃsa,* assert about the eighteen schools:

> 51. Seventeen are the heretical sects, and there is one orthodox sect [us: the Mahāvihāra]; together with the orthodox sect they are eighteen in all.
> 52. Of the traditions, that of the Elders, which resembles a large banyan tree, is the best; it is the doctrine of the Jina *in full, with nothing lacking or added.* The other schools arose as thorns grow on a tree.[44]

The Insight movement leans more toward textual pluralism but does so within a universalizing narrative ("one Dharma") that places itself at the center. The Pali canon, however, may be invoked when a practitioner seeks to exclude Asian and Asian American practice. By making use of textual authority while downplaying or rejecting the authority of tradition or of the monastic community, Asian American Buddhist practices that are uncomfortable for convert Buddhists can be rejected as inauthentic or shallow. For example, one person said to me, "I don't visit those [Asian American Theravada] temples because they're mostly about cultural practices and socializing, not deep practice [i.e., meditation]." Asian American Buddhist ritual, mostly in the form of merit practice, is rejected as both noncanonical and superficial. The person quoted above added, "The Buddha said [in the Pali suttas] that ritual is useless." Similarly, a teacher in the Insight community characterized merit practice as "not really Buddhist" and likened beliefs in the spiritual efficacy of merit practice to belief in American folk figures like Santa Claus.

Of course, merit practice is mentioned throughout the sutta literature. When the canon contradicts a sectarian identity built on white middle-class religious norms (i.e., Insight does not practice ritual or merit), the American tradition of hyper-individualism, the authority of the "self," may be invoked to reject those passages as later additions or merely as skillful means for backward or ignorant laypeople. Both forms of authority—scriptural authority and the authority of the individual (who has attained knowledge via the spiritual "experience"[45] of meditation)—are employed to add legitimacy to the sectarian rejection of merit practice. I would argue that this stems from Orientalist assumptions and prejudices about backward, childish, irrational, superstitious, and/or ignorant Asians and Asian Americans. Predominantly white convert practice is considered "deep," and Insight practitioners are keen to use scientific findings to characterize their chosen practices as highly rational. At the same time, Asian American practice is described as "cultural" or, as suggested by a local sitting group's name ("No Nonsense Buddhism"), as *nonsense*. Ultimately the authority for rejecting these practices as false is white authority: we (white convert Buddhists) know better than you (heritage Buddhists) do about authentic Buddhism.

Another way white convert sectarianism is justified is through labeling Asian American Theravada as hopelessly patriarchal. When asked why s/he didn't visit any non-white-majority temples or communicate with their leaders, another Insight teacher told me, "There's no outlet for women to be in positions of authority in Asian Theravada." I asked, "What about precepts nuns like *dasa sil* and *mae chi*?" to which this teacher responded that they "aren't really nuns."[46] The rejection of Asian authority based on its assumed universal toxic patriarchy runs deep, to such a degree that most of those with whom I've discussed patriarchy in Theravada are completely unaware that certain Asian American *bhikkhus* and their Asian American lay supporters spearheaded the *bhikkhunī* movement in the United States, and that many Asian Americans (by no means a monolithic group) support women's higher ordination. There is certainly no lack of patriarchal attitudes and constrictions to be found in non-Insight (as well as Insight) Theravada centers, but by labeling *all* Asian and Asian American-led groups as irredeemably patriarchal they can be safely excluded, ignored, and ultimately erased.

Another way the Insight movement has justified maintaining a separate existence from other American Theravada groups is by tacitly describing Asian Americans as foreign. One teacher explained to me that "we [white founders of Insight] wanted to bring Buddhism to this country in a way that appealed to American sensibilities." In other words, expunging "superstitious" practices was part of a calculated move to align with liberal, white (coded here as "American") culture. Asian American temples are subtly or overtly criticized as being more "foreign" than American. By creating a practice community from which Asian Americans have been edited out, racial stress brought on by the mere presence of Asian American Buddhists in positions of authority could be avoided, and the authority of white converts could remain unopposed. The authenticity of Insight Buddhism, with all its intentional and calculated discontinuities with Asian tradition, could stand unchallenged, even while retreat materials or spoken discourse invoke the "ancient origins" of Insight's chosen practices.

Is encountering Asian or Asian American Theravada valuable? Based on my findings, I suggest that many, if not most, white Insight practitioners think not.

Consider the words of Jack Kornfield, the highest-ranking member of the Insight community and founder of the Bay Area's Spirit Rock Meditation Center:

> Americans [i.e., non-Asian Americans] have visions of a mysterious Orient, incense-filled temples inhabited by serene, wise Buddhist monks. But just as only a small minority of Christians in this country really understand and practice their religion, so too do only a small minority of Asian Buddhists understand and practice theirs. Even among Buddhist monks, only a small percentage, perhaps less than ten percent, meditate. What do the rest do? They study, teach, and perform [merit-making] ceremonies, and some just sit around and enjoy not working.[47]

This invokes rather familiar derogatory Orientalist characterizations: Asians don't understand Buddhism; Asians practice superstitious ritual instead of "real" practice like meditation; Asians are lazy. As well, here again is the claim that convert (mostly white) Buddhists, unlike most Asians, apprehend "real" Buddhism. Cheah notes in his important book *Race and Religion in American Buddhism:*

> The Buddhism presented by white Buddhists who regard themselves as true Buddhists assume overarching postulates of what constitutes true Buddhism and use them as the sole standard by which to evaluate the cultural elements and nonnormative aspects of ethnic Buddhism. This is nothing short of the reinscription of the racial ideology of white supremacy internalized in the Orientalist interpretation of Buddhism.[48]

In the year or so I spent querying various Bay Area white Insight members about why they do or don't attend non-white-majority Theravada temples (spoiler alert: they don't), the responses I received included:

- Applying childlike features to Asians and Asian Americans, such as being irrational or prone to believing in superstition;
- Asserting that meditation is "deep" while merit practice is shallow, superstitious, or self-centered;
- Claiming that popular Asian, and by extension Asian American, Theravada is largely a perversion of the pure Buddhism taught by the Buddha;
- Suggesting that Asians and Asian Americans are collectivist, that is, "group-oriented," and thus are either incapable of or unwilling to engage in individual, rational thought that challenges traditional practices and authority;
- Describing Asians and Asian Americans as inherently patriarchal or conservative;

- Suggesting that popular Asian and Asian American perspectives on their own religion can be safely dismissed as ignorant (sometimes the word "villagers" and its tropes of backwardness and ignorance are used to make this claim);
- Judging practice and doctrine against Pali canon textual norms and ignoring or rejecting later Asian developments, such as the commentarial traditions and vernacular literature, as corrupted;
- Rejecting the authority of Asian American monastics;
- Claiming authority over the Buddhist tradition, asserting ownership and entitlement.

While many Bay Area Theravada temples can be characterized as multi-ethnic and largely inclusive, the Insight tradition draws sharp boundaries around itself along racial lines, appealing to those who, for various reasons outlined above, do not wish to practice alongside Asian American heritage Buddhists. Insight is a sect built on (1) the authority of whiteness: we know what real Buddhism is, while Asian Americans do not, and cannot therefore be considered authorities; and (2) the safety of whiteness, shielding practitioners from the racial stress of being a minority and losing their "natural" authority.[49] To press this further, I am inclined to believe that many white converts in the Insight tradition are unwilling for their white authority to be challenged through real, constructive discussions with co-religionists on the nature of merit or the value of ritual. Instead, they simply avoid and ignore Asian American Theravada while repeating prejudicial notions about Asians and Asian Americans, asserting their own interpretations as "true" Buddhism and passively or actively participating in the deprecation of Asian American heritage Theravada.

In response to American studies scholar Dr Funie Hsu's important article published online in *Buddhadharma* magazine,[50] which revealed a pattern of exclusion, appropriation, and erasure of Asian American Buddhism by white Buddhists, a number of readers expressed outrage or condemned the writer as *not really Buddhist*. Rather than publish those letters to the editor, the white Theravadin *bhikkhu* Ajahn Amaro published a response in which he writes:

> Over the years, particularly during my time in the USA, I have interacted a lot with both of these groups [converts and heritage Buddhists]. It is sad to say, but in conversations with Western-born Buddhist teachers and practitioners, at formal meetings and conferences as much as in informal dialogues, I have regularly encountered the kind of white cultural conceit that speaks of practicing "real Buddhism" rather than "folk Buddhism" weighed down with so called "cultural baggage." As one whose lifestyle is devotedly built around

> such "baggage" (preferably understood as "skillful means") such comments and discussions come across bearing the ugliness and conceit of the unconscious racism of: "Some of my best friends are. . . ."[51]

The Insight movement has in recent years made considerable strides to address some of the unconscious racial bias highlighted above. Some small groups have formed to meet and discuss white privilege and racism, and a curriculum to address white supremacy (called WAIC UP, an acronym for White Awareness Insight Curriculum for Uprooting Privilege) has been developed. A task force at Spirit Rock Meditation Center focuses on inclusivity and welcoming/empowering people of color, and retreats for people of color are now held regularly. There has been a move to train more people of color to be teachers; the East Bay Meditation Center in Oakland has developed policies and practices to ensure that participation in its programs reflect the racial demographics of the city. A Buddhist studies scholar was invited to give a talk to white members of Spirit Rock's teachers' council on issues of Orientalism in Western Buddhist traditions. All of these efforts are commendable, but by setting itself apart from and above Asian traditions the Insight community's sectarianism, built on the authority of whiteness, remains. Rather than envisioning their centers as part of a larger Theravada community and visiting temples established by heritage Buddhists, Insight satisfies its own notions of developing inclusivity by working on issues of inclusion and white supremacy *within its own bounded realm of "authentic" Buddhism*, with little regard for reaching out to Asian American Theravada groups or visiting their temples.

While it's true that some heritage temples have been largely mono-ethnic (indeed, two of the three Sri Lankan monastic-led temples in the Bay Area follow this model), many, if not most, of these temples are *multi-ethnic*. In other words, a temple's monastics may be from one national background (e.g., Thailand, Sri Lanka), but its lay supporters come from a variety of ethnic and racial backgrounds (Khmer, Sinhalese, Thai, Indian, Vietnamese, white, etc.).[52] Monastics from various Bay Area temples frequently attend other temples as guests during Kathina season, displaying a shared sense of identity despite their varied ethnic backgrounds. They recognize their co-religionists' temples as "real" Buddhism in more or less the same lineage. Laypeople often patronize the closest Theravada temple rather than a specifically Thai or Lao temple.[53] To be clear: of all the many and varied Bay Area Theravada centers I've visited, among the most mono-ethnic are, in fact, in the Insight tradition.[54] This is reflective of this community's sectarian identity originally developed through a logic of exclusion and Orientalism, and made possible through the assumption of white authority.

## Conclusions

The rhetoric of authenticity, as a rhetoric of exclusion that is prone to being used in the service of social power, is not an appropriate framework for use in Buddhist studies. As embodied, subjective individuals, scholars, too, fall into excluding some Buddhists, using authenticity claims for financial, political, religious, or even personal motivations. This is how the rhetoric of authenticity serves to shroud the scholar's personal stake in who is considered worthy of study as a "real" Buddhist.[55] As the history of Orientalism in Western scholarship has demonstrated, one's positionalities and subjectivities, such as being white or male, or having particular economic or institutional privilege, produce specific biases. Further, competition for scarce resources (tenured appointments, prestigious university jobs, research funding) often provides fuel for contention around the legitimacy of modernist or Western Buddhisms when funding for such research diverts scarce resources from the more institutionally sanctioned locus of Buddhist studies (e.g., philology, philosophy, and area studies) in prestigious universities.[56]

Engaging in more in-depth personal reflection on our own biases suggests to me that how we define Buddhists in our research (and who is excluded from this definition) cannot be separated from our social positions and personal identities, though this recognition need not prevent us from pointing out discontinuities and continuities in traditions, as well as Buddhist rhetoric that may be harmful for the environment, people of color, women, and others. As I have sought to demonstrate in this case study, we can still engage in ethics; for example, in pointing toward how white authority operates in the sectarian formation of the Insight movement, this criticism can be used constructively by both researchers and Buddhists. If I simply ignored American Insight Buddhism or cut them out from Buddhist studies altogether because they aren't "authentic" enough, a valuable opportunity for constructive reimagining would be lost.

Recognizing that I inherit white authority as one of the "flows" of Western Buddhist scholarship and practice outlined in this chapter compels me to ask myself difficult questions. From what source do I legitimize my own authority to "speak" for Buddhism? Is it due to my academic degrees, and do white privilege and racial bias play a role in my access to academia? In what ways does white authority operate in my scholarship? In my classrooms? In my writing? In my choice of textbooks? Whose funds support my scholarship? How am I part of a culture that systematically degrades non-whites? How do I behave toward people of color at conferences? Do I listen more than I speak? Do I feel entitled to monopolize conversations because I know better? How does the embodiment of cultural habits of white supremacy, manifesting as assumptions of authority, affect how I see myself in relation to Buddhists or other scholars? Answering these questions doesn't require separating real Buddhists from fake ones; it *does* require seeing my embeddedness in communities of academics, Buddhists, and other humans.

And this is the crux of it: Metcalf asks us what responsibility we as scholars have to Buddhism, a fair and important question for which I am grateful. My response is that I feel no responsibility to Buddhism at all: I feel responsible to *people*. I feel responsible for how my own ideas of authenticity or authority shape the ways I practice academia, and how that practice impacts the well-being of Buddhists, other academics, students, my family, and humans writ large. To concern ourselves with the ethics of scholarship is to expose our human embodiment, our commitments to values that animate our daily lives and that can be so easily hidden behind a façade of "objective" scholarship or a bland and empty rhetoric of "contribution to the field."

Finally, I want to expose my own biases and subjectivities in this particular study. I would be remiss if I did not also recognize that Insight Buddhists are, demographically, very close to my own identity. This comes with its own set of concerns, least of which involves the human desire to set oneself above the rest, to be a greater authority than others. How do Insight Buddhists threaten my sense of being an authority on Buddhism? In what ways might I experience them as rivals and thus as more likely targets for critique? Additionally, my field studies are usually in Sri Lankan American and, to a lesser extent, Thai American and multi-ethnic Asian American Theravada communities; given this, in what ways might I be more likely to negatively characterize the Insight movement?

# Notes

## Introduction

1 Richard K. Payne, "Buddhism and the Powers of the Mind," in David L. McMahan, ed., *Buddhism in the Modern World* (New York: Routledge, 2012), p. 234.

2 Richard K. Payne, "Individuation and Awakening: Romantic Narrative and the Psychological Interpretation of Buddhism," in Mark Unno, ed., *Buddhism and Psychotherapy: Across Cultures* (Boston, MA: Wisdom Publications, 2006), p. 51.

3 Ann Gleig, *American Dharma: Buddhism beyond Modernity* (New Haven, CT: Yale University Press, 2019).

4 Richard K. Payne, "Realizing Inherent Enlightenment: Ritual and Self-Transformation in Shingon Buddhism," in Michael B. Aune and Valerie DeMarinis, eds., *Religious and Social Ritual: Interdisciplinary Explorations* (Albany, NY: State University of New York [SUNY] Press, 1996), p. 72.

5 Ibid.

6 See Richard K. Payne, "Why 'Buddhist Theology' Is Not a Good Idea: Keynote Address for the Fifteenth Biennial Conference of the International Association of Shin Buddhist Studies, Kyoto, August 2011," *The Pure Land* 27 (2012): 1–35. In his critique of the neologism "Buddhist theology," Payne suggests "Buddhist praxis" not so much as a one-to-one alternative but as a category of critical analyses of both Buddhist doctrine and practice in which Buddhists have long been engaged, work that represents a "dialectic relation between doctrinal claims and the practices (and the experiences those practices lead to) of the Buddhist tradition" (p. 33).

7 Oliver Freiberger, "The Disciplines of Buddhist Studies—Notes on Religious Commitment as Boundary-maker," *Journal of the International Association of Buddhist Studies* 30/1–2 (2007): 299–318.

8 Paul Harrison, "Experimental Core Samples of Chinese Translations of Two Buddhist Sūtras Analysed in the Light of Recent Sanskrit Manuscript Discoveries," *Journal of the International Association of Buddhist Studies* 13/1–2 (2010): 205.

9 Zachary Lockman, *Field Notes: The Making of Middle East Studies in the United States* (Stanford: Stanford University Press, 2016); Freiberger, "The Disciplines of Buddhist Studies," p. 317, suggests, among other things, that Buddhist studies is structured like other area studies such as Asian studies.

10 Richard Payne, "Buddhism or Buddhisms? Rhetorical Consequences of Geo-political Categories," OUPBlog (2012): https://blog.oup.com/2012/08/buddhism-rhetorical-consequence-geo-political-category/.
11 Thomas A. Tweed, *Crossing and Dwelling: A Theory of Religion* (Cambridge, MA: Harvard University Press, 2008), pp. 13–20.
12 Freiberger, "The Disciplines of Buddhist Studies," pp. 300–301.
13 Charles S. Prebish, *Luminous Passage: The Practice and Study of Buddhism in America* (Berkeley, CA: University of California Press, 1998), p. 75; Natalie E. Quli, "Western Self, Asian Other: Modernity, Authenticity, and Nostalgia for 'Tradition' in Buddhist Studies," *Journal of Buddhist Ethics* 16 (2009): 22.
14 Richard K. Payne, "Traditionalist Representations of Buddhism," *Pacific World: Journal of the Institute of Buddhist Studies* 10 (2008): 180.
15 Donald S. Lopez, "Developments in Buddhist Studies, 2015: A Report on the Symposium 'Buddhist Studies Today,'" *Canadian Journal of Buddhist Studies* 11 (2016): 7.
16 Ibid., p. 34.
17 Richard K. Payne, "Aparimitāyus: 'Tantra' and 'Pure Land' in Medieval Indian Buddhism?" *Pacific World: Journal of the Institute of Buddhist Studies* 9 (2007): 237.
18 Richard K. Payne and Michael Witzel, eds., *Homa Variations: The Study of Ritual Change across the Longue Durée* (New York: Oxford University Press, 2016), p. 17.
19 Richard K. Payne, "Afterword: Buddhism beyond Borders: Beyond the Rhetorics of Rupture," in Scott A. Mitchell and Natalie E. F. Quli, eds., *Buddhism beyond Borders: New Perspectives on Buddhism in the United States* (Albany: State University of New York Press, 2015), p. 217.
20 Quli, "Western Self."
21 Payne, "Why 'Buddhist Theology' Is Not a Good Idea."
22 See Quli's contribution to this volume and Elizabeth Cullen Dunn, "The Problem with Assholes," *Public Anthropologist*, June 20, 2018, http://publicanthropologist.cmi.no/2018/06/20/the-problem-with-assholes.

## Chapter 1

1 Parts of this chapter dealing with Suwa draw from my PhD dissertation, Lisa Grumbach, "Sacrifice and Salvation in Medieval Japan: Hunting and Meat in Religious Practice at Suwa Jinja" (Stanford University, 2005).
2 On how Buddhist institutions used hunting and logging bans to limit the economic activities of local people, see Fabio Rambelli, *Buddhist Materiality: A Cultural History of Objects in Japanese Buddhism* (Stanford: Stanford University Press, 2007), pp. 156–61.

3 Robert Morrell, *Sand and Pebbles (Shasekishū): The Tales of Mujū Ichien, A Voice for Pluralism in Kamakura Buddhism* (Albany, NY: State University of New York Press, 1985), p. 92.

4 Miyasaka Yūshō, "Kami to hotoke no yūgō: Mikkyō shisō kara no kaishaku," in Ueda Masaaki, Miyasaka Kōshō, Ōbayashi Taryō, Miyasaka Yūshō, and Gorai Shigeru, eds., *Onbashira matsuri to Suwa Taisha* 御柱祭と諏訪大社 (Tokyo: Chikuma Shobō, 1987), pp. 151–52. See also Inoue Takami, "The Interaction between Buddhist and Shinto Traditions at Suwa Shrine," in Mark Teeuwen and Fabio Rambelli, eds., *Buddhas and Kami in Japan: Honji Suijaku as a Combinatory Paradigm* (London and New York: RoutledgeCurzon, 2003), pp. 288–91.

5 The hunts are the *Satsuki-e mikari* 五月会御狩 in the fifth month; the *misakuta mikari* 御作田御狩 in the sixth month; the *Misayama mikari* 御射山御狩 in the seventh month; and the *Akio mikari* 秋尾御狩 in the ninth month. See Grumbach, "Sacrifice and Salvation in Medieval Japan," p. 40.

6 Kanai Tenbi 金井典美, *Suwa shinkō shi* 諏訪信仰史 (Tokyo: Meicho Shuppan, 1982), pp. 59–61.

7 *Nennai kamigoto shidai kyūki* 年内神事次第旧記. Cited in Miyasaka Yūshō, "Suwa Taisha Kamisha no mikari to otō" 諏訪大社上社の御狩と御頭, 3 parts, Shinano 信濃 46 (1994), no. 5: 73–85; no. 7: 73–86; no. 8: 45–57: part 1: 83.

8 *Azuma kagami* 吾妻鏡, edited by Nagahara Keiji 永原慶二, modern translation by Kishi Shōzō 貴志正造 (Tokyo: Shinjinbutsu Ōraisha, 1976–79), record of Kenryoku 建暦2 (1212)/8/19: vol. 3, 189.

9 *Suwa Kamisha monoimirei*, in *Shintō taikei*, Jinjahen 30 Suwa (Tokyo: Shintō taikei hensankai, 1982), pp. 255–56.

10 *Kōgizuiketsu-shū* 廣疑瑞決集, by Kyōsaibō Shinzui 敬西房信瑞, Kokubun Tōhō Bukkyō sōsho 国文東方仏教叢書, Hōgobu jō 法語部上 (Tokyo: Tōhō Shoin, 1931), p. 16.

11 Ibid., p. 21.

12 Ibid., p. 70.

13 Ibid.

14 Ibid., p. 74.

15 Ibid., pp. 19–20.

16 Ibid., p. 70.

17 *Suwa Kamisha monoimirei*, 256.

18 This version of the phrase, the one most cited in work on Suwa's hunting rituals, is found in the *Suwa engi* 諏訪縁起, included in the *Shintōshū* 神道集 (comp. 1352–1360). The *Monoimirei* and *Suwa daimyōjin ekotoba* 諏訪大明神絵詞, discussed below, have slightly different versions, respectively, using the terms *ninchū* 人中 and *ninshin* 人身 in the third line, instead of the term *ninten* 人天. On the significance of these variations, see Grumbach, "Sacrifice and Salvation in Medieval Japan," pp. 206–13.

19 *Suwa daimyōjin ekotoba*, in *Shintō taikei*, Jinjahen 30: Suwa, 48.

20 *Ekotoba*, 49–50.

21 Enchū provides some explanation of what the local people believed about the god. In his description of the fifth-month Satsukie hunt, he again states that only two or three deer are hit by the hunters' arrows, adding, "The village elders say that [this is because] the deer in the Suwa fields have holes in them. But isn't it rather due to the [deity's] original vow of *gōjin ushō*?" (*Ekotoba*, 43) While Enchū pushes the Buddhist doctrine of the god's original vow, the local people seem to have legends that explain the hunts without reference to Buddhism.

22 Extant copies of the *kajikimen*, which were stamped-paper *fuda* 札, date to the Muromachi (1336–1573) and Edo (1603–1868) periods. The stamp used to make the *fuda* is displayed at the Suwa Kamisha as a shrine treasure. See Kanai, *Suwa shinkō shi*, p. 19.

23 *Nihon kōki* 日本後紀, scroll 21, Kōnin 2 (811)/7/17, in *Shinto taikei* 神道大系, Jinja-hen 神社編 40: Itsukushima (Tokyo: Shintō taikei hensankai, 1987), p. 123.

24 *Nihon sandai jitsuroku* 日本三代実録, scroll 14, Jōgan 貞観 9 (867)/10/13. Cited in *Shinto taikei* 神道大系, Jinja-hen 神社編 40: Itsukushima, 123. The record uses the alternate characters 宗形. The three Munakata goddesses are Ichikishima-hime no mikoto 市杵島姫命, Togori-hime no mikoto 田心姫命, and Tagitsu-hime no mikoto 湍津姫命.

25 On the role of the Munakata clan in early Japanese politics and trade, see Michael Como, *Shōtoku: Ethnicity, Ritual, and Violence in the Japanese Buddhist Tradition* (New York: Oxford University Press, 2008), pp. 66–69.

26 In 701 one of the Munakata goddesses, Ichikishima-hime, was enshrined at the Matsunoo Jinja. This shrine was controlled by the Hata clan in the area that later became the Heian capital. The Hata clan, another immigrant kinship group, was instrumental in Yamato politics and trade, acting as a go-between with other immigrant clans and tasked with building the Naniwa Canal that formed a main artery for Yamato trade and transport. See Como, *Shōtoku*, p. 67.

27 Kishida Hiroshi 岸田裕之, ed., *Hiroshima-ken no rekishi* 広島県の歴史 (Tokyo: Yamakawa Shuppan, 1999), pp. 27–29.

28 Ibid., p. 30.

29 Ibid.

30 Ibid., pp. 37–8.

31 Ibid., pp. 40–2.

32 *Angen ninen Aki-no-kuni no tsukasa marōdo miya kinen norito* 安元二年安芸国司客人宮祈念祝詞 (Itsukushima monjo 厳島文書, document 109), cited in *Shintō taikei*, 40: Itsukushima, 135.

33 Kishida, *Hiroshima-ken no rekishi*, pp. 56–58.

34 Ibid., p. 59.

35 *Shintō taikei* 40: Itsukushima, Introduction, 19–20.

36 This story is in the "Nyūdō shin Itsukushima suijaku no koto" 「入道信厳島垂迹事」 section of the *Genpei seisuiki*, scroll 13. See *Shintō taikei* 40: Itsukushima, 5.

37 *Itsukushima shidai no koto*, in *Shintō taikei*, Jinjahen 40: Itsukushima, 9–10.

38 *Itsukushima shidai no koto*, 11. The text states that this is the first of thirty-three vows (*daigan* 大願) made by the Itsukushima deities, although neither this text nor any other elaborates on the content of other vows. The *honji* of the Itsukushima deities are various forms of Kannon; thus the idea of thirty-three vows is likely a device based on Kannon's thirty-three forms.

39 On the genealogy of the Utsunomiya clan and the problems with crediting Sōen as the progenitor, see Ichimura Takao 市村高男, "Chūsei Utsunomiyashi no seiritsu to tenkai: Shimotsuke, Buzen, Iyo no sanryū no kankei wo saguru" 中世宇都宮氏の成立と展開一下野・豊前・伊予の三流の関係を探る, in Ichimura Takao, ed., *Chūsei Utsunomiyashi no sekai: Shimotsuke, Buzen, Iyo no jikū wo sakanoboru* 中世宇都宮氏の世界一下野・豊前・伊予の時空を遡る (Tokyo: Sairyūsha, 2013), pp. 17–73, especially pp. 19–20.

40 Ibid., p. 26.

41 Ibid., pp. 54–9.

42 *Tochigi-ken no rekishi* 栃木県の歴史, edited by Abe Akira, Hashimoto Sumio, Chida Kōmyō, and Otake Hiroyoshi (Tokyo: Yamakawa Shuppan, 1998), pp. 97–98.

43 See Nagamatsu Atsushi 永松敦, *Shuryō minzoku kenkyū: Kinsei ryōshi no jitsuzō to denshō* 狩猟民俗研究：近世猟師の実像と伝承 (Kyoto: Hozokan, 2005).

44 *Utsunomiya daimyōjin daidai kizui no koto*, in *Shintō taikei* 神道大系: Jinja-hen 神社編 31 Nikkō, Futarasan 日光・二荒山 (Tokyo: Shintō taikei hensankai, 1988), p. 84.

45 Ibid., pp. 115–16.

46 Ibid., p. 116.

47 *Utsunomiya Kōan shikijō* 宇都宮弘安式条, in *Utsunomiya Futarasan Jinja-shi* 宇都宮二荒山神社誌, Shiryō-hen 資料編 (Utsunomiya-shi: Utsunomiya Jinja, 1988), p. 15.

48 Ibid., pp. 7–8. The annual observances mentioned in the *Shikijō* item are the two seasonal festivals (*niki gosai* 二季御祭) in spring and winter, the Third Month Rite (*Yayoi-e* 三月会), the *issaikyō-e* 一切経会, the Fifth Month Rite (*Satsuki-e* 五月会), the Sixth Month *rinjisai* (*Minazuki rinjisai* 六月臨時祭), and the Ninth Month Rite (*Kugatsu-e* 九月会).

49 *Shikijō*, 14 (items 59, 60).

50 *Shikijō*, 14 (item 61).

51 *Shikijō*, 13 (item 49).

52 *Futarasan shinden*, in *Shintō taikei* 神道大系: Jinja-hen 神社編 31 Nikkō, Futarasan 日光・二荒山, 131. On the composition and date of the text, see p. 26.

## Chapter 2

1 See, for example, Nishimura Ryō, "Tokumon fujaku: Sono shōgai" (1701–1781) 徳門普寂：その生涯 (1701–1781), *Indotetsugaku Bukkyōgaku kenkyū* インド哲学仏教学研究 14 (2007): 87–99.

2 See Sueki Fumihiko, *Meiji shisōka ron* 明治思想家論 (Tokyo: Transview, 2004); Hayashi Makoto, "General Education and the Modernization of Japanese Buddhism," *The Eastern Buddhist,* 43 (1/2) (2012): 133–52, and "Religious Studies and Religiously Affiliated Universities," in Hayashi Makoto, Ōtani Eiichi, and Paul Swanson, eds., *Modern Buddhism in Japan* (Nagoya: Nanzan Institute for Religion and Culture, 2014), pp. 163–93; Jacqueline Stone, "A Vast and Grave Task: Interwar Buddhist Studies as an Expression of Japan's Envisioned Global Role," in J. Thomas Rimer, ed., *Culture and Identity: Japanese Intellectuals during the Interwar Years* (Princeton, NJ: Princeton University Press, 1990), pp. 217–33; Kathleen M. Staggs, "'Defend the Nation and Love the Truth.' Inoue Enryō and the Revival of Meiji Buddhism," *Monumenta Nipponica* 38/3 (1983): 251–81; Orion Klautau, "Against the Ghosts of Recent Past: Meiji Scholarship and the Discourse on Edo-Period Buddhist Decadence," *Japanese Journal of Religious Studies* 35/2 (2008): 263–303, and *Kindai nihon shisō to shite no bukkyō shigaku* 近代日本思想として仏教史学 (Kyoto: Hōzōkan, 2012).

3 Klautau, "Against the Ghosts of Recent Past."

4 Ejima Naotoshi 江島 尚俊, Miura Shū 三浦周, and Matsuno Tomoaki 松野智章, eds., *Kindai nihon no daigaku to shūkyō* 近代日本の大学と宗教 (Kyoto: Hōzōkan, 2014), p. 307.

5 These universities were Ōtani (Jōdo Shinshū), Ryūkoku (Jōdo Shinshū), Risshō (Nichirenshū), Komazawa (Sōtōshū), Taishō (trans-sectarian: Jōdoshū, Shingonshū Buzan-ha, Shingonshū Shingi-ha, and Tendai), and Kōyasan (Shingonshū).

6 Hayashi Makoto, "The Birth of Buddhist Universities," *Japanese Religions Special Issue: "The Politics of Buddhist Studies in Early Twentieth-Century Japan,"* 39 (1/2) (2013): 11–29.

7 An example of a major difference between the treatment of Buddhism between the two types of universities is that Buddhist studies in the imperial universities was taught within Literature and Philosophy departments; see Hayashi, "Religious Studies and Religiously Affiliated Universities."

8 Ejima, Miura, and Matsuno, eds., *Kindai nihon no daigaku to shūkyō.*

9 Ishida Kazuhiro 石田一裕, "Shūkyō Daigaku ni okeru kindai bukkyōgaku—Watanabe Kaikyoku no toō to kōgi wo chūshin ni" 教大学における近代仏教学—渡辺海旭の渡欧と講義を中心に, in Ejima Naotoshi, Miura Shū, and Matsuno Tomoaki, eds., *Kindai nihon no daigaku to shūkyō* (Kyoto: Hōzōkan, 2014), pp. 279–304.

10 *Ōtani daigaku hyakunenshi* 大谷大学百年史 (Kyoto: Ōtani daigaku, 2001), p. 46.

11 Adapted from traditional Indian monastic retreats during the monsoon season, *ango* is a concentrated period of intense study for priests.

12 *Ōtani daigaku hyakunenshi*, p. 42.

13 Ibid., p. 44.

14 This kind of practice is not a modern innovation but stretches back to Buddhism's Indian roots. It is noteworthy that this ancient tradition was employed at the Gohōjō to tackle Japanese Buddhism's modern critics.

15 Nanjō Bunyū 南条文雄, *Kaikyūroku* 懐旧録 (Tokyo: Daiyūkaku, 1927), p. 17.

16 *Ōtani daigaku hyakunenshi*, p. 47.

17 Ibid., p. 48.

18 Ibid., p. 49.

19 Ibid.

20 Ibid., p. 53.

21 This incident actually began in the 1830s and was only resolved with Kūkaku's expulsion in 1851.

22 *Ōtani daigaku hyakunenshi*, p. 69.

23 See Inoue Takami, "Shūmon hakusho wo megutte: Ishikawa Shuntai no kadai" 『宗門白書』をめぐって:石川舜台の話題, *Kyōka kenkyū* 教化研究 151 (2012): 47–56.

24 James Edward Ketelaar, *Of Heretics and Martyrs in Meiji Japan* (Princeton, NJ: Princeton University Press, 1993), p. 85.

25 Combined with Buddhism, this was known as the Three Teachings. Robert F. Rhodes points out that this was also an effort to end the criticism of Buddhism from Shintō and Confucianism by "reconciling it"; Rhodes, "Introduction to 'A Translation of "Otani Daigaku's Founding Spirit" by Sasaski Gessho,'" Michael Conway, Takami Inoue, and Robert F. Rhodes, trans., *Shinshū Sōgō Kenkyūjo Kenkyūkiyō* 真宗総合研究所研究紀要 30 (2011): 5.

26 One exception to this was Shingon, which was relatively slow to reform. See Abe Takako 阿部貴子, "Meijiki shingonshū no daigakurin kyōiku—futsūgaku dōnyū wo meguru giron to jissai" 明治期真言宗の大学林教育—普通学導入をめぐる議論と実際, in Ejima, Miura, and Matsuno, eds., *Kindai nihon no daigaku to shūkyō* (Kyoto: Hōzōkan, 2014), pp. 169–202.

27 Ketelaar, *Of Heretics and Martyrs in Meiji Japan*, p. 83.

28 *Ōtani daigaku hyakunenshi*, p. 46.

29 See Jon H. Roberts and James Turner, *The Sacred and the Secular University* (Princeton, NJ: Princeton University Press, 2000), Kindle Edition.

30 Ibid., location 980.

31 Hayashi, "Religious Studies and Religiously Affiliated Universities."

## Chapter 3

1 I examined the cult of Kōen and the ritual calendar of the Renge-in in "Kōen the Dragon Bodhisattva: History and Hagiography, A Translation and Analysis of the *Fuso ryūjinden,*" MA thesis (University of Colorado-Boulder, 2008).

2 Regarding the institutional responses to this rather widespread tendency among some Shin Buddhists to engage in practices that are officially unorthodox, see Sasaki Shoten, "Shinshu and Folk Religion: Toward a Post-Modern 'Shinshu Theology,'" *Bulletin of the Nanzan Institute for Religion and Culture* 12 (Spring 1988): 13–35.

3 The *kechien kanjō* 結縁灌頂 is a kind of Esoteric initiation ritual wherein one establishes a karmic tie via the mandalas of the Shingon tradition. On Kōyasan, these rituals are carried out once a year for each mandala. In Tendai and other Esoteric traditions, other schedules are followed. The *Taizōkai mandara* 胎藏界曼荼羅 (Skt. *Mahākaruṇā-garbhodbhava maṇḍala*, sometimes rendered as *Garbhadhātu maṇḍala*), is paired with the *Kongōkai mandara* 金剛界曼荼羅 (Skt. *Vajradhātu maṇḍala*). These two mandalas are understood to represent two nondual aspects of reality, the fundamental buddhahood of reality (corresponding to the Taizōkai) and the wisdom through which this reality is grasped (corresponding to the Kongōkai). For more on this, see Shingen Takagi and Thomas Eijo Dreitlein, *Kukai on the Philosophy of Language* (Tokyo: Keio University Press, 2010), pp. 356, 374, 401–2.

4 Richard K. Payne, "Aparamitāyus: 'Tantra' and 'Pure Land' in Late Medieval Indian Buddhism?" *Pacific World: Journal of the Institute of Buddhist Studies*, 3rd Series, No. 9 (2007): 273–308.

5 Aaron Proffitt, "Mysteries of Speech and Breath: Dōhan's 道範 (1179–1252) *Himitsu nenbutsu shō* 秘密念仏抄 and Esoteric Pure Land Buddhism," PhD dissertation (University of Michigan, 2015).

6 George Tanabe, "Kōyasan in the Countryside: The Rise of Shingon in the Kamakura Period," in Richard K. Payne, ed., *Re-Visioning "Kamakura" Buddhism* (Honolulu: University of Hawaii Press, 1998), pp. 43–55.

7 Mark T. Unno, "Recommending Faith in the Sand of the Mantra of Light," in Richard K. Payne, ed., *Re-Visioning "Kamakura" Buddhism* (Honolulu: University of Hawaii Press, 1998), pp. 167–218.

8 Richard K. Payne, "*Ajikan*: Ritual and Meditation in the Shingon Tradition," in Richard K. Payne, ed., *Re-Visioning "Kamakura" Buddhism* (Honolulu: University of Hawaii Press, 1998), pp. 219–48.

9 While it is commonly asserted that the Pure Land movement was inspired as a rejection of Esoteric Buddhist culture, several scholars in Japan have been arguing

against this for some time. See Kuroda Toshio 黒田俊雄, *Nihon chūsei no kokka to shūkyō* 日本中世の国家と宗教 (Tokyo: Iwanami Shōten, 1975), pp. 436–41; 280–99; Hayami Tasuku 速水侑, *Jōdo shinkō ron* 浄土信仰論 (Tokyo: Yūzankaku Shuppan 雄山閣出版, 1978); and Kakehashi Nobuaki 梯信暁, *Jōdokyō shisōshi: Indo, Chūgoku, Chōsen, Nihon* 浄土教思想史：インド・中国・朝鮮・日本 (Kyoto: Hōzōkan, 2012). Kakehashi's work is a textbook on the history of Pure Land thought up to Shinran, based on his earlier work, *Nara, Heianki jōdokyō tenkairon* 奈良・平安期浄土教展開論 (Kyoto: Hōzōkan, 2008). See also Proffitt, "Mysteries of Speech and Breath," pp. 22, 195–7.

10 Payne argues that these boundaries often enough lend themselves to ahistorical and teleological narrative constructions, in his "Introduction," to Richard K. Payne and Kenneth K. Tanaka, eds., *Approaching the Land of Bliss, Religious Praxis in the Cult of Amitābha* (Honolulu: University of Hawai'i Press, 2004), pp. 1–15.

11 Sanford's approach to Kakuban is similar to Hendrick Van der Veere, *A Study into the Thought of Kōgyo Daishi Kakuban* (Leiden: Hotei Publishing, 2000). Both seem to see the Pure Land elements as secondary to Kakuban's thought. Conversely, in his critical review of Van der Veere's approach to Kakuban, Brian Ruppert, in his "Review of Van der Veere's *A Study into the Thought of Kōgyō Daishi Kakuban: With a Translation of His Gorin kuji myō himitsushaku*," *Monumenta Nipponica* 56/3 (2001): 422–4, argues that Pure Land elements were central to Kakuban's thought. See also Proffitt, "Mysteries of Speech and Breath," pp. 279–89; Jacqueline I. Stone, "By the Power of One's Last Nenbutsu: Deathbed Practices in Early Medieval Japan," in Richard K. Payne and Kenneth K. Tanaka, eds., *Approaching the Land of Bliss* (Honolulu: University of Hawai'i Press, 2004), pp. 77–120. Of the many articles Stone has written on this topic I would direct the reader to "The Secret Art of Dying, Esoteric Deathbed Practices in Heian Japan," in Bryan J. Cuevas and Jacqueline I. Stone, eds., *The Buddhist Dead: Practices, Discourses, Representations* (Honolulu: University of Hawai'i Press, 2007), pp. 134–74. Her recent monograph, *Right Thoughts at the Last Moment: Buddhism and Deathbed Practices in Early Medieval Japan* (Honolulu: University of Hawai'i Press, 2016), should be required reading for anyone interested in Esoteric Pure Land thought or practice. See my recent review of Stone's *Right Thoughts*, "Multiple Logics and Multiple Paths in Medieval Japanese Deathbed Practice," H-Japan, H-Net Reviews, November 2017, http://www.h-net.org/reviews/showrev.php?id=50791.

12 James H. Sanford, "Breath of Life: The Esoteric Nembutsu," in Richard K. Payne, ed., *Tantric Buddhism in East Asia* (Boston, MA: Wisdom Publications, 2006), pp. 161–90. In this article Sanford draws heavily on Kushida Ryōkō 櫛田良洪, "Himitsu nenbutsu shisō no bokkō" 秘密念仏思想の勃興, *Taishō daigaku kenkyū*

*kiyō tsūgō* 大正大学研究紀要 通号 48 (1963): 43–80. See also Nakamura Honnen 中村本然, "Dōhan no Jōdo kan" 道範の浄土観, *Kōyasan daigaku ronsō* 高野山大学論叢 29 (1994): 149–202; Satō Mona 佐藤もな, "Chūsei Shingonshū ni okeru jōdo shisō kaishaku: Dōhan Himitsu nenbutsu shō o megutte" 中世真言宗における浄土思想解釈--道範『秘密念仏抄』をめぐって, *Indo tetsugaku bukkyōgaku kenkyū* インド哲学仏教学研究 9 (2002): 80–92; Proffitt, "Mysteries of Speech and Breath."

13 Brian Ruppert, "Review of Thomas Conlan, *From Soverign to Symbol: An Age of Ritual Determinism in Fourteenth-Century Japan*," *Japanese Journal of Religious Studies* 40/2 (2013): 391n6; Ryūichi Abe, *The Weaving of Mantra: Kūkai and the Construction of Esoteric Buddhist Discourse* (New York: Columbia University Press, 1999), pp. 375–76, 399–415.

14 See, for example, Kakuban's *Gorin kuji myo himitsu shaku* 五輪九字明秘密釋 (*T.* 2514) and the *Amida hishaku* 阿弥陀秘釋 (*T.* 2522); translated in full in James H. Sanford, "Amida's Secret Life: Kakuban's Amida hisaku," in Richard K. Payne and Kenneth K. Tanaka, eds., *Approaching the Land of Bliss: Religious Praxis in the Cult of Amitābha* (Honolulu: University of Hawai'i Press, 2004), pp. 120–39.

15 Proffitt, "Mysteries of Speech and Breath," pp. 272–84.

16 Sanford, "Breath of Life: The Esoteric Nembutsu," p. 170.

17 Stone, *Right Thoughts at the Last Moment*, p. 4.

18 Stone, "The Secret Art of Dying," p. 162; *Original Enlightenment and the Transformation of Medieval Japanese Buddhism* (Honolulu: University of Hawaii Press, 1999), pp. 191–2.

19 Nakamura, "Dōhan no Jōdo kan."

20 Richard K. Payne, "The Shingon Subordinating Fire Offering for Amitābha: 'Amida Kei Ai Goma,'" *Pacific World: Journal of the Institute of Buddhist Studies*, 3rd Series, No. 8 (2006): 191–236.

21 See, for example, Payne's article on the *ajikan* ritual, "The Shingon Ajikan: Diagrammatic Analysis of Ritual Syntax," *Religion* 29 (1999): 215–29. A comparison of this ritual with the *Amida keiai goma* would reveal that the basic structure is fairly similar.

22 The first complete English language translation of Amoghavajra's *Wuliangshou rulai guanxing gongyang yigui* will be published in a forthcoming anthology: Thomas Eijo Dreitlein, "Amoghavajra's Amitāyus Ritual Manual," in Georgios T. Halkias and Richard K. Payne, eds., *Pure Lands in Asian Texts and Contexts: An Anthology* (Honolulu: University of Hawaii Press, 2019).

23 Charles D. Orzech, "A Tang Esoteric Manual for Rebirth in the Pure Land," in Richard K. Payne, ed., *Path of No Path: Contemporary Studies in Pure Land Buddhism Honoring Roger Corless* (Berkeley, CA: Institute of Buddhist Studies and Numata Center for Buddhist Translation and Research, 2009), pp. 31–55. See also Proffitt, "Mysteries of Speech and Breath," pp. 178–9, 236–9.

24 Regarding Pure Land thought and practice in Chinese Esoteric Buddhist texts, see Proffitt, "Mysteries of Speech and Breath," pp. 105–92, and on the Pure Land content of the *Dhāraṇīsaṃgraha*, pp. 166–71. For more information on the *Dhāraṇīsaṃgraha*, see Charles D. Orzech, "Esoteric Buddhism in the Tang: From Atikūṭa to Amoghavajra (651–780)," in Charles D. Orzech, Henrik H. Sørensen, and Richard K. Payne, eds., *Esoteric Buddhism and the Tantras in East Asia* (Leiden: Brill, 2011), pp. 263–85; Ronald M. Davidson, "Some Observations on the Usṇīsa Abhiṣeka Rites in Atikūṭa's *Dhāraṇīsaṃgraha*," in István Keul, ed., *Transformations and Transfer of Tantra: Tantrism in Asia and Beyond* (Berlin and New York: Walter de Gruyter, 2012), pp. 77–98; Koichi Shinohara, *Spells, Images and Maṇḍalas: Tracing the Evolution of Esoteric Buddhist Rituals* (New York: Columbia University Press, 2014).

25 See note 3.

26 Payne, "The Shingon Ajikan," pp. 229n3.

27 Payne, "Introduction," p. 3; cited in Proffitt, "Mysteries of Speech and Breath," pp. 49–50.

# Chapter 4

1 Bhikṣuṇī Vinītā, *A Unique Collection of Twenty Sūtras in a Sanskrit Manuscript from the Potala, Vol. I, 1. Editions and Translations: 5. Anityatāsūtra* (Beijing and Vienna: China Tibetology Publishing House and Austrian Academy of Sciences Press, 2010), pp. 169–206.

2 Charles Willemen, *A Collection of Important Odes of the Law: The Chinese Udānavarga* (Berkeley: Institute of Buddhist Studies and BDK America, 2013), pp. 16, 32. Śāntideva writes *youwei* 有为 ("the formed," *saṃskṛta*) *pin* 品 (*varga*). All concordances have *Wuchang* 无常, *Anitya*°. The *Fa ji yao song jing* 法集要颂经, *Udānavarga,* collects stanzas from the *Chuyao* (*Udāna*) *jing* 出曜经; see Willemen, *A Collection of Important Odes of the Law,* p. 16. This is reminiscent of Avalokitasiṃha's *Dharmasamuccaya* (*T.* 728), translated by Richeng 日称 (Sūryakīrti?, d. 1078), stanzas collected from the *Saddharmasmṛtyupasthānasūtra, Zhengfa nianchu jing* 正法念处经 (*T.* 721), translated by Prajñāruci in Yecheng 邺城 between 538 and 541. Perhaps Avalokitasiṃha followed the example of the *Udānavarga*?

3 Wang Bangwei 王邦维, *Nanhai jigui neifa zhuan jiaozhu* 南海寄归内法传校注 (Beijing: Zhonghua Shuju, 1995), p. 109. The Chinese text was translated into Japanese by Izumi Hōkei 泉芳璟, "Bussetsu Mujōkyō. Mata Sankeikyō to nazuku" 佛说无常经. 亦三启经と 名く, in *Kokuyaku Issai Kyō. Kyōjū-bu* 国译一切经. 经集部 (Tokyo: Daitō Shuppansha, 1932), vol. 12, pp. 53–60.

4 The terms Mūlasarvāstivāda, Dārṣṭāntika, Vaibhāṣika, and Sautrāntika have often been explained; for a recent treatment, see Charles Willemen, "Remarks about the History of Sarvāstivāda Buddhism," *Journal of Buddhist Studies* 11 (2013): 129–45.

5 *Anuttara*, one of the ten appellations of a buddha. See Nakamura Hajime 中村元, *Bukkyōgo Daijiten* 佛教语大辞典 (Tokyo: Tōkyō Shoseki Kabushiki Kaisha, 1981), p. 653, s.v. *jūgō* 十号; Wogihara Unrai, *The Sanskrit-Chinese Dictionary of Buddhist Technical Terms: Based on the Mahāvyutpatti* (Tokyo: Sankibo, 1959), part I, mentions all the appellations of a buddha.

6 "Safe," *anyin* 安隐; *kṣema.*

7 The six *pāramitās* ("perfections") are meant here: generosity (*dāna*), morality (*śīla*), patient acceptance (*kṣānti*), vigorous effort, (*vīrya*), meditation (*dhyāna*) (*fangbian* 方便, i.e., *yoga, yukta*), and wisdom (*prajñā*).

8 Two of the ten appellations of a buddha: *puruṣadamyasārathi* ("guide of those who have to be restrained") and *śāstā devamanuṣyāṇām.* See also note 5.

9 The thirty-seven *bodhipakṣikā* or *bodhipakṣyā dharmā*, factors that contribute to awakening: the four applications of mindfulness, (*smṛtyupasthāna*), the four right rejections (*samyakprahāṇa*), and the four bases of psychic power (*ṛddhipāda*)—3 × 4 = 12. The five faculties (*indriya*), and the five powers (*bala*)—2 × 5 = 10. The seven members of awakening (*saṃbodhyaṅga*) and the Noble Eightfold Path (*āryāṣṭāṅga mārga*)—7 + 8 = 15. An early explanation and use (probably first century BCE) is found in Dharmaśreṣṭhin's Bactrian *Abhidharmahṛdaya;* see Charles Willemen, *The Essence of Scholasticism. Abhidharmahṛdaya. T. 1550* (Delhi: Motilal Banarsidass, 2006), pp. 234–35. The explanation in Vasubandhu's *Abhidharmakośabhāṣya,* an elaborate Gandhāran Sautrāntika *Miśrakābhidharmahṛdaya*, goes back to this early *Hṛdaya.* As there was no Vaibhāṣika Sarvāstivāda in the first century BCE the *Hṛdaya* must have existed before the word Sautrāntika existed; "Sautrāntika" makes sense only if you have Vaibhāṣikas. For a recent overview of Sarvāstivāda literature, see Willemen, "Remarks about the History of Sarvāstivāda Buddhism." For the explanation in the *Kośa*, see Louis de La Vallée Poussin, *L'Abhidharmakośa de Vasubandhu*, Tomes I–VI (Bruxelles: Institut Belge des Hautes Études Chinoises, 1971), Vol. IV, Chapter 6, pp. 282–92.

10 *Asaṃskṛta.*

11 The eight stages of the fruitions of the *śramaṇa* path (*śrāmaṇyaphala*): in the path of cultivation (*bhāvanāmārga*) progress is made toward the first fruition, *phalapratipanna*, that is, entering the stream (*srotāpattiphala*). This is followed by the fruition of once-returning (*sakṛdāgāmiphala*), the fruition of nonreturning (*anāgāmiphala*), and the fruition of arhatship (*arhattvaphala*). After accomplishing each of these progressive stages, one abides in fruition (*phalastha*) and is then

called *srotāpanna, sakṛdāgāmin, anāgāmin,* or arhat, respectively. See Willemen, *The Essence of Scholasticism*, pp. 127–29.

12 The first sermon, turning the wheel of the Dharma, took place in the Deer Park near Benares. The Buddha then preached for about forty-five years until his death in Kuśinagara, between the twin *śāla* trees. See Charles Willemen, *Buddhacarita: In Praise of Buddha's Acts* (Berkeley: Numata Center for Buddhist Translation and Research, 2009), p. 196, stanza 64.

13 Meaning both body and mind. See Nakamura, *Bukkyōgo Daijiten*, p. 294, s.v. *keshin metsuchi* 灰身灭智.

14 *Varia lectio,* three eds., 證.

15 Mount Sumeru, the *axis mundi* of traditional Indian cosmology.

16 Being born; *varia lectio,* 3 eds., 生. *Naivasaṃjñānāsaṃjñāyatana*, the sphere of neither perception nor nonperception, is the highest stage of the formless realm (*ārūpyadhātu*). See Willemen, *The Essence of Scholasticism*, pp. 81, 131, etc.

17 *Cakravartirāja,* often translated as "wheel-turning king," is a righteous worldly ruler.

18 *Saptaratna*. There are several series of seven precious things; see, for example, Nakamura, *Bukkyōgo Daijiten,* p. 587, s.v. *shichihō* 七宝. Kumārajīva, in his translation of the *Lotus Sutra,* mentions gold, silver, lapis lazuli, crystal, red pearls, agate, and mother-of-pearl. The *Larger Sukhāvatīvyūha* (*Wuliangshou jing* 无量寿经, *T.* 360), translated by Baoyun 宝云 in 421, has two different sets of seven precious things; this text is of Bactrian, non-Vaibhāṣika origin. See Charles Willemen, "Early Yogācāra and Visualization (*Bhāvanā*)," in Sarah F. Haynes and Michelle J. Sorensen, eds., *Wading into the Stream of Wisdom: Essays in Honor of Leslie Kawamura* (Berkeley: Institute of Buddhist Studies and BDK America, 2013), pp. 211–14.

19 That is, *kāmadhātu*, *rūpadhātu*, and *ārūpyadhātu*: the realm of desire, the realm of form or matter, and the formless realm.

20 Only the Chinese *Udānavarga,* the *Fa ji yao song jing* 法集要颂经 (*T*. 213, I 24), and the Tibetan Uv have this stanza in the *Anityavarga*. Both versions are known to be Mūlasarvāstivāda. The *Chuyao jing* 出曜经, *Udāna* (*T*. 212) does not have it, and it is not extant in Sanskrit. Willemen, *The Essence of Scholasticism,* pp. 31, 36.

21 The first three of the ten appellations of a buddha: Tathāgata, Arhat, Samyaksaṃbuddha. See also notes 5 and 8.

22 *Varia lectio,* three eds., 桩彩 *zhuangcai.*

23 *Variae lectiones,* three eds., 停 *ting*, not 住 *zhu*; 成枯悴 *cheng kucui*, not 见枯羸 *jian kulei.*

24 *Jīvitendriya.*

25 *Varia lectio,* three eds., *ye* 噎, not *duan* 短.

26 All six consciousnesses (*vijñāna*) from the eye consciousness (*cakṣurvijñāna*) to mental consciousness (*manovijñāna*).
27 The fortress of the king of death, Yamarāja.
28 Physical, verbal, and mental actions (*karma*).
29 Merit (*puṇya*) and knowledge (*jñāna*); that is, moral and intellectual qualities. In the oldest *Abhidharma*, the *Abhidharmahṛdaya*, they do not form a preparatory path, *saṃbhāramārga*, the path of equipment. In the stages of the *Kośa,* however, they constitute this path. See de La Vallée Poussin, *L'Abhidharmakośa de Vasubandhu*, Vol. V, Chapter 7, pp. 80–81.
30 Most likely Aśvaghoṣa. This final stanza is reminiscent of the final stanza of Aśvaghoṣa's *Buddhacarita*, XXVIII 80. See Willemen, *Buddhacarita,* p. 208.
31 See note 29.
32 That is, may the practitioner be endowed with morality (*śīla*), concentration (*samādhi*), and wisdom (*prajñā*).
33 Willemen, "Remarks about the History of Sarvāstivāda Buddhism," pp. 130–31, 134–36.
34 Willemen, *The Essence of Scholasticism,* p. 10.
35 Sylvain Lévy and J. Takakusu, "Bombai," in *Hōbōgirin*, Fascicle I: 93–Fascicle II: 112 (Tokyo: Maison Franco-Japonaise, 1929–1930), p. 94.
36 Li Rongxi, *Buddhist Monastic Traditions of Southern Asia: A Record of the Inner Law Sent Home from the South Seas* (Berkeley: Numata Center for Buddhist Translation and Research, 2000), p. 139.
37 Kanakura Enshō 金苍円照, *Memyō no Kenkyū* 马鸣の研究 (Kyoto: Heiraku-ji Shoten, 1966), pp. 46–50.
38 Willemen, *Buddhacarita*, p. 148.
39 Ibid., p. 42.
40 Ibid., p. 208.
41 Li, *Buddhist Monastic Traditions of Southern Asia,* p. 79.
42 Willemen, *The Essence of Scholasticism,* p. 13.

## Chapter 5

1 *The Oni no shikogusa* is revised and annotated in three books: Hashimoto Fumio, Ariyoshi Tamotsu, and Fujiwara Haruo, eds., *Shinpen Nihon Koten Bungaku Zenshū 87: Karonshū* (Tokyo: Shōgakukan, 2002), pp. 99–102; Mabuchi Kazuo, Kunisaki Fumimaro, and Inagaki Taiichi, eds., *Shinpen Nihon Koten Bungaku Zenshū 38: Konjaku monogatarishū 4* (Tokyo: Shōgakukan, 2002), pp. 559–61; Moriyama Shōshin, *Tachikawa jakyō to sono shakaiteki haikei no kenkyū* (Tokyo: Kanōen, 1965), pp. 530–71.

2 Kazuaki Komine, "Toshiyori zuinō no uta to katari," *Chūsei bungaku kenkyū* 9 (1983): 1–24.
3 Kazuaki Komine, *Inseiki bungakuron* (Tokyo: Kasama Shoin, 2006), pp. 448–56.
4 Keiko Takanose, *Minamoto no Toshiyori* (Tokyo: Kasama Shoin, 2012), p. 60.
5 Tomoko Akase, *Inseikiigo no kagakusho to utamakura* (Osaka: Seibundo Shuppan, 2006), pp. 8–32.
6 Fumito Ikura, "Oni no shikogusa to oni no koshigusa: Toshiyori to hon josetsu," *Mita kokubun* 29 (1999): 1–14.
7 Mareo Okada, "Toshiyori Mumyōshō no chosha to sono chojutsu nendai ge," *Geimon* 12, no. 7 (1921): 20–37.
8 Ibid., pp. 8–35.
9 Hitaku Kyūsojin, "Shunpishō ni tsuite," *Kokugo to kokubungaku* 16, no. 3 (1939): 52–67.
10 *Konjaku monogatarishū*, 31:26, in *Shinpen nihon koten bungaku zenshū* (Tokyo: Shōgakkan, 1994–2002), 38:4, pp. 559–61.
11 Kenji Tachibana, "Konjaku monogatari to Toshiyori zuinō tono kankei," *Kenkyūkiyō: Nara joshidaigaku bungakubu fuzoku chūgakkō kōtōgakkō* 5 (1962): 1–8.
12 Moriyama Shōshin, *Tachikawa jakyō to sono shakaiteki haikei no kenkyū*, pp. 530–71. See also Tomomi Yoshino, "Oni no shikogusa setsuwa wo megutte: Tokyo daigaku kokubungaku kenkyūshitsuzō Oni no shikogusa no shōkai to kōsatsu," *Tokyo daigaku kokubungaku ronshū* 1 (2006): 17–31.
13 Fumihiko Sueki, "Kōzanjibon juhōyōjinshū ni tsuite," *Kōzanji tenseki bunsho sōgō chōsadan kenkyū hōkoku ronshū*, ed. Kōzanji tenseki bunsho chōsadan (2007): 5–11.
14 *Gukanshō*, 7, in *Nihon koten bungaku taikei*, ed. Takagi Ichinosuke et al. (Tokyo: Iwanami Shoten, 1957–1968), 86:337–39.
15 *Nihon kiryaku zenpen*, 17, in *Shintei zōho, Kokushi taikei, Nihon kiryaku zenpen*, ed. Kuroita Katsumi et al. (Tokyo: Yoshikawa Kōbunkan, 1979-1980), 2:420.
16 *Honchō seiki* 2, in *Shintei zōho, Kokushi taikei* (Tokyo: Yoshikawa Kōbunkan, Shōwa 4, 1929–1964), 9:12. Similar descriptions appear in the *Fusō ryakki* (Abbreviated History of Japan) entry for the second day of the ninth month of the second year of Tengyō (939). *Fusō ryakki*, 25 in *Shintei zōho, Kokushi taikei*, 12:214.
17 *Nihon kiryaku kōhen*, 1, in *Shintei zōho, Kokushi taikei, Nihon kiryaku kōhen*, ed. Kuroita Katsumi et al. (Tokyo: Yoshikawa Kōbunkan, 1979–1980), 3:19. Similar description of holding the spirits' sign festival can be found in the *Nihon kiryaku* entry for (1) the twenty-fourth day of the first month of the ninth year of Jōgan (867) (*Nihon kiryaku zenpen*, 2, in *Shintei zōho, Kokushi taikei, Nihon kiryaku zenpen*, 2:435) and (2) the fourteenth day of the eighth month of the first year of Tenryaku (947) (*Nihon kiryaku kōhen*, 3, in *Shintei zōho, Kokushi taikei, Nihon kiryaku kōhen*, 3:53).

18 *Nihon kiryaku kōhen*, 9, in *Shintei zōho, Kokushi taikei, Nihon kiryaku kōhen*, 3:178. Similar descriptions of holding the assembly for the honorific spirits can be found in the *Nihon kiryaku* entries for (1) the first day of the fifth month of the third year of Chōhō 長保 (1001) (*Nihon kiryaku kōhen*, 10, in *Shintei zōho, Kokushi taikei, Nihon kiryaku kōhen*, 3:197), (2) the eighteenth day of the seventh month of the second year of Kankō 寛弘 (1005) (*Nihon kiryaku kōhen*, 11, in *Shintei zōho, Kokushi taikei, Nihon kiryaku kōhen*, 3:209), and (3) the ninth day of the fifth month of the fifth year of Kankō (1008) (*Nihon kiryaku kōhen*, 11, in *Shintei zōho, Kokushi taikei, Nihon kiryaku kōhen*, 3:216).

19 *Nihon kiryaku zenpen*, 2, in *Shintei zōho, Kokushi taikei, Nihon kiryaku zenpen*, 2:541. Similar descriptions of holding the assembly for the recitation of the *Humane Kings Sutra* due to the popularity of a pestilence can be found in the *Nihon kiryaku* entries for (1) the twenty-sixth day of the fourth month of the ninth year of Engi 延喜 (908) (*Nihon kiryaku kōhen*, 1, in *Shintei zōho, Kokushi taikei, Nihon kiryaku kōhen*, 3:13), (2) the twenty-ninth day of the eighth month of the second year of Ten-en 天延 (974) (*Nihon kiryaku kōhen*, 6, in *Shintei zōho, Kokushi taikei, Nihon kiryaku kōhen*, 3:125), (3) the twenty-ninth day of the third month of the fourth year of Chōwa 長和 (1015) (*Nihon kiryaku kōhen*, 12, in *Shintei zōho, Kokushi taikei, Nihon kiryaku kōhen*, 3:234), (4) the fifteenth day of the fifth month of the fourth year of Chōwa (*Nihon kiryaku kōhen*, 12, in *Shintei zōho, Kokushi taikei, Nihon kiryaku kōhen*, 3:235), (5) the twenty-third day of the sixth month of the fourth year of Chōwa (*Nihon kiryaku kōhen*, 12, in *Shintei zōho, Kokushi taikei, Nihon kiryaku kōhen*, 3:235), and (6) the twenty-third day of the fourth month of the fourth year of Kannin 寛仁 (1015) (*Nihon kiryaku kōhen*, 13, in *Shintei zōho, Kokushi taikei, Nihon kiryaku kōhen*, 3:254).

20 *Himitsu mandala jūjūshinron*, 1, in *Nihon shisō taikei,* ed. Hayashiya Tatsusaburō et al., 67 vols. (Tokyo: Iwanami Shoten, 1970-1982), 5:48.

21 *Nihon kiryaku zenpen* 13, in *Shintei zōho, Kokushi taikei, Nihon kiryaku zenpen*, 2:282.

22 The descriptions of the spirits of the dead can be found in the *Nihon kiryaku* entries for (1) the twenty-fourth day of the intercalary twelfth month of the seventh year of Tenchō 天長 (830) (*Nihon kiryaku zenpen* 14, in *Shintei zōho, Kokushi taikei*, 5:464) and (2) the twenty-sixth day of the sixth month of the eighth year of Tenchō (831) (*Nihon kiryaku zenpen* 14, in *Shintei zōho, Kokushi taikei*, 5:466).

23 *Honchō seiki,* 13, in *Shintei zōho, Kokushi taikei*, 9:181–82.

24 Ibid., 9:163–93.

25 Many descriptions of holding the special assemblies of the *Humane Kings Sutra* can be found in the *Honchō seiki.* These appear in the entries for: (1) the eleventh day of the eighth month of the fourth year of Shōryaku (994) (*Honchō seiki* 12 in *Shintei zōho, Kokushi taikei*, 9:165), (2) the twenty-fourth day of the second month

of the fifth year of Shōryaku (995) (*Honchō seiki* 12, in *Shintei zōho, Kokushi taikei*, 13:179–180), (3) the fifteenth day of the fifth month of the fifth year of Shōryaku (995) (*Honchō seiki* 12, in *Shintei zōho, Kokushi taikei*, 13:188), and (4) the twenty-second day of the sixth month of the fifth year of Shōryaku (995) (*Honchō seiki* 12, in *Shintei zōho, Kokushi taikei*, 13:192). In addition, similar descriptions of holding special assemblies of the *Humane Kings Sutra* can be found in the *Nihon kiryaku kōhen* entry for (1) the twenty-eighth day of the first month of the first year of Chian 治安 (1021) (*Nihon kirayku kōhen*, 13, in *Shintei zōho, Kokushi taikei, Nihon kiryaku kōhen*, 3:255), (2) the tenth day of the seventh month of the first year of Chian (*Nihon kirayku kōhen*, 13, in *Shintei zōho, Kokushi taikei, Nihon kiryaku kōhen*, 3:256), and (3) the twentieth day of the sixth month of the third year of Chōgen 長元 (1030) (*Nihon kirayku kōhen*, 14, in *Shintei zōho, Kokushi taikei, Nihon kiryaku kōhen*,, 3:277).

26 *Honchō seiki* 13 in *Shintei zōho, Kokushi taikei*, 9:191. The same descriptions can be found in the *Honchō seiki* entries for (1) the sixteenth day of the sixth month of the fifth year of Shōryaku (994) (*Hochō seiki* 13, in *Shintei zōho, Kokushi taikei* 9:192) and (2) the twenty-fifth day of the sixth month of the first year of Kōwa 康和 (1099) (*Hochō seiki 22,* in *Shintei zōho, Kokushi taikei* 9: 305–06).

27 *Manyōshū*, 727 and 3062, in *Shinpen nihon koten bungaku zenshū*, 6:357 and 8:343.

28 *Honzō wamyō jōkan*, in *Nihon koten zenshū Honzō wamyō* (Tokyo: Gendai shichōsha, 1978), 82.

29 *Dazhidulun*, in *Taishō shinshū Daizōkyō*, ed. Junjirō Takakusu and Kaigyoku Watanabe, 100 vols. (Tokyo: Taisho Issaikyo Kankokai, 1924–1934), *T.* 1509.25.0637b19–20.

30 *Unjigi*, *T.* 2430.77.0406a29–b01.

31 *Niepan jing*, *T.* 0374.12.0402c08–09.

32 *Himitsu mandala jūjūshinron*, 1, in *Nihon shisō taikei*, 5:58.

## Chapter 6

1 For translation I follow Paul Harrison, "Vajracchedikā Prajñāpāramitā: A New English Translation of the Sanskrit Text Based on Two Manuscripts from Greater Gandhāra," in *Buddhist Manuscripts in the Schøyen Collection* (Oslo: Hermes Publishing, 2006), vol. 3, pp. 133–60; https://www2.hf.uio.no/polyglotta/index.php?page=fulltext&view=fulltext&vid=22. The site offers parallel text and translation of the Gilgit/Bamiyan manuscripts, Kumārajīva's Chinese translation, the Tibetan text, and Harrison's English translation. The passage is Vaj H 148, 18–22. Cf. Edward Conze's translation, *Buddhist Wisdom Books: The Diamond and the Heart Sutra* (New York: Harper and Row, 1972), p. 52. Similar passages can be found at Vaj H 154, 18–23 and Vaj H 156, 8–20. The Sanskrit reads, *tat kiṃ manyase*

*subhūte dvātṛṃśadbhir mahāpuruṣalakṣaṇaiḥ tathāgato 'rhan samyaksaṃbuddho draṣṭavyaḥ | subhūtir āha | no hīdaṃ bhagavan | tat kasya hetoḥ | yāni tāni bhagavan dvātṛṃśanmahāpuruṣa lakṣaṇāni tathāgatena bhāṣitāny alakṣaṇāni tathāgatena bhāṣitāni tasmād ucyaṃte dvātṛṃśanmahāpuruṣalakṣaṇānīti.* The rhetorical question in Kumārajīva's Chinese reads,「於意云何 可以三十二相見如來不」(*T.* 235.8:750a21).

2 Alan Cole has recently analyzed the scripture's logic in *Text as Father: Paternal Seductions in Early Mahāyāna Buddhist Literature* (Berkeley: University of California Press, 2005), pp. 160–96. This is one of the few modern critical analyses of the text, though it does not engage the possibility that the scripture is critiquing specific practices.

3 For instance, Vaj H 145, 1–9: "Furthermore, the Lord said this to the Venerable Subhūti, 'What do you think, Subhūti? Is there anything whatsoever that the Realized One has fully awakened to, or any dharma whatsoever that the Realized One has taught, as supreme and perfect awakening?'"

4 Vaj H 142, 13–28. Kumārajīva's text reads: 云何住云何降伏其心, "How should one abide; how should one subdue the mind?" (*T.* 235.8:748c24–749a6).

5 Vaj H 143, 6–11; "fixing" here is *pratiṣṭhitena,* or 住.

6 The Chinese is less specific here than the Sanskrit.

7 Vaj H 144, 5–31.

8 See James Egge, "Interpretive Strategies for Seeing the Body of the Buddha," in John Clifford Holt, Jacob N. Kinnard, and Jonathan S. Walters, eds., *Constituting Communities: Theravada Buddhism and the Religious Cultures of South and Southeast Asia* (Albany, NY: State University of New York Press, 2003), pp. 191–92. Buddhism was not alone in developing such prognosticatory systems. See also Nathan McGovern, "On the Origins of the 32 Marks of the Great Man," *Journal of the International Association of Buddhist Studies* 39 (2016): 207–47; Kenneth Zysk, *The Indian System of Human Marks* (Leiden: E. J. Brill, 2016). The origins of the thirty-two marks remain obscure. McGovern argues that the particular number is probably a Buddhist invention.

9 Egge, "Interpretive Strategies for Seeing the Body of the Buddha," pp. 190–91. The originals are *Majjhima Nikāya* II, 146; *Saṃyutta Nikāya* 548–67; and *Theragāthā* 818–41.

10 These are found notably in the *Brahmāyu-sutta* (*Majjhima Nikāya* II, 133–46), the *Lakkhaṇa-sutta* (*Dīgha Nikāya* III, 142–79), and the *Mahāpadāna-sutta* (*Dīgha Nikāya* II, 1–54).

11 See Egge, "Interpretive Strategies for Seeing the Body of the Buddha," pp. 193–96.

12 See Nobumi Yamabe, "The Paths of Śrāvakas and Bodhisattvas in Meditative Practices," *Meditative Buddhism: Its Origins and Reality*, special issue, *Acta Asiatica* 96 (2009): 47–75.

13 The term *ta* 塔 used here might be meant literally or it might refer to images on the gates of stupas. However, it can also be a metonymic designation for a temple, and that is most likely what is meant here.

14 *T.* 643.15:689a24–b3. The *Guan Fo sanmei hai jing* 観佛三昧海經, attributed as a translation by Buddhabhadra, belongs to a family of texts that includes the *Guan Wuliangshou Fo jing* 觀無量壽佛經 (*T.* 365), which is regarded as a core text of Pure Land Buddhist schools. For a slightly different translation, see Yamabe, "The Paths of Śrāvakas and Bodhisattvas in Meditative Practices," pp. 50–51.

15 The term *chan* here refers to early manuals focused on meditation techniques 禪, not to classical Chan formulations of later periods. For an analysis of the visionary techniques set out in these texts, see Eric Greene, "Meditation, Repentance, and Visionary Experience in Early Medieval Chinese Buddhism" (PhD dissertation, University of California, Berkeley, 2012), especially Chapter 1: "Chinese Meditation Texts of the Fifth Century (I)," pp. 15–76. Greene also traces the genealogy of the use of the term "visualization" in modern English and cautions against its ubiquitous use in translating Buddhist technical vocabulary; see Chapter 3: "Vision and Visualization," especially pp. 144–58.

16 *T.* 614.15:276a8–13. Yamabe's rendering is in "The Paths of Śrāvakas and Bodhisattvas in Meditative Practices," p. 51.

17 Yamabe, "The Paths of Śrāvakas and Bodhisattvas in Meditative Practices," p. 52, points to the *Maitreya-mahāsiṃhanāda-sūtra* as one piece of evidence that such techniques as described in the *Ocean Sutra* and other Central and East Asian sources were found in South Asia.

18 Classical forms of "mindfulness" involve mental fixation or attentiveness: "Its property is not losing; its manifestation is guarding or the state of being face to face with an object; its basis is strong noting of the *satipaṭṭhānas* of the body and so on. It should be seen as like a post due to its state of being firmly set in the object, and as like a gatekeeper because it guards the gate of the eye and so on"; translation of *Visuddhimagga* XIV, 141, in Rupert Gethin, *The Buddhist Path to Awakening: A Study of the Bodhi-Pakkhiyā Dhammā* (Leiden: E. J. Brill, 1992), p. 40.

19 *Visuddhimagga* IV, 28–30. Bhikkhu Ñāṇamoli, trans., *Visuddhimagga: The Path of Purification* (Kandy: Buddhist Publication Society, 2010, fourth ed.), pp. 119–20.

20 For what has become one of the most influential discussions of the tantric distinction and "deity yoga," see H. H. the Dalai Lama, Tsong-ka-pa, and Jeffrey Hopkins, *Deity Yoga in Action and Performance Tantra* (Boston, MA and London: Snow Lion, 1987; reprint of *The Yoga of Tibet*, London: George Allen & Unwin, Ltd., 1981). The concept is designated by the term *yidam* in Tibetan, but *iṣṭadevatā* apparently does not appear in Buddhist Sanskrit sources and there is no corresponding term in Chinese.

21 See Michel Strickmann's treatment of this text, "The *Consecration Sūtra*: A Buddhist Book of Spells," in Robert E. Buswell, Jr., ed., *Chinese Buddhist Apocrypha* (Honolulu: University of Hawai'i Press, 1990), pp. 75–118. Koichi Shinohara has suggested rethinking our understanding of such texts in his article, "Rethinking the Category of Chinese Buddhist Apocrypha," *Studies in Chinese Religions* 1/1 (2015): 70–81.

22 *T*. 365.12:343a18–21; 343b2. For an introduction to the *Guan jing* and its context in China, see Julian F. Pas, *Visions of Sukhāvatī: Shan-Tao's Commentary on the Kuan Wu-Liang-Shou-Fo ching* (New York: State University of New York Press, 1995); and Jonathan A. Silk, "The Composition of the 'Guan Wuliangshoufo-jing': Some Buddhist and Jaina Parallels to Its Narrative Frame," *Journal of Indian Philosophy* 25/2 (1997): 181–256.

23 On *abhiṣeka,* see Ronald M. Davidson, "*Abhiṣeka*," in Charles D. Orzech, Henrik H. Sørensen, and Richard K. Payne, eds., *Esoteric Buddhism and the Tantras in East Asia,* (Leiden: E. J. Brill, 2011), pp. 71–75. For the construction of the subject in *abhiṣeka,* see Charles D. Orzech, "On the Subject of Abhiṣeka," *Pacific World: Journal of the Institute of Buddhist Studies*, 3rd Series, No. 13 (Fall 2011): 113–128. For a full treatment of *āveśa,* see Fredrick M. Smith, *The Self Possessed: Deity and Spirit Possession in South Asian Literature and Civilization* (New York: Columbia University Press, 2006). Michel Strickmann and others have discussed *āveśa* rituals for inducing possession of children by a deity for oracular purposes. See Michel Strickmann, *Mantras et mandarins: Le bouddhisme tantrique en Chine* (Paris: Gallimard, 1996), pp. 213–229. Like Strickmann, both the *Bukkyō daijiten* (50c–51a) and the *Mikkyō daijiten* (32c–33b) treat the induction of possession states for oracular purposes while ignoring its use in *abhiṣeka*. Alexis Sanderson argues that the appearance of *āveśa* in *T*. 865 and other Buddhist texts is the result of borrowing from Śaiva Kaula systems; see Alexis Sanderson, "The Śaiva Age: The Rise and Dominance of Śaivism during the Early Medieval Period," in S. Einoo, ed., *Genesis and Development of Tantrism* (Tokyo: Institute of Oriental Culture, 2009), pp. 133, 133n311. As Smith demonstrates, the notion of *āveśa* appeared early and was widespread in Indian literature and it is probably premature to claim direct causality. Gavin Flood has also treated the Hindu tantras, *The Tantric Body: The Secret Tradition of the Hindu Religion* (London: I. B. Tauris, 2006), pp. 87–96.

24 *T*. 1796.39:713a1–2, 次出外向第三院 畫牟尼王釋迦種姓。著袈裟衣具足三十二相。There are numerous examples. See, for instance, *T*. 952.19:267b4–7.

25 *T*. 1018.19:704a6–10, 出生無邊門陀羅尼經.

26 *T*. 930.19:68a20. The scripture has been the subject of analysis in Robert Sharf, "Thinking Through Shingon Ritual," *Journal of the International Association of Buddhist Studies* 26 (2003): 51–96; Charles D. Orzech, "A Tang Esoteric Manual for Rebirth in the Pure Land," in Richard K. Payne, ed., *Path of No Path: Contemporary*

*Studies in Pure Land Buddhism Honoring Roger Corless* (Berkeley: Institute of Buddhist Studies and Numata Center for Buddhist Research and Translation, 2009), pp. 31–55. Similar passages are found elsewhere, for instance, in the *Regulations for the Practice and Cultivation of the Dhāraṇī of the Great Compassionate Heart* 大悲心陀羅尼修行念誦略 (*T*. 1066.20:127b12–17) and the *Scripture of the Dhāraṇī of Zhunti Enunciated by the Buddha-Mother of Seven Koṭīs*, 七俱胝佛母所說准提陀羅尼經 (*T*. 1076.20:181a3–7).

27 The passage is from a manual attributed to Amoghavajra, *Regulations for Siddhi through Worship and Recitation of Amṛtakuṇḍalin Bodhisattva* 甘露軍荼利菩薩供養念誦成就儀軌 (*T*. 1211 21.47a1, 由結此印誦密言加持故。速獲三十二相). Similar passages can be found in *T*. 1332, *T*. 1336, *T*. 1339, and so forth.

28 This passage is from the *Buddha's Discourse on the Great Dhāraṇī Scripture of the Buddha-Mother of the Seven Koṭīs*, 佛說七俱胝佛母准提大明陀羅尼經 : 即如畫像法觀也。若求三十二相。當觀三十二臂。 若求八萬四千法門者。應觀八十四臂 (*T*. 1075.20:177c10–11), a text attributed to Amoghavajra. For more on this cult, see Robert M. Gimello, "Icon and Incantation: The Goddess Zhunti and Role of Images in the Occult Buddhism of China," in Phyllis Granoff and Koichi Shinohara, eds., *Images in Asian Religions: Text and Contexts* (Vancouver: University of British Columbia Press, 2004), pp. 225–6. A similar process is also described in *T*. 904.18:905c8.

29 *T*. 932.19:76c29–77a2. The text is attributed to Vajrabodhi. An almost identical passage is found in *T*. 1112.20:492b23–25, and similar passages can be found elsewhere, for example, in *T*. 946, *T*. 1331, *T*. 1340, etc.

## Chapter 7

1 *Xinhua News Agency*, "Police Advise: Beware Fake Monks Cheat" (jingfang tixing: dangxin jia senglu jietou xing pian), February 1, 2007. http://www.gov.cn/fwxx/sh/2007-02/01/content_514779.htm. 2017.

2 *Bloomburg News*, "The Rise and Fall of Shaolin's CEO Monk," December 28, 2015. https://www.bloomberg.com/news/features/2015-12-28/the-rise-and-fall-of-shaolin-s-ceo-monk.

3 *Guanghua Daily*, "Buddhism Involved in Provoking Songshan Shaolin Annual Income of More Than 100 Million" (fomen she shang re yi songshan shaolin nian shouru yu yi), November 22, 2017. http://www.kwngwah.com.my/?p=429019.2017.

4 Deng Xiaoping, *Selected Works, 1975–1982* (Beijing: Foreign Languages Press, 1984), pp. 154, 160.

5 Michael E. Mari, *China and the Legacy of Deng Xiaoping: From Communist Revolution to Capitalist Evolution* (Dulles, VA: Potomac Books, 2001).

6 Siegfried G. Karsten, "China's Approach to Social Market Economics: The Chinese Variant of Market Socialism Seeks to Escape from the Difficulties of Central Command Planning," *The American Journal of Economics and Sociology* 47/2 (1988): 131.

7 Ibid., p. 133.

8 Ibid., p. 135.

9 For more, see the company profile of the Putuoshan Tourism Development Company Limited 普陀山旅游发展股份有限公司, http://www.zsptsgs.com/Tmp/Content.aspx?ChannelID=0d5f2b16-dd2c-403b-a8c6-68161c995d4a.

10 For more, see the Mount Putuo Tourism Group Company Profile 普陀山旅游集团有限公司, http://www.putuoshan.gov.cn/Enterprise/Index_38.html. Profile of the Putuo Tianhua Souvenirs Limited 中国旅游纪念品网, http://www.lyjnp.cn/Member.asp?id=485#cpzs.

11 Xuecheng is now the former abbot of Longquang and was president of the Buddhist Association of China from 2015 to 2018. In 2018 he was removed from these leadership positions because of allegation of sexual misconduct.

12 Phoenix Satellite Television, "Face-to-face with Faith: An Exclusive Interview with Ven. Master Xuecheng," 2016.

13 Phoenix Satellite Television, "Face-to-face with Faith."

14 Shi Huikong, *Stories of Ven. Master Xuecheng* (Beijing: China Fortune Press, 2016), p. 93.

15 "Longquan si shi ruhe liyong gao keji hongyang fofa de" ("How Longquan Temple Uses High-Tech to Promote Buddhism"), *Fayin* (*Voice of Dharma*) 10: (2016): 72.

16 "Exclusive Interview with Venerable Master Xuecheng: Buddhists Need to Advance with the Times," CCTV, October 25, 2015.

17 "Happiness Lies Inside," *Voice of Longquan,* September 3, 2016. http://eng.longquanzs.org/xuecheng/writings/73109.htm.

18 "Relieving Our Mental Stress," *Voice of Longquan,* August 24, 2016. http://eng.longquanzs.org/xuecheng/writings/72922.htm.

19 "Setting Mind at Peace for the Present," *Voice of Longquan,* July 15, 2016. http://eng.longquanzs.org/xuecheng/writings/72054.htm.

20 "Feeling Other People's Emotions Wholeheartedly," *Voice of Longquan,* August 9, 2016. http://eng.longquanzs.org/xuecheng/writings/72102.htm.

21 Xuecheng, "Zhongguo fojiao xianzhuang" ("Current State of Chinese Buddhism"), *Voice of Longquan*, June 18, 2017. http://eng.longquanzs.org/xuecheng/writings/77389.htm.

22 "Do Not Seek From Without," *Voice of Longquan*, August 25, 2016. http://eng.longquanzs.org/xuecheng/writings/72935.htm.

23 Yang Piaowei, *A Roaming AI Xian'er, the Robot Monk* (Beijing: Zhanlu Culture, 2006), p. vi.

24 Joseph Campbell, "Robot Monk Blends Science and Buddhism at Chinese Temple," *Reuters*, April 21, 2016.

25 Ke Yun, "Finding Robot Monk Xian'er: Understanding Buddhism in Longquan Animation," *Journal of Visual and Media Anthropology* 2/1 (2016): 16.
26 Longquan Animation, "Real Success," April 4, 2016. http://longquanzs.org/sj/lqdm/jhty/73334.htm 2016.
27 Longquan Animation, "Angry is Like Drinking Poison," June 26, 2015. http://longquanzs.org/sj/lqdm/jhty/65101.htm
28 Cui Jia, "Robot Monk Learns to 'Speak' English," *China Daily*, August 18, 2017.
29 Shi Huikong, *Stories of Ven. Master Xuecheng* (Beijing: China Fortune Press, 2016), p. 244.
30 *Voice of Longquan*. "A Summary of Beijing Longquan Monastery," August 12, 2017, http://eng.longquanzs.org/monastery/introduction%20/77832.htm.
31 Xuecheng. "On the Belt and Road: The Spiritual Footprints of Buddhism and the Construction of a New World Civilization," *Voice of Longquan*, June 29, 2017, http://eng.longquanzs.org/xuecheng/writings/76775.htm.
32 "Nuli kaichuang fojiao zhongguo hua de xin jingjie" ("Efforts to Create Chinese Buddhism's New Realm"), *Fayin* (*Voice of Dharma*) 8 (2016): 16–20.
33 State Department of the People's Republic of China, "Zongjiao shiwu tiaoli" ("Religious Affairs Regulation"), September 7, 2017. http://www.gov.cn/zhengce/content/2017-09/07/content_5223282.htm
34 Xuecheng, "Zhongguo fojiao xianzhuang" ("Current State of Chinese Buddhism"), *Voice of Longquan*, June 18, 2017. http://eng.longquanzs.org/xuecheng/writings/77389.htm.
35 Richard Payne, "Afterword," in Scott A. Mitchell and Natalie E. F. Quli, eds., *Buddhism beyond Borders: New Perspectives on Buddhism in the United States* (Albany, NY: State University of New York Press, 2015), p. 217.
36 Michael J. Walsh, *Sacred Economies: Buddhist Monasticism and Territoriality in Medieval China*, Sheng Yen Series in Chinese Buddhist Studies (New York: Columbia University Press, 2010), p. 3.

## Chapter 8

1 Peter N. Gregory, "Describing the Elephant: Buddhism in America," *Religion and American Culture* 11/2 (2001): 240.
2 Ibid., p. 239.
3 Ibid., p. 236; emphasis added.
4 Ibid., p. 240.
5 Joanna Cook, James Laidlaw, and Jonathan Mair, "What If There Is No Elephant? Towards a Conception of an Un-Sited Field," in Mark-Anthony Falzon, ed., *Multi-Sited Ethnography: Theory, Praxis and Locality in Contemporary Research* (London: Routledge, 2012), p. 48.
6 Ibid., p. 68.

7 Pew Research Center, "Asian Americans: A Mosaic of Faiths" (Washington, DC, 2012). http://www.pewforum.org/files/2012/07/Asian-Americans-religion-full-report.pdf.
8 Paul David Numrich, *Old Wisdom in the New World: Americanization in Two Immigrant Theravada Buddhist Temples* (Knoxville: University of Tennessee Press, 1996).
9 Ibid., p. xii.
10 Ibid., p. 45.
11 Ibid., p. 80.
12 Kenneth K. Tanaka, "Epilogue: The Colors and Contours of American Buddhism," in Charles S. Prebish and Kenneth K. Tanaka, eds., *The Faces of Buddhism in America* (Berkeley: University of California Press, 1998), pp. 287–8.
13 For example, Charles S. Prebish, "Two Buddhisms Reconsidered," *Buddhist Studies Review* 10/2 (1993): 187–206; Jan Nattier, "Visible and Invisible: On the Politics of Representation in America," *Tricycle: The Buddhist Review* (Fall 1995): 42–9; Gregory, "Describing the Elephant"; Paul David Numrich, "Two Buddhisms Further Considered," *Contemporary Buddhism* 4/1 (2003): 55–78; Christine L. Walters, "American Buddhism as Identity and Practice: Scholarly Classifications of Buddhists in the United States" (Master's thesis, University of Hawai'i, 2009); Jeff Wilson, "Mapping the American Buddhist Terrain: Paths Taken and Possible Itineraries," *Religions Compass* 3/5 (2009): 836–46; Wakoh Shannon Hickey, "Two Buddhisms, Three Buddhisms, and Racism," *Journal of Global Buddhism* 11 (2010): 1–25; Mihiri Uthpala Tillakaratne, "Multiculturalism, Ethnicity, Religious Identity and the 1.5 and Second Generation in Two Los Angeles-Area Sri Lankan Buddhist Temples" (MA thesis, University of California Los Angeles, 2012).
14 Charles S. Prebish, *American Buddhism* (North Scituate, MA: Duxbury Press, 1979), p. 51.
15 Numrich, *Old Wisdom in the New World*, pp. 65–7.
16 For example, Natalie E. Quli, "Western Self, Asian Other: Modernity, Authenticity, and Nostalgia for 'Tradition' in Buddhist Studies," *Journal of Buddhist Ethics* 16 (2009): 1–38; Hickey, "Two Buddhisms, Three Buddhisms, and Racism"; Joseph Cheah, *Race and Religion in American Buddhism: White Supremacy and Immigrant Adaptation* (New York: Oxford University Press, 2011); Anne C. Spencer, "Diversification in the Buddhist Churches of America: Demographic Trends and Their Implications for the Future Study of U.S. Buddhist Groups," *Journal of Global Buddhism* 15 (2014): 35–61; Jiemin Bao, *Creating a Buddhist Community: A Thai Temple in Silicon Valley* (Philadelphia: Temple University Press, 2015), pp. 8–10; Adeana McNicholl, "Buddhism and Race," in Paul Harvey and Kathryn Gin Lum, eds., *The Oxford Handbook of Religion and Race in American History* (New York: Oxford University Press, 2018), pp. 223–40.
17 Numrich, *Old Wisdom in the New World*, p. 140.

18 Ibid., p. 146.

19 Scott A. Mitchell, *Buddhism in America: Global Religion, Local Contexts* (New York: Bloomsbury Academic, 2016), p. 81.

20 Jeff Wilson, "Review of *Heartwood: The First Generation of Theravada Buddhism in America* by Wendy Cadge (Chicago: University of Chicago Press, 2004)," *Journal of Global Buddhism* 6 (2005): 7–11.

21 Wendy Cadge, *Heartwood: The First Generation of Theravada Buddhism in America* (Chicago: University of Chicago Press, 2005).

22 Ibid., p. 13.

23 Linda Learman, "Introduction," in Linda Learman, ed., *Buddhist Missionaries in the Era of Globalization* (Honolulu: University of Hawai'i Press, 2005), p. 19fn30; Hickey, "Two Buddhisms, Three Buddhisms, and Racism"; Arun, "American Buddhism's 'Ethnic' Problem," *Angry Asian Buddhist* (blog), May 2, 2012, http://www.angryasianbuddhist.com/2012/05/american-buddhisms-ethnic-problem.html; "Who Are Non-Ethnic Asian Westerners?," *Angry Asian Buddhist* (blog), March 21, 2014, http://www.angryasianbuddhist.com/2014/03/who-are-non-ethnic-asian-westerners.html.

24 Cadge, *Heartwood*, p. 205; Bao, *Creating a Buddhist Community*, p. x.

25 Bao, *Creating a Buddhist Community*, p. 5, emphasis in original.

26 Wilson, "Mapping the American Buddhist Terrain."

27 Bao, *Creating a Buddhist Community*, p. 145.

28 Tillakaratne, "Multiculturalism, Ethnicity, Religious Identity," p. 18.

29 Bao, *Creating a Buddhist Community*, p. 137–43.

30 Ibid., p. 143.

31 Sharon A. Suh, *Being Buddhist in a Christian World: Gender and Community in a Korean American Temple* (Seattle: University of Washington Press, 2004); Carolyn Chen, *Getting Saved in America: Taiwanese Immigration and Religious Experience* (Princeton, NJ: Princeton University Press, 2008).

32 Suh, *Being Buddhist in a Christian World*, p. 11.

33 Ibid., pp. 9, 10.

34 Ibid., p. 175.

35 Chen, *Getting Saved in America*, pp. 109, 189.

36 Lisa Lowe, *Immigrant Acts: On Asian American Cultural Politics* (Durham, NC: Duke University Press, 1996), p. 65.

37 Amos Yong, "Review Essay: Asian American Religions," *Nova Religio: The Journal of Alternative and Emergent Religions* 9/3 (2006): 92–107.

38 Wendy Cadge and Elaine Howard Ecklund, "Immigration and Religion," *Annual Review of Sociology* 33/1 (2007): 359–79.

39 Ibid., p. 360; emphasis added.

40 Chenxing Han, "Diverse Practices and Flexible Beliefs among Young Adult Asian American Buddhists," *Journal of Global Buddhism* 18 (2017): 1–24.

41 Asian Pacific American Legal Center, "A Community of Contrasts: Asian Americans in the United States," 2011. http://www.advancingjustice.org/pdf/Community_of_Contrast.pdf.

42 Thomas A. Tweed, "Night-Stand Buddhists and Other Creatures," in Duncan Ryuken Williams and Christopher S. Queen, eds., *American Buddhism: Methods and Findings in Recent Scholarship* (Surrey: Curzon Press, 1999).

43 Anne C. Spencer and Scott Draper, "Introducing the Sort-of Buddhist: Or, 'If There Is No "I" to Have a Religious Identity, Then How Do I Fill Out This Survey?,'" *Interdisciplinary Journal of Research on Religion* 14 (2018): 1–34.

44 Kenneth K. Tanaka, "The Individual in Relation to the Sangha in American Buddhism: An Examination of 'Privatized Religion,'" *Buddhist-Christian Studies* 27/1 (2007): 115–27.

45 Mario Luis Small, "'How Many Cases Do I Need?': On Science and the Logic of Case Selection in Field-Based Research," *Ethnography* 10/1 (2009): 14.

46 Martin A. Mills, *Identity, Ritual and State in Tibetan Buddhism: The Foundations of Authority in Gelukpa Monasticism* (New York: Routledge, 2003); Ingrid Jordt, *Burma's Mass Lay Meditation Movement: Buddhism and the Cultural Construction of Power* (Athens: Ohio University Press, 2007); Joanna Cook, *Meditation in Modern Buddhism: Renunciation and Change in Thai Monastic Life* (Cambridge: Cambridge University Press, 2010); Mark Rowe, *Bonds of the Dead: Temples, Burial, and the Transformation of Contemporary Japanese Buddhism* (Chicago: University of Chicago Press, 2011); Alexander Soucy, *The Buddha Side: Gender, Power, and Buddhist Practice in Vietnam* (Honolulu: University of Hawai'i Press, 2012); Guillaume Rozenberg, *The Immortals: Faces of the Incredible in Buddhist Burma*, trans. Ward Keeler (Honolulu: University of Hawai'i Press, 2015); Brooke Schedneck, *Thailand's International Meditation Centers: Tourism and the Global Commodification of Religious Practices* (New York: Routledge, 2015); Erik W. Davis, *Deathpower: Buddhism's Ritual Imagination in Cambodia* (New York: Columbia University Press, 2016); Thomas A. Borchert, *Educating Monks: Minority Buddhism on China's Southwest Border* (Honolulu: University of Hawai'i Press, 2017).

47 Thomas A. Tweed, "Between the Living and the Dead: Fieldwork, History, and the Interpreter's Position," in James V. Spickard, J. Shawn Landres, and Meredith B. McGuire, eds., *Personal Knowledge and Beyond: Reshaping the Ethnography of Religion* (New York: New York University Press, 2002), p. 65.

48 Richard K. Payne, "Afterword: Buddhism beyond Borders: Beyond the Rhetorics of Rupture," in Scott A. Mitchell and Natalie E. F. Quli, eds., *Buddhism beyond Borders: New Perspectives on Buddhism in the United States* (Albany, NY: State University of New York [SUNY] Press, 2015), p. 217; quoted in Mitchell, *Buddhism in America*, p. 209.

49 Quli, "Western Self, Asian Other."

50 Numrich, *Old Wisdom in the New World*, p. xxii.

51 David K. Yoo, "Introduction: Reframing the U.S. Religious Landscape," in David K. Yoo, ed., *New Spiritual Homes: Religion and Asian Americans* (Honolulu: University of Hawaii Press, 1999), pp. 8–10.

52 Irene Lin, "Journey to the Far West: Chinese Buddhism in America," in David K. Yoo, ed., *New Spiritual Homes: Religion and Asian Americans* (Honolulu: University of Hawaii Press, 1999), p. 136.

53 Pew Research Center, "Asian Americans: A Mosaic of Faiths," p. 8.

54 For example, Fenggang Yang, "The Growing Literature of Asian American Religions: A Review of the Field, with Special Attention to Three New Books," *Journal of Asian American Studies* 3/2 (2000): 251–6; Jane Naomi Iwamura and Paul Spickard, eds., *Revealing the Sacred in Asian and Pacific America* (New York: Routledge, 2003); David K. Yoo and Ruth H. Chung, eds., *Religion and Spirituality in Korean America* (Urbana, IL: University of Illinois Press, 2008); Carolyn Chen and Russell Jeung, eds., *Sustaining Faith Traditions: Race, Ethnicity, and Religion among the Latino and Asian American Second Generation* (New York: New York University Press, 2012).

55 Rudy V. Busto, "The Gospel According to Rice: The Next Asian American Christianity," *Amerasia Journal* 40/1 (2014): 65.

56 Richard Hughes Seager, *Buddhism in America* (New York: Columbia University Press, 1999); Tanaka, "The Individual in Relation to the Sangha."

57 Jeff Wilson, "'All Beings Are Equally Embraced by Amida Buddha': Jodo Shinshu Buddhism and Same-Sex Marriage in the United States," *Journal of Global Buddhism* 13 (2012): 37.

58 For example, Isao Horinouchi, "Americanized Buddhism: A Sociological Analysis of Protestantized Japanese Religion" (PhD dissertation, University of California, Davis, 1973); Emma McCloy Layman, *Buddhism in America* (Chicago: Nelson-Hall, 1976), pp. 33–51; Tetsuden Kashima, *Buddhism in America: The Social Organization of an Ethnic Religious Institution* (Westport, CT: Greenwood Press, 1977), and "The Buddhist Churches of America: Challenges for Change in the Twenty-First Century," in Richard K. Payne, ed., *Shin Buddhism: Historical, Textual, and Interpretive Studies* (Berkeley: Institute of Buddhist Studies and Numata Center for Buddhist Translation and Research, 2007) pp. 321–40; Prebish, *American Buddhism*, pp. 57–69; Alfred Bloom, "The Unfolding of the Lotus: A Survey of Recent Developments in Shin Buddhism in the West," *Buddhist-Christian Studies* 10 (1990): 157–64, and "Shin Buddhism in America: A Social Perspective," in Charles S. Prebish and Kenneth K. Tanaka, eds., *The Faces of Buddhism in America* (Berkeley: University of California Press, 1998), pp. 31–48; David K. Yoo, "Enlightened Identities: Buddhism and Japanese Americans of California, 1924–1941," *The Western Historical Quarterly* 27/3

(1996): 281–301; Seager, *Buddhism in America*, pp. 51–69; Kenneth K. Tanaka, "Issues of Ethnicity in the Buddhist Churches of America," in Duncan Ryuken Williams and Christopher S. Queen, eds., *American Buddhism: Methods and Findings in Recent Scholarship* (Surrey: Curzon Press, 1999), pp. 3–19; Duncan Ryuken Williams, "Camp Dharma: Japanese-American Buddhist Identity and the Internment Experience of World War II," in Charles S. Prebish and Martin Baumann, eds., *Westward Dharma: Buddhism beyond Asia* (Berkeley: University of California Press, 2002), pp. 191–200; Tara K. Koda, "Aloha with Gassho: Buddhism in the Hawaiian Plantations," *Pacific World*, Third Series, No. 5 (2003): 237–54; Michael K. Masatsugu, "'Beyond This World of Transiency and Impermanence': Japanese Americans, Dharma Bums, and the Making of American Buddhism during the Early Cold War Years," *Pacific Historical Review* 77/3 (2008): 423–51; Lori Pierce, "Buddha Loves Me This I Know: Nisei Buddhists in Christian America, 1889–1942," in Gary Storhoff and John Whalen-Bridge, eds., *American Buddhism as a Way of Life* (Albany, NY: State University of New York [SUNY] Press, 2010), pp. 167–82; Duncan Ryuken Williams and Tomoe Moriya, eds., *Issei Buddhism in the Americas* (Urbana, IL: University of Illinois Press, 2010); Michihiro Ama, *Immigrants to the Pure Land: The Modernization, Acculturation, and Globalization of Shin Buddhism, 1898–1941* (Honolulu: University of Hawai'i Press, 2011); Michiro Ama, "'First White Buddhist Priestess': A Case Study of Sunya Gladys Pratt at the Tacoma Buddhist Temple," in Scott A. Mitchell and Natalie E. F. Quli, eds., *Buddhism beyond Borders: New Perspectives on Buddhism in the United States* (Albany, NY: State University of New York [SUNY] Press, 2015), pp. 59–74.

59 Scott Mitchell, "Locally Translocal American Shin Buddhism," *Pacific World*, Third Series, No. 12 (2010): 112.

60 Patricia Kanaya Usuki, "American Women in Jodo Shin Buddhism Today: Tradition and Transition," *Pacific World*, Third Series, No. 7 (2005): 159–75.

61 Spencer, "Diversification in the Buddhist Churches of America."

62 For example, S. J. Tambiah, *Buddhism and the Spirit Cults in North-East Thailand* (Cambridge: Cambridge University Press, 1970); Melford E. Spiro, *Buddhism and Society: A Great Tradition and Its Burmese Vicissitudes* (Berkeley: University of California Press, 1982, second ed.); David N. Gellner, *Monk, Householder, and Tantric Priest: Newar Buddhism and Its Hierarchy of Ritual* (New York: Cambridge University Press, 1992).

63 C. Julia Huang, *Charisma and Compassion: Cheng Yen and the Buddhist Tzu Chi Movement* (Cambridge, MA: Harvard University Press, 2009).

64 Respectively, Bao, *Creating a Buddhist Community;* Tillakaratne, "Multiculturalism, Ethnicity, Religious Identity and the 1.5 and Second Generation"; Cheah, *Race and Religion in American Buddhism*, pp. 105–7.

65 Respectively, Carol A. Mortland, *Cambodian Buddhism in the United States* (Albany, NY: State University of New York [SUNY] Press, 2017); Penny Van Esterik, *Taking Refuge: Lao Buddhists in North America* (Tempe, AZ: Program for Southeast Asian Studies, Arizona State University, 2003).

66 "About Wake Up," *Wake Up International* (blog), April 23, 2013. https://wkup.org/about/.

67 Gregory Price Grieve, "The Middle Way Method: A Buddhist-Informed Ethnography of the Virtual World of Second Life," in Gregory Price Grieve and Daniel M. Veidlinger, eds., *Buddhism, the Internet, and Digital Media: The Pixel in the Lotus* (New York: Routledge, 2015), pp. 23–39.

68 Dhiraj Murthy, "Digital Ethnography: An Examination of the Use of New Technologies for Social Research," *Sociology* 42/5 (2008): 841–3. https://doi.org/10.1177/0038038508094565.

69 Rashmi Sadana, "Reading Delhi, Writing Delhi: An Ethnography of Literature," in Shalini Puri and Debra A. Castillo, eds., *Theorizing Fieldwork in the Humanities* (New York: Palgrave Macmillan US, 2016), p. 160. https://doi.org/10.1057/978-1-349-92834-7_8.

70 Mindy McAdams, "Finding American Buddhism in Blogs," paper presented at the conference "Buddhism without Borders: Contemporary Buddhism in the West," p. 21, Institute of Buddhist Studies, Berkeley, CA, March 18–21, 2010. http://www.researchgate.net/publication/266557128_Finding_American_Buddhism_in_Blogs.

71 Thomas A. Tweed, "Theory and Method in the Study of Buddhism: Toward 'Translocative' Analysis," *Journal of Global Buddhism* 12 (2011): 24.

72 Ally Ostrowski, "Buddha Browsing: American Buddhism and the Internet," *Contemporary Buddhism* 7/1 (2006): 91–103; Charles S. Prebish, *An American Buddhist Life: Memoirs of a Modern Dharma Pioneer* (Richmond Hill, Ontario: Sumeru Press, 2015), p. 250, and "The Buddhist Sangha: Buddhism's Monastic and Lay Communities," in John Powers, ed., *The Buddhist World* (New York: Routledge, 2016), p. 414.

73 Wanwan Lu, *Youth Group,* 2015. http://www.cool939.wixsite.com/mva2015/youth-group.

74 Cook, Laidlaw, and Mair, "What If There Is No Elephant?," p. 69.

75 Michael M. J. Fischer, "Ethnicity and the Post-Modern Arts of Memory," in James Clifford and George E. Marcus, eds., *Writing Culture: The Poetics and Politics of Ethnography* (Berkeley: University of California Press, 1986), p. 199.

76 Jeff Wilson, *Dixie Dharma: Inside a Buddhist Temple in the American South* (Chapel Hill, NC: University of North Carolina Press, 2012).

77 Janet McLellan, *Many Petals of the Lotus: Five Asian Buddhist Communities in Toronto* (Toronto: University of Toronto Press, 1999).

## Chapter 9

1 Einar Thomassen, "Some Notes on the Development of Christian Ideas about a Canon," in Einar Thomassen, ed., *Canon and Canonicity: The Formation and Use of Scripture* (Copenhagen: Museum Tusculanum Press, 2010), p. 9, note 3.

2 Wilfred Cantwell Smith, "Scripture as Form and Concept: Their Emergence for the Western World," in Miriam Levering, ed., *Rethinking Scripture: Essays from a Comparative Perspective* (Albany, NY: State University of New York (SUNY) Press, 1998), p. 295. See also the following definition from the Oxford English Dictionary: "The collection or list of books of the Bible accepted by the Christian Church as genuine and inspired. Also transf., any set of sacred books; also, those writings of a secular author accepted as authentic." (www.oed.com)

3 Tomas Hägg, "Canon Formation in Greek Literary Culture," in Einar Thomassen, ed., *Canon and Canonicity: The Formation and Use of Scripture* (Copenhagen: Museum Tusculanum Press, 2010), p. 109.

4 Smith, "Scripture as Form and Concept," p. 305.

5 Ibid., pp. 29–57.

6 Gregory Schopen, "Archaeology and Protestant Presuppositions in the Study of Indian Buddhism," *History of Religions* 31/1 (1991): 1–23.

7 Kendall Folkert, "The 'Canons' of 'Scripture,'" in Miriam Levering, ed., *Rethinking Scripture: Essays from a Comparative Perspective* (Albany, NY: State University of New York [SUNY] Press, 1989), pp. 170–9.

8 Thomassen, "Some Notes on the Development of Christian Ideas about a Canon," pp. 12–13.

9 Jiang Wu and Lucille Chia, eds., *Spreading Buddha's Word in East Asia: The Formation and Transformation of the Chinese Buddhist Canon* (New York: Columbia University Press, 2016). pp. 16, 17.

10 Tanya Storch, *The History of Chinese Buddhist Bibliography* (Amherst: Cambria Press, 2014), p. 24.

11 Ibid., pp. 32, 36.

12 Stefano Zacchetti, "Notions and Visions of the Canon in Early Chinese Buddhism," in Jiang Wu and Lucille Chia, eds., *Spreading Buddha's Word in East Asia: The Formation and Transformation of the Chinese Buddhist Canon* (New York: Columbia University Press, 2016), pp. 90–92.

13 Storch, *The History of Chinese Buddhist Bibliography*, p. 51.

14 Ibid., p. 118.

15 Ibid., p. 112.

16 Guangchang Fang, "Defining the Chinese Buddhist Canon: Its Origin, Periodization, and Future," *Journal of Chinese Buddhist Studies* 28 (2015): 5–7.

17 Storch, *The History of Chinese Buddhist Bibliography*, p. 132.

18 Lianbin Dai, "The Economics of the Jiaxing Edition of the Buddhist Tripitaka," *T'oung Pao*, Second Series, 94, Fasc. 4/5 (2008): 320–21.

19 Smith,"Scripture as Form and Concept," p. 305.

20 Ibid., p. 307.

21 Miriam Levering, "Scripture and its Reception: A Buddhist Case," in Miriam Levering, ed., *Rethinking Scripture: Essays from a Comparative Perspective* (Albany, NY: State University of New York (SUNY) Press, 1989), pp. 58–101.

22 Stefania Travagnin, "The Mādhyamika Dimension of Yinshun: A Restatement of the School of Nāgārjuna in 20th Century Chinese Buddhism" (PhD dissertation, SOAS University of London, 2009), pp. 43–47.

23 Raoul Birnbaum, "Buddhist China at the Century's Turn," *The China Quarterly* 174 (2003): 434.

24 See Jones, "Apologetic Strategies in Late Imperial Chinese Pure Land Buddhism."

25 Robert F. Campany, "Notes on the Devotional Uses and Symbolic Functions of Sutra Texts as Depicted in Early Chinese Buddhist Miracle Tales and Hagiographies," *Journal of the International Association of Buddhist Studies* 14/1 (1991): 28–72.

26 Beverly Foulks McGuire, *Living Karma: the Religious Practices of Ouyi Zhixu* (New York: Columbia University Press, 2014), pp. 111–12.

27 Ouyi Zhixu, "Guan quan Kaishi xueshu Fahua jing ba" 觀泉開士血書法華經跋, in *Ouyi dashi quanji* 藕益大師全集 (Taipei: Fojiao shuju 1989), p. 18: 11267.

28 Levering, "Scripture and its Reception: A Buddhist Case," p. 71.

29 Ibid., p. 69.

30 Holmes Welch, *The Practice of Chinese Buddhism 1900–1950* (Cambridge, MA: Harvard University Press, 1967), p. 210.

31 Jiang Wu, "From the 'Cult of the Book' to the 'Cult of the Canon': A Neglected Tradition in Chinese Buddhism," in Jiang Wu and Lucille Chia, eds., *Spreading Buddha's Word in East Asia: The Formation and Transformation of the Chinese Buddhist Canon* (New York: Columbia University Press, 2016), pp. 53–58.

32 Peter Berger, *The Sacred Canopy: Elements of a Sociological Theory of Religion* (New York: Anchor, 1967), "Chapter 1. Religion and World-Construction," pp. 3–28.

33 Fang, "Defining the Chinese Buddhist Canon," pp. 29–32.

## Chapter 10

1 Karen Derris and Natalie Gummer, *Defining Buddhism(s)* (London: Equinox Publishing, 2007), p. 5.

2 Ibid., p. 10.

3 Stephen Batchelor, *After Buddhism: Rethinking the Dharma for a Secular Age* (New Haven and London: Yale University Press, 2015), pp. 333–34, quoting the *Ariyapariyesanā Sutta.*

4 Hillary Rodrigues, "An Instance of Dependent Origination: Are Krishnamurti's Teachings Buddhadharma?," *Pacific World,* Third Series, No. 9 (2007): 99.

5 Jiddu Krishnamurti, speech on the dissolution of The Order of the Star, August 3, 1929. http://www.jkrishnamurti.org/about-krishnamurti/dissolution-speech.php.

6 Jiddu Krishnamurti, *Freedom from the Known* (San Francisco: HarperSanFrancisco, 1975), p. 10.

7 Jonathan A. Silk, "What, If Anything, Is Mahāyāna Buddhism? Problems of Definitions and Classifications," *Numen* 49/4 (2002): 355–405.

8 To be precise, I should say that my cousin was Charles Dodgson, who used the pen name Lewis Carroll.

9 Lewis Carroll (Charles Lutwidge Dodgson), *Sylvie and Bruno Concluded* (1893). http://etc.usf.edu/lit2go/211/sylvie-and-bruno-concluded/4652/chapter-11-the-man-in-the-moon.

10 Speaking of doing nearly as well, or better, I here had originally intended to use the example of Jorges Luis Borges's "On Exactitude in Science." In that very short short story, Borges relates that in a specific empire "the Cartographers Guilds struck a Map of the Empire whose size was that of the Empire, and which coincided point for point with it. The following Generations, who were not so fond of the Study of Cartography as their Forebears had been, saw that that vast Map was Useless, and not without some Pitilessness was it, that they delivered it up to the Inclemencies of Sun and Winters"—a parable of *avijja* and *anatta* if there ever was one. For the full story in English, see Jorge Luis Borges, *Collected Fictions* (New York: Viking Press, 1998), p. 325; http://www.sccs.swarthmore.edu/users/08/bblonder/phys120/docs/borges.pdf. I chose Dodgson's map over Borges's not merely for family pride, but also because the Borges story, being written after Dodgson's, seemed to me itself merely a map of the earlier territory. But perhaps that makes me a bit pitiless, myself.

11 I critique Thomas Tweed below. Here I want to explicitly express my appreciation of his Buddhist-inflected theory of religion: Thomas A. Tweed, "Theory and Method in the Study of Buddhism: Toward 'Translocative' Analysis," *Journal of Global Buddhism* 12 (2011): 22–3.

12 Here I adapt then secretary of defense Donald Rumsfeld's line, "As you know, you go to war with the army you have, not the army you might want or wish to have at a later time." Reported by Wolf Blitzer for CNN, "Troops Put Rumsfeld in the Hot Seat," December 8, 2004. http://www.cnn.com/2004/US/12/08/rumsfeld.kuwait/index.html.

13 Jonathan Z. Smith, *Map Is Not Territory: Studies in the History of Religions* (Chicago: University of Chicago Press, 1978).

14 Tweed, "Theory and Method in the Study of Buddhism," p. 23.

15 Ibid., p. 28.

16 Quoted from W. H. Auden, "In Memory of W. B. Yeats," written (among other things) to express Auden's frustration with other poets' infatuation with socialism (it was 1939, and Auden was already breaking away from Brecht and returning to Christianity) and its roots in the Romantic age. But can poetry, in the end, stand apart from the flow of culture? And does that flow not, at times, wear away even institutional stone? To experience the sweep of Auden's poetry, see W. H. Auden, *Collected Poems*, Edward Mendelson, ed. (New York: Modern Library, 2007).

17 Thomas A. Tweed, "Crabs, Crustaceans, Crabiness, and Outrage: A Response," *Journal of the American Academy of Religion* 77/2 (2009): 456.

18 *Pirkei Avot*, 1:14 (part of the Mishnah, the first collection of commentary on the Talmud). Note that though this is a Buddhist-inflected translation, I believe it is supported in the original Hebrew.

19 For a provocative examination of these issues, see the *Journal of Global Buddhism*'s special issue on "Blurred Genres," Vol. 9 (2008). Naturally, I find myself standing with John Makransky's article, "The Emergence of Buddhist Critical-Constructive Reflection in the Academy as a Resource for Buddhist Communities and for the Contemporary World" (pp. 113–53) and against Ian Reader's "Buddhism and the Perils of Advocacy" (pp. 83–112). http://www.globalbuddhism.org/contents9.html.

20 Charles Prebish, "Studying the Spread and Histories of Buddhism in the West," in Charles S. Prebish and Martin Baumann, eds., *Westward Dharma: Buddhism beyond Asia* (Berkeley and Los Angeles: University of California Press, 2002), pp. 78–9.

21 Natalie E. F. Quli, "Western Self, Asian Other: Modernity, Authenticity, and Nostalgia for 'Tradition' in Buddhist Studies," *Journal of Buddhist Ethics* 16 (2009): 15; http://www.buddhistethics.org/16/quli-article.html.

## Chapter 11

1 By "heritage Buddhist" I mean a person who self-identifies as Buddhist and was raised in a Buddhist household by parents whose family heritage also includes Buddhism (three generations or more). I have adopted this term, using it with an admittedly arbitrary three generations, from Jan Nattier, "Who Is a Buddhist? Charting the Landscape of Buddhist America," in Charles S. Prebish and Kenneth K. Tanaka, eds., *The Faces of Buddhism in America* (Berkeley: University of California Press, 1998). By "convert" I mean a person who self-identifies as Buddhist but was not raised in a Buddhist household. I use Tweed's notion here of "sympathizers" as seekers who do not consider themselves Buddhists but who engage with Buddhist people or materials. See Thomas A.

Tweed, "Nightstand Buddhists and Other Creatures: Sympathizers, Adherents, and the Study of Religion," in Christopher Queen and Duncan Ryuken Williams, eds., *American Buddhism: Methods and Findings in Recent Scholarship* (London: Routledge, 1998). Note that while these terms "convert," "heritage," and "sympathizer" have no inherent ethnicity attached to them, historically, "heritage" Buddhists in the United States have been (and currently are) Asian American. This will undoubtedly change in a generation, with converts' offspring eventually becoming heritage Buddhists themselves. Clarity in our language here is valuable, as it reveals dimensions of time beyond a single lifetime and is connected to larger issues of cultural and social change ("flows" to use Tweed's aquatic metaphor for the malleability of tradition). This is especially useful when analyzing authenticity discourse, which is often built on assumptions about continuity and rupture.

2 The Protestant assumptions I had are notable. Even non-Protestant Christians are exposed to and absorb these ideas due to their ubiquity in American culture. Orientalist themes of a mystic East are also evident.

3 See Charles Hallisey, "Roads Taken and Not Taken in the Study of Theravāda Buddhism," in Donald S. Lopez, Jr., ed., *Curators of the Buddha: The Study of Buddhism under Colonialism* (Chicago: University of Chicago Press, 1995), p. 43.

4 See Richard K. Payne, *Critical Reflections on Buddhist Thought*, "on not capitalizing (on) the dharma," July 27, 20018, https://rkpayne.wordpress.com/reflections-on-buddhist-thought-posts.

5 Steven C. Berkwitz has studied this authorizing discourse of authenticity in the context of contemporary Sri Lanka in "The Rhetoric of Authenticity: Modernity and 'True Buddhism' in Sri Lanka," in *Theravāda Buddhist Encounters with Modernity*, ed. Juliane Schober and Steven Collins (New York: Routledge, 2018), pp. 103–17.

6 See Thomas A. Tweed, "Theory and Method in the Study of Buddhism: Toward a 'Translocative' Analysis," in Scott Mitchell and Natalie Quli, eds., *Buddhism beyond Borders: New Perspectives on Buddhism in the United States* (Albany, NY: State University of New York [SUNY] Press, 2015), pp. 3–20.

7 Hallisey, "Roads Taken and Not Taken," pp. 33, 36.

8 I've previously written on the subject of authenticity in terms of how "Buddhist modernism" can be weaponized as a means for excluding Asian Americans and other contemporary Buddhist groups from the area of Buddhist studies; see Natalie E. F. Quli, "Western Self, Asian Other: Modernity, Authenticity, and Nostalgia for 'Tradition' in Buddhist Studies," *Journal of Buddhist Ethics* 16 (2009): 1–38.

9 Tweed, "Nightstand Buddhists and Other Creatures," p. 79.

10 Thomas A. Tweed, *The American Encounter with Buddhism, 1844–1912* (Bloomington, IN: University of Indiana Press, 1992), especially Chapter 3:

"Esoterics, Rationalists, and Romantics: A Typology of Euro-American Buddhist Sympathizers and Adherents, 1875–1912," pp. 48–77.

11 Ibid., p. 54.

12 Ibid., p. 63.

13 See, for example, Stephen Prothero, *The White Buddhist: The Asian Odyssey of Henry Steel Olcott* (Bloomington, IN: University of Indiana Press, 1996); Judith Snodgrass, *Presenting Japanese Buddhism to the West: Orientalism, Occidentalism, and the Columbian Exposition* (Chapel Hill, NC: University of North Carolina Press, 2003), Chapter 7: "Deploying Western Authority I: Henry Steel Olcott in Japan," pp. 155–71; Anne M. Blackburn, *Locations of Buddhism: Colonialism and Modernity in Sri Lanka* (Chicago: University of Chicago Press, 2010), Chapter 4: "Engaging the Adventurers," pp. 104–42.

14 See George Bond, *The Buddhist Revival in Sri Lanka: Religious Tradition, Interpretation, and Response* (1988) (Delhi: Motilal Banarsidass, 1996, reprint).

15 See Donald S. Lopez, Jr., "Introduction," in Donald S. Lopez, Jr., ed., *Curators of the Buddha: The Study of Buddhism under Colonialism* (Chicago: University of Chicago Press, 1995), pp. 1–29.

16 Henry Steel Olcott, *A Buddhist Catechism: According to the Sinhalese Canon* (London: Theosophical Publication Society, 1887); see also Henry Steel Olcott, preface to *The Golden Rules of Buddhism* (1887) (Madras: Theosophical Publishing House, 1902).

17 Edward Said, *Orientalism* (New York: Pantheon, 1978). See also, among many others, Philip C. Almond, *The British Discovery of Buddhism* (Cambridge and New York: Cambridge University Press, 1988) and Richard King, *Orientalism and Religion: Postcolonial Theory, India, and "The Mystic East"* (New York: Routledge, 1999). On contemporary Buddhism and Orientalism, see Joseph Cheah, *Race and Religion in American Buddhism: White Supremacy and American Adaptation* (Oxford and New York: Oxford University Press, 2011); Jane Naomi Imamura, *Virtual Orientalism: Asian Religions and American Popular Culture* (Oxford and New York: Oxford University Press, 2011); Sharon A. Suh, *Silver Screen Buddha: Buddhism in Asian and Western Film* (New York: Bloomsbury, 2015). Cheah, as far as I can ascertain, is the first to use the words "white supremacy" in reference to the Orientalism of white Insight attitudes. I am deeply indebted to his ideas and those of countless other Asian American scholars who have been pointing out racism for a very, very long time. Finally, I am deeply indebted to the writings of the late Aaron Lee, who laid bare white supremacy in contemporary American Buddhism. His blog "Angry Asian Buddhist," http://www.angryasianbuddhist.com, is required reading, including the comments of offended whites.

18 See Donald S. Lopez, Jr., "Buddha," in Donald S. Lopez, Jr., ed., *Critical Terms for the Study of Buddhism* (Chicago: University of Chicago Press, 2005), pp. 13–34.

19 This idea of the primacy of texts over praxis is likely inherited from Protestantism, as Gregory Schopen notes in "Archaeology and Protestant Presuppositions in the Study of Indian Buddhism," in *Bones, Stones, and Buddhist Monks: Collected Papers on the Archaeology, Epigraphy, and Texts of Monastic Buddhism in India* (Honolulu: University of Hawai'i Press, 1997), pp. 1–22. See also Donald S. Lopez, Jr., *The Scientific Buddha: His Short and Happy Life* (New Haven, CT: Yale University Press, 2012).

20 This seems to be Prothero's conclusion in *The White Buddhist,* where he describes Olcott's Buddhism as a "creole of Protestantism with a Buddhist syntax."

21 See Thomas A. Tweed, *Crossing and Dwelling: A Theory of Religion* (Cambridge and London: Cambridge University Press, 2006) and Tweed, "Theory and Method in the Study of Buddhism."

22 Peter Moran, "Introduction," in Peter Moran, ed., *Buddhism Observed: Travellers, Exiles and Tibetan Dharma in Kathmandu* (New York and London: Curzon Press, 2004), p. 10.

23 See Richard K. Payne, "Why 'Buddhist Theology' Is Not a Good Idea: Keynote Address for the Fifteenth Biennial Conference of the International Association of Shin Buddhist Studies, Kyoto, August 2011," *The Pure Land: Journal of the International Association of Shin Buddhist Studies*, New Series, 27 (2012–2013): 66; see also Tomoko Masuzawa, Chapter 4: "Buddhism, A World Religion," in *The Invention of World Religions: Or, How Universalism Was Preserved in the Language of Pluralism* (Chicago: University of Chicago Press, 2005), pp. 121–46.

24 For Buddhism and "tradition" as shifting discourses with no essence, see Ananda Abeysekara, *Colors of the Robe: Religion, Identity, and Difference* (Columbia, SC: University of South Carolina Press, 2002).

25 Franz Metcalf, "Our *Buddhadharma*, Our Buddhist Dharma," pp. 144–53.

26 Payne notes somewhat humorously in "Why 'Buddhist Theology' Is Not a Good Idea," p. 63: "Sometimes it feels like everybody but me knows what the Buddha said, thought, and felt. Person A says, 'This is what the Buddha taught.' Then I read Person B, who claims just the opposite of what Person A says, claiming that 'this is what the Buddha taught.' I get so confused so that sometimes it all seems like everyone is making up their own Buddha. If people would only say, 'According to text XYZ, which I choose to accept as authoritative, the Buddha taught PQR,' then we could avoid so many acts of Sartrean bad faith."

27 Peter Skilling, "Scriptural Authenticity and the Śrāvaka Schools: An Essay toward an Indian Perspective," *The Eastern Buddhist,* New Series 41/2 (2010): 1–47. Skilling notes that for East Asian Buddhists the question of authenticity has rested on whether or not a text was translated from an Indic original, a different criteria than what is used in Theravada (and Mahāvihāra) contexts.

28 Charles B. Jones, "Is a *Dazang jing* a Canon? On the Nature of Chinese Buddhist Textual Anthologies," pp. 129–43.

29 Skilling, "Scriptural Authenticity and the Śrāvaka Schools," p. 22.

30 Robert Sharf, *Coming to Terms with Chinese Buddhism: A Reading of the Treasure Store Treatise* (Honolulu: University of Hawai'i Press, 2002), p. 16.

31 On the exclusion of Buddhists from non-Asian locales from the study of Buddhism, see Quli, "Western Self, Asian Other."

32 Gil Fronsdal, "Insight Meditation in the United States: Life, Liberty, and the Pursuit of Happiness," in Charles S. Prebish and Kenneth K. Tanaka, eds., *The Faces of Buddhism in America* (Berkeley: University of California Press, 1998), p. 178. In this chapter Fronsdal also provides an excellent overview of the history and development of American Insight. For an excellent in-depth study of East Coast Insight, see Wendy Cadge, *Heartwood: The First Generation of Theravada Buddhism in America* (University of Chicago Press, 2005). Many of her observations apply to Bay Area Insight communities as well.

33 A notable exception to this pattern is the East Bay Meditation Center, which strives to be radically inclusive. See Ann Gleig, "Queering Buddhism or Buddhist De-Queering? Reflecting on Differences Amongst Western LGBTQI Buddhists and the Limits of Liberal Convert Buddhism," *Theology & Sexuality* 18/3 (2012): 198–214; Scott Mitchell, *Buddhism in America: Global Religion, Local Contexts* (New York: Bloomsbury, 2016), p. 158; East Bay Meditation Center, "Diversity Practices," https://eastbaymeditation.org/resources/diversity.

34 Given Chenxing Han's warning that many young Asian American Buddhists do not attend Buddhist temples or groups, there may be more Asian Americans who identify with Insight groups and teachings yet do not regularly attend community activities. See Chenxing Han, "Describing the (Nonexistent?) Elephant: Ethnographic Methods in the Study of Asian American Buddhists," pp. 109–25 in this volume; see also Chenxing Han, "Engaging the Invisible Majority: Conversations with Young Adult Asian American Buddhists" (MA thesis, Graduate Theological Union, 2014), p. 7.

35 For a valuable discussion of this see Charles S. Prebish, *Luminous Passage: The Practice and Study of Buddhism in America* (Berkeley: University of California Press, 1999), pp. 242 *passim*.

36 Emphasis added. These particular passages are included in Prebish's analysis in *Luminous Passage*, noted above. Jacob Needleman, *The New Religions* (Garden City, NY: Doubleday, 1970), pp. 226, 227.

37 Paul Numrich, *Old Wisdom in the New World: Americanization in Two Immigrant Theravada Buddhist Temples* (Knoxville, TN: University of Tennessee Press, 1996), p. 78.

38 See Ofelia Villero, Natalie Fisk (Quli), and Emily Wu, "New Religious Movements Project Report: For the Area of Cultural and Historical Studies of Religions," unpublished report, September 2006. In this paper my colleagues and I conclude:

"As we perused through the NRM archives, we came to realize the implicit racism in the Center's perspective must be addressed and articulated. What the Center seemed to be really researching was why new religious movements were attractive to White Christians. . . . The exclusion of NRMs among African Americans, immigrant communities, and Asian Buddhist groups support our argument that the Center's study focused on those groups perceived to be threats to the purity of White ideologies. As these omitted groups did not attract a significant number of White followers, they were not seen as invaders or competitors in the spiritual marketplace of mainline Christianity" (p. 19).

39 For an overview of new religious movements and sects according to the framework of two sociologists of religion, see Rodney Stark and William Sims Bainbridge, *The Future of Religion: Secularization, Revival and Cult Formation* (Berkeley: University of California Press, 1985). In *A Theory of Religion* (New York: P. Lang, 1987), p. 124, they write, "A sect movement is a deviant religious organization with traditional beliefs and practices," and "a cult movement is a deviant religious organization with novel beliefs and practices." According to this definition, sects maintain many traditional features of their parent organizations (in this case the use of the Pali canon, dedication to the Buddha, the use of statuary, *vipassanā* practice, acceptance of established Buddhist doctrine, reverence of Buddhist masters, etc.), but they present themselves as authentic, purged, purified, and so forth. Of course, all traditions are constantly in flux, with novel elements constantly being introduced, which makes the task of defining them tremendously problematic.

40 One example is the purification that led to the *Thammayutika-nikāya* in nineteenth-century Siam and neighboring Cambodia and Laos. Hansen's work on textualization and the Pali canon is particularly informative here; see Anne Hansen, *How to Behave: Buddhism and Modernity in Colonial Cambodia, 1860–1930* (Honolulu: University of Hawaii Press, 2007).

41 Steven Collins, "On the Very Idea of the Pāli Canon," in Paul Williams, ed., *Buddhism: Critical Concepts in Religious Studies* (London: Routledge, 2005), vol. 1, p. 72.

42 Skilling, "Scriptural Authenticity and the Śrāvaka Schools," p. 6.

43 As mentioned previously, almost all of this literature is now lost; many of the texts cited in Indian monastic scholarship are totally unknown to us today. Skilling, "Scriptural Authenticity and the Śrāvaka Schools," p. 22.

44 The translation here combines portions of Hermann Oldenberg, trans., *Dīpavaṃsa, The Chronicle of the Island: An Ancient Buddhist Historical Record* (London: Williams and Norgate, 1879), pp. 142 for verse 51; Rupert Gethin, "Was Buddhaghosa a Theravādin? Buddhist Identity in Pali Commentaries and Chronicles," in Peter Skilling, Jason Carbine, Claudia Cicuzza, and Santi Pakdeekham, eds., *How Theravāda Is Theravāda? Exploring Buddhist Identities*

(Chiang Mai, Thailand: Silkwork Books, 2012), p. 43 for verse 52. Gethin's translation emphasizes the textual exclusivity of the fourth- to fifth-century writer of the *Dīpavaṃsa*; italics added for emphasis. For the Pali, see Oldenberg, *Dīpavaṁsa,* p. 37.

45 See Robert Sharf, "The Rhetoric of Experience and the Study of Religion," *Journal of Consciousness Studies* 7, no. 11–12 (2000): pp. 267–87 as well as his "Buddhist Modernism and the Rhetoric of Meditative Experience," *Numen* 42(3): 228-83.

46 For an overview of attitudes of white superiority among white liberal Buddhist feminists toward Asian Buddhist nuns, see Nirmala S. Salgado, *Buddhist Nuns and Gendered Practice: In Search of the Female Renunciant* (New York: Oxford University Press, 2013); see also Justine Semmens, "Ten-Precept Mothers in the Buddhist Revival of Sri Lanka," in John Holt, ed., *The Sri Lanka Reader: History, Culture, Politics* (Durham, NC: Duke University Press, 2011), pp. 364–75.

47 Jack Kornfield, *Modern Buddhist Masters* (1977) (Kandy, Sri Lanka: Buddhist Publication Society, 2007), p. 7.

48 Cheah, *Race and Religion in American Buddhism*, p. 135.

49 As an interesting aside, I've also observed the behaviors of whites in heritage Theravada temples in the United States. One noticeable pattern is the tendency for white men to be given special attention and treated as authorities by monastics and laypeople alike. Another is white men giving spontaneous and patronizing lectures on Buddhism in the context of community gatherings and dhamma groups, essentially monopolizing the conversation and painting themselves as authorities. A friend confided that she grew tired of inevitably being lectured by each new white Buddhist male who arrived at her own temple, usually in a discourse that begins, "*Actually,* the Buddha taught . . . ." This, too, is the authority of whiteness.

50 Funie Hsu, "We've Been Here All Along," *Buddhadharma: The Practioner's Quarterly* (Winter 2016); https://www.lionsroar.com/weve-been-here-all-along.

51 "Ajahn Amaro, "A Response to Critics of 'We've Been Here All Along,'" https://www.lionsroar.com/a-response-to-critics-of-weve-been-here-all-along-from-the-winter-2016-buddhadharma.

52 See Natalie Quli, "Laicization in Four Sri Lankan Buddhist Temples in Northern California" (PhD dissertation, Graduate Theological Union, Berkeley, 2010), especially Chapter 5: "Issues in Lay-Monastic Relationships," pp. 165–257, and Chapter 6: "Conclusions: Laicization and Americanization," pp. 258–77.

53 While Insight members tended to view Asian American Theravada as inauthentic, several Sinhalese American Buddhists have expressed to me their appreciation for American Insight, which they regard as part of their own Pali tradition.

54 Yes, we should consider whiteness an ethnicity in our studies. All Buddhism is cultural Buddhism: all Buddhists are human, and all humans have culture, including whites. See Quli, "Western Self, Asian Other," p. 16.

55 I am indebted to Scott Mitchell for his observations in "Scrambled Eggs: At the Intersection of Buddhist Economies and Knowledge Economies," paper presented at the American Academy of Religion Conference, November 19–22, 2016, San Antonio, TX.

56 See Prebish, *Luminous Passage*, p. 75. Laura Harrington has noted that Area Studies, along with Asian Buddhist studies, were funded in part by the CIA, which hoped to gain useful material for influencing Asian subjects in locations of military interest; this relationship drove the field in the direction of studies deemed useful. Laura Harrington, "Cold War Karma: A Brief History of Buddhist Studies and the CIA 1951–1967," paper presented at the American Academy of Religion Conference, November 18–21, Boston, MA. I'd also like to draw attention to the culture of exclusion and bullying encouraged in the academy, poignantly and intelligently described by Elizabeth Cullen Dunn, "The Problem with Assholes," *Public Anthropologist*, June 20, 2018, http://publicanthropologist.cmi.no/2018/06/20/the-problem-with-assholes: "Assholery structures the entire discipline from top to bottom, shaping the goals and dreams of graduate students, allowing faculty at every rank to sneer at those in lesser positions (or, God forbid, working outside academia), and determining our formal criteria for hiring, promotion and tenure." Assholery, too, is deeply embedded in Buddhist studies departments: in a field in which there is intense competition for very limited funding, the exclusion of studies of Asian American and convert Buddhism, which has been rationalized by arguments made through a rhetoric of authenticity, has the practical benefit of eliminating rival scholars who study such groups; see Quli, "Western Self, Asian Other."

# Bibliography


Abe, Ryūichi. *The Weaving of Mantra: Kūkai and the Construction of Esoteric Buddhist Discourse*. New York: Columbia University Press, 1999.

Abe, Takako 阿部貴子. "Meijiki shingonshū no daigakurin kyōiku—futsūgaku dōnyū wo meguru giron to jissai" 明治期真言宗の大学林教育—普通学導入をめぐる議論と実際, in Ejima Naotoshi 江島尚俊, Miura Shū 三浦周, and Matsuno Tomoaki 松野智章, eds., *Kindai nihon no daigaku to shūkyō* 近代日本の大学と宗教, pp. 169–202. Kyoto: Hōzōkan, 2014.

Abeysekara, Ananda. *Colors of the Robe: Religion, Identity, and Difference*. Columbia, SC: University of South Carolina Press, 2002.

Akase, Tomoko. *Inseikiigo no kagakusho to utamakura*. Osaka: Seibundo Shuppan, 2006.

Almond, Philip C. *The British Discovery of Buddhism*. Cambridge and New York: Cambridge University Press, 1988.

Ama, Michihiro. *Immigrants to the Pure Land: The Modernization, Acculturation, and Globalization of Shin Buddhism, 1898–1941*. Honolulu: University of Hawai'i Press, 2011.

Ama, Michihiro. "'First White Buddhist Priestess': A Case Study of Sunya Gladys Pratt at the Tacoma Buddhist Temple," in Scott A. Mitchell and Natalie E. F. Quli, eds., *Buddhism beyond Borders: New Perspectives on Buddhism in the United States*, pp. 59–74. Albany, NY: State University of New York (SUNY) Press, 2015.

Amaro, Ajahn. "A Response to Critics of 'We've Been Here All Along,'" https://www.lionsroar.com/a-response-to-critics-of-weve-been-here-all-along-from-the-winter-2016-buddhadharma.

Arun. "American Buddhism's 'Ethnic' Problem," *Angry Asian Buddhist* (blog), May 2, 2012. http://www.angryasianbuddhist.com/2012/05/american-buddhisms-ethnic-problem.html.

Arun. "Who Are Non-Ethnic Asian Westerners?" *Angry Asian Buddhist* (blog), March 21, 2014. http://www.angryasianbuddhist.com/2014/03/who-are-non-ethnic-asian-westerners.html.

Asian Pacific American Legal Center. "A Community of Contrasts: Asian Americans in the United States," 2011. http://www.advancingjustice.org/pdf/Community_of_Contrast.pdf.

Auden, W. H. *Collected Poems*. Edward Mendelson, ed. New York: Modern Library, 2007.

Bao, Jiemin. *Creating a Buddhist Community: A Thai Temple in Silicon Valley*. Philadelphia: Temple University Press, 2015.

Batchelor, Stephen. *After Buddhism: Rethinking the Dharma for a Secular Age*. New Haven, CT and London: Yale University Press, 2015.

Bender, Courtney. *The New Metaphysicals: Spirituality and the American Religious Imagination*. Chicago: University of Chicago Press, 2010.

Berger, Peter. *The Sacred Canopy: Elements of a Sociological Theory of Religion*. New York: Anchor, 1967.

Birnbaum, Raoul. "Buddhist China at the Century's Turn," *The China Quarterly* 174 (2003): 428–50.

Blackburn, Anne M. *Locations of Buddhism: Colonialism and Modernity in Sri Lanka*. Chicago: University of Chicago Press, 2010.

Blitzer, Wolf. "Troops Put Rumsfeld in the Hot Seat," interview with Secretary of Defense Donald Rumsfeld, December 8, 2004. http://www.cnn.com/2004/US/12/08/rumsfeld.kuwait/index.html.

Bloom, Alfred. "The Unfolding of the Lotus: A Survey of Recent Developments in Shin Buddhism in the West," *Buddhist-Christian Studies* 10 (1990): 157–64.

Bloom, Alfred. "Shin Buddhism in America: A Social Perspective," in Charles S. Prebish and Kenneth K. Tanaka, eds., *The Faces of Buddhism in America*, pp. 31–48. Berkeley, CA: University of California Press, 1998.

Bloomburg News. "The Rise and Fall of Shaolin's CEO Monk," December 28, 2015. https://www.bloomberg.com/news/features/2015-12-28/the-rise-and-fall-of-shaolin-s-ceo-monk.

Bond, George. *The Buddhist Revival in Sri Lanka: Religious Tradition, Interpretation, and Response* (1988). Delhi: Motilal Banarsidass, 1996, reprint.

Borchert, Thomas A. *Educating Monks: Minority Buddhism on China's Southwest Border*. Honolulu: University of Hawaiʻi Press, 2017.

Borges, Jorges Luis. "On Exactitude and Science," in Andrew Hurley, trans., *Collected Fictions*, p. 325. New York: Viking Press, 1998.

Busto, Rudy V. "The Gospel According to Rice: The Next Asian American Christianity," *Amerasia Journal* 40/1 (2014): 59–79.

Cadge, Wendy. *Heartwood: The First Generation of Theravada Buddhism in America*. Chicago: University of Chicago Press, 2005.

Cadge, Wendy and Elaine Howard Ecklund. "Immigration and Religion," *Annual Review of Sociology* 33/1 (2007): 359–79.

Campany, Robert F. "Notes on the Devotional Uses and Symbolic Functions of Sutra Texts as Depicted in Early Chinese Buddhist Miracle Tales and Hagiographies," *Journal of the International Association of Buddhist Studies* 14/1 (1991): 28–72.

Campbell, Joseph. "Robot Monk Blends Science and Buddhism at Chinese Temple," *Reuters*, April 21, 2016.

Carroll, Lewis (Charles Lutwidge Dodgson). *Sylvie and Bruno Concluded* (1893). http://etc.usf.edu/lit2go/211/sylvie-and-bruno-concluded/4652/chapter-11-the-man-in-the-moon/.

CCTV. "Exclusive Interview with Venerable Master Xuecheng: Buddhists Need to Advance with the Times," October 25, 2015. www.CCTV.com.

Cheah, Joseph. *Race and Religion in American Buddhism: White Supremacy and American Adaptation*. Oxford and New York: Oxford University Press, 2011.

Chen, Carolyn. *Getting Saved in America: Taiwanese Immigration and Religious Experience*. Princeton, NJ: Princeton University Press, 2008.

Chen, Carolyn and Russell Jeung, eds. *Sustaining Faith Traditions: Race, Ethnicity, and Religion among the Latino and Asian American Second Generation*. New York: New York University Press, 2012.

Cole, Alan. *Text as Father: Paternal Seductions in Early Mahāyāna Buddhist Literature*. Berkeley, CA: University of California Press, 2005.

Collins, Steven. "On the Very Idea of the Pāli Canon," in Paul Williams, ed., *Buddhism: Critical Concepts in Religious Studies*, vol. 1, pp. 72–95. London: Routledge, 2005.

Como, Michael. *Shōtoku: Ethnicity, Ritual, and Violence in the Japanese Buddhist Tradition*. New York: Oxford University Press, 2008.

Conlan, Thomas. *From Sovereign to Symbol: An Age of Ritual Determinism in Fourteenth Century Japan*. Oxford: Oxford University Press, 2011.

Conze, Edward, trans. *Buddhist Wisdom Books: The Diamond and the Heart Sutra*. New York: Harper and Row, 1972.

Cook, Joanna. *Meditation in Modern Buddhism: Renunciation and Change in Thai Monastic Life*. Cambridge: Cambridge University Press, 2010.

Cook, Joanna, James Laidlaw, and Jonathan Mair. "What If There Is No Elephant? Towards a Conception of an Un-Sited Field," in Mark-Anthony Falzon, ed., *Multi-Sited Ethnography: Theory, Praxis, and Locality in Contemporary Research*, pp. 47–72. London: Routledge, 2012.

Cui, Jia. "Robot Monk Learns to 'Speak' English," *China Daily*, August 18, 2017.

Dai, Lianbin. "The Economics of the Jiaxing Edition of the Buddhist Tripitaka," *T'oung Pao*, Second Series, vol. 94, Fasc. 4/5 (2008): 306–59.

Davidson, Ronald M. *Indian Esoteric Buddhism: A Social History of the Tantric Movement*. New York: Columbia University Press, 2002.

Davidson, Ronald M. "Abhiṣeka," in Charles D. Orzech, Henrik H. Sørensen, and Richard K. Payne, eds., *Esoteric Buddhism and the Tantras in East Asia*, pp. 71–75. Leiden: E. J. Brill, 2011.

Davidson, Ronald M. "Some Observations on the Usṇīsa Abhiṣeka Rites in Atikūṭa's Dhāraṇīsaṃgraha," in István Keul, ed., *Transformations and Transfer of Tantra: Tantrism in Asia and Beyond*, pp. 77–98. Berlin and New York: Walter de Gruyter, 2012.

Davis, Erik W. *Deathpower: Buddhism's Ritual Imagination in Cambodia*. New York: Columbia University Press, 2016.

Deng, Xiaoping. *Selected Works, 1975–1982*. Beijing: Foreign Languages Press, 1984.

Derris, Karen and Natalie Gummer. *Defining Buddhism(s)*. London: Equinox Publishing, 2007.

Devereux, George. *From Anxiety to Method in the Behavioral Sciences*. New Babylon Studies in the Behavioral Sciences Book 3. The Hague, Paris: Mouton, 1967.

Dreitlein, Thomas Eijo. "Amoghavajra's Amitāyus Ritual Manual," in Georgios T. Halkias and Richard K. Payne, eds., *Pure Lands in Asian Texts and Contexts: An Anthology*. Honolulu: University of Hawai'i Press, 2019.

Dunn, Elizabeth Cullen. "The Problem with Assholes," *Public Anthropologist*, June 20, 2018. http://publicanthropologist.cmi.no/2018/06/20/the-problem-with-assholes.

Egge, James. "Interpretive Strategies for Seeing the Body of the Buddha," in John Clifford Holt, Jacob N. Kinnard, and Jonathan S. Walters, eds., *Constituting Communities: Theravada Buddhism and the Religious Cultures of South and Southeast Asia*, pp. 189–208. Albany, NY: State University of New York Press, 2003.

Ejima, Naotoshi 江島 尚俊, Miura Shū 三浦周, and Matsuno Tomoaki 松野智章, eds. *Kindai nihon no daigaku to shūkyō* 近代日本の大学と宗教. Kyoto: Hōzōkan, 2014.

Ejima, Naotoshi 江島 尚俊. "Kindai nihon no kōtō kyōiku ni okeru kyōiku to kyōka" 近代日本の高等教育における教育と教化, in Ejima Naotoshi 江島尚俊, Miura Shū 三浦周, and Matsuno Tomoaki 松野智章, eds., *Kindai nihon no daigaku to shūkyō* 近代日本の大学と宗教, pp. 3–32. Kyoto: Hōzōkan, 2014.

Fang, Guangchang. "Defining the Chinese Buddhist Canon: Its Origin, Periodization, and Future," *Journal of Chinese Buddhist Studies* 28 (2015): 1–34.

Fischer, Michael M. J. "Ethnicity and the Post-Modern Arts of Memory," in James Clifford and George E. Marcus, eds., *Writing Culture: The Poetics and Politics of Ethnography*, pp. 194–233. Berkeley, CA: University of California Press, 1986.

Flood, Gavin. *The Tantric Body: The Secret Tradition of the Hindu Religion*. London: I. B. Tauris, 2006.

Foard, James, Michael Solomon, and Richard K. Payne, eds. *The Pure Land Tradition: History and Development*. Berkeley Buddhist Studies Series, 1996. Fremont, CA: Jain Publishing Co., 2006.

Folkert, Kendall. "The 'Canons' of 'Scripture,'" in Miriam Levering, ed., *Rethinking Scripture: Essays from a Comparative Perspective*, pp. 170–79. Albany, NY: State University of New York (SUNY) Press, 1989.

Foulks McGuire, Beverly. *Living Karma: the Religious Practices of Ouyi Zhixu*. New York: Columbia University Press, 2014.

Freiberger, Oliver. "The Disciplines of Buddhist Studies—Notes on Religious Commitment as Boundary-Maker," *Journal of the International Association of Buddhist Studies* 30/1–2 (2007): 299–318.

Fronsdal, Gil. "Insight Meditation in the United States: Life, Liberty, and the Pursuit of Happiness," in Charles S. Prebish and Kenneth K. Tanaka, eds., *The Faces of Buddhism in America*, pp. 163–80. Berkeley, CA: University of California Press, 1998.

Fumio, Hashimoto, Ariyoshi Tamotsu, and Fujiwara Haruo, eds., *Shinpen Nihon Koten Bungaku Zenshū 87: Karonshū*. Tokyo: Shōgakukan, 2002.

Gellner, David N. *Monk, Householder, and Tantric Priest: Newar Buddhism and Its Hierarchy of Ritual*. New York: Cambridge University Press, 1992.

Gethin, Rupert. *The Buddhist Path to Awakening: A Study of the Bodhi-Pakkhiyā Dhammā*. Leiden: E. J. Brill, 1992.

Gethin, Rupert. "Was Buddhaghosa a Theravādin? Buddhist Identity in Pāli Commentaries and Chronicles," in Peter Skilling, Jason Carbine, Claudia Cicuzza, and Santi Pakdeekham, eds., *How Theravāda is Theravāda? Exploring Buddhist Identities*, pp. 1–63. Chiang Mai, Thailand: Silkwork Books, 2012.

Gimello, Robert M. "Icon and Incantation: The Goddess Zhunti and Role of Images in the Occult Buddhism of China," in Phyllis Granoff and Koichi Shinohara, eds., *Images in Asian Religions: Text and Contexts*, pp. 225–56. Vancouver: University of British Columbia Press, 2004.

Gleig, Ann. "Queering Buddhism or Buddhist De-Queering? Reflecting on Differences amongst Western LGBTQI Buddhists and the Limits of Liberal Convert Buddhism," *Theology & Sexuality* 18/3 (2012): 198–214.

Gleig, Ann. *American Dharma: Buddhism beyond Modernity*. New Haven, CT: Yale University Press, 2019.

Greene, Eric. "Meditation, Repentance, and Visionary Experience in Early Medieval Chinese Buddhism," PhD dissertation, University of California, Berkeley, CA, 2012.

Gregory, Peter N. "Describing the Elephant: Buddhism in America," *Religion and American Culture* 11/2 (2001): 233–63.

Grieve, Gregory Price. "The Middle Way Method: A Buddhist-Informed Ethnography of the Virtual World of Second Life," in Gregory Price Grieve and Daniel M. Veidlinger, eds., *Buddhism, the Internet, and Digital Media: The Pixel in the Lotus*, pp. 23–39. New York: Routledge, 2015.

Grumbach, Lisa. "Sacrifice and Salvation in Medieval Japan: Hunting and Meat in Religious Practice at Suwa Jinja," PhD dissertation, Stanford University, 2005.

Guanghua Daily. "Buddhism Involved in Provoking Songshan Shaolin Annual Income of More than 100 Million" (*fomen she shang re yi songshan shaolin nian shouru yu yi)*, November 22, 2017. http://www.kwongwah.com.my/?p=429019.

H. H. the Dalai Lama, Tsong-ka-pa, and Jeffrey Hopkins. *Deity Yoga in Action and Performance Tantra*. Boston, MA and London: Snow Lion, 1987.

Habermas, Jürgen. *The Theory of Communicative Action*, vol. 1. Thomas McCarthy, trans. Boston, MA: Beacon Books, 1984.

Hägg, Tomas. "Canon Formation in Greek Literary Culture," in Einar Thomassen, ed., *Canon and Canonicity: The Formation and Use of Scripture*, pp. 109–28. Copenhagen: Museum Tusculanum Press, 2010.

Hallisey, Charles. "Roads Taken and Not Taken in the Study of Theravāda Buddhism," in Donald S. Lopez, Jr., ed., *Curators of the Buddha: The Study of Buddhism under Colonialism*, pp. 31–61. Chicago: University of Chicago Press, 1995.

Han, Chenxing. "Engaging the Invisible Majority: Conversations with Young Adult Asian American Buddhists," MA thesis, Graduate Theological Union, Berkeley, CA, 2014.

Han, Chenxing. "Diverse Practices and Flexible Beliefs among Young Adult Asian American Buddhists," *Journal of Global Buddhism* 18 (2017): 1–24.

Hansen, Anne. *How to Behave: Buddhism and Modernity in Colonial Cambodia, 1860–1930*. Honolulu: University of Hawai'i Press, 2007.

Harrington, Laura. "Cold War Karma: A Brief History of Buddhist Studies and the CIA 1951–1967," paper presented at the American Academy of Religion (AAR) Conference, November 18–21, 2017, Boston, MA.

Harrison, Paul. "Vajracchedikā Prajñāpāramitā: A New English Translation of the Sanskrit Text Based on Two Manuscripts from Greater Gandhāra," in *Buddhist Manuscripts in the Schøyen Collection*, vol. 3, pp. 133–60. Oslo: Hermes Publishing, 2006. https://www2.hf.uio.no/polyglotta/index.php?page=fulltext&view=fulltext&vid=22.

Harrison, Paul. "Experimental Core Samples of Chinese Translations of Two Buddhist Sūtras Analysed in the Light of Recent Sanskrit Manuscript Discoveries," *Journal of the International Association of Buddhist Studies* 13/1–2 (2010): 205–49.

Hayami, Tasuku 速水侑. *Jōdo shinkō ron* 浄土信仰論. Tokyo: Yūzankaku Shuppan, 1978.

Hayashi, Makoto 林 淳. "Kindai ni okeru bukkyōgaku to shūkyōgaku" 近代における仏教学と宗教学, *Shūkyō kenkyū* 宗教研究 333 (2002): 29–53.

Hayashi, Makoto 林 淳. "Shūkyō kei daigaku to shūkyōgaku" 宗教系大学と宗教学, *Kikan Nihon Shisōshi* 季刊日本思想史 72 (2002): 71–88.

Hayashi, Makoto 林 淳. "Gakumonshi kara mita bukkyōshigakkai" 学問史から見た仏教史学会, *Bukkyōshigaku kenkyū* 仏教史学研究 53/1 (2010): 103–14.

Hayashi, Makoto 林 淳. "General Education and the Modernization of Japanese Buddhism," *The Eastern Buddhist* 43/1–2 (2012): 133–52.

Hayashi, Makoto 林 淳. "The Birth of Buddhist Universities," *Japanese Religions*, Special Issue: "The Politics of Buddhist Studies in Early Twentieth-Century Japan," 39/1–2 (2013): 11–29.

Hayashi, Makoto 林 淳. "Religious Studies and Religiously Affiliated Universities," in Hayashi Makoto, Ōtani Eiichi, and Paul Swanson, eds., *Modern Buddhism in Japan*, pp. 163–93. Nagoya: Nanzan Institute for Religion and Culture, 2014.

Hickey, Wakoh Shannon. "Two Buddhisms, Three Buddhisms, and Racism," *Journal of Global Buddhism* 11 (2010): 1–25.

Horinouchi, Isao. "Americanized Buddhism: A Sociological Analysis of Protestantized Japanese Religion," PhD dissertation, University of California, Davis, 1973.

Hsu, Funie. "We've Been Here All Along," *Buddhadharma: The Practitioner's Quarterly* (Winter 2016); https://www.lionsroar.com/weve-been-here-all-along.

Huang, C. Julia. *Charisma and Compassion: Cheng Yen and the Buddhist Tzu Chi Movement*. Cambridge, MA: Harvard University Press, 2009.

Ichimura, Takao 市村高男. "Chūsei Utsunomiyashi no seiritsu to tenkai: Shimotsuke, Buzen, Iyo no sanryū no kankei wo saguru" 中世宇都宮氏の成立と展開—下野·豊前·伊予の三流の関係を探る, in Ichimura Takao, ed., Chūsei *Utsunomiyashi no sekai: Shimotsuke, Buzen, Iyo no jikū wo sakanoboru* 中世宇都宮氏の世界—下野·豊前·伊予の時空を遡る. Tokyo: Sairyūsha, 2013.

Ikura, Fumito. "Oni no shikogusa to oni no koshigusa: Toshiyori to hon josetsu," *Mita kokubun* 29 (1999): 1–14.

Inoue, Takami. "Shūmon hakusho wo megutte: Ishikawa Shuntai no kadai"『宗門白書』をめぐって:石川舜台の話題, *Kyōka kenkyū* 教化研究 151 (2012): 47–56.

Inoue, Takami. "The Interaction between Buddhist and Shinto Traditions at Suwa Shrine," in Mark Teeuwen and Fabio Rambelli, eds., *Buddhas and Kami in Japan: Honji Suijaku as a Combinatory Paradigm*. London and New York: RoutledgeCurzon, 2003.

Ishida, Kazuhiro 石田一裕. "Shūkyō Daigaku ni okeru kindai bukkyōgaku—Watanabe Kaikyoku no toō to kōgi wo chūshin ni" 教大学における近代仏教学—渡辺海旭の渡欧と講義を中心に, in Ejima Naotoshi 江島尚俊, Miura Shū 三浦周, and Matsuno Tomoaki 松野智章, eds., *Kindai nihon no daigaku to shūkyō* 近代日本の大学と宗教, pp. 279–304. Kyoto: Hōzōkan, 2014.

Iwamura, Jane Naomi. *Virtual Orientalism: Asian Religions and American Popular Culture*. Oxford and New York: Oxford University Press, 2011.

Iwamura, Jane Naomi, and Paul Spickard, eds. *Revealing the Sacred in Asian and Pacific America*. New York: Routledge, 2003.

Izumi, Hōkei 泉芳璟. "Bussetsu Mujōkyō. Mata Sankeikyō to nazuku" 佛说无常经. 亦三启经と 名く, in *Kokuyaku Issai Kyō. Kyōjū-bu* 国译一切经. 经集部, vol. 12, pp. 53–60. Tokyo: Daitō Shuppansha, 1932.

Jaffe, Richard M. *Neither Monk nor Layman: Clerical Marriage in Modern Japanese Buddhism*. Princeton, NJ: Princeton University Press, 2001.

Jansen, Marius B. and Gilbert Rozman. *Japan in Transition, from Tokugawa to Meiji*. Princeton, NJ: Princeton University Press, 1986.

Jones, Charles B. "Apologetic Strategies in Late Imperial Chinese Pure Land Buddhism," *Journal of Chinese Religions* 29 (2001): 69–90.

Jordt, Ingrid. *Burma's Mass Lay Meditation Movement: Buddhism and the Cultural Construction of Power*. Athens: Ohio University Press, 2007.

Josephson, Jason Ananda. *The Invention of Religion in Japan*. Chicago: University of Chicago Press, 2012.

Kakehashi, Nara. *Heianki jōdokyō tenkairon* 奈良・平安期浄土教展開論. Kyoto: Hōzōkan, 2008.

Kakehashi, Nobuaki 梯信暁. *Jōdokyō shisōshi: Indo, Chūgoku, Chōsen, Nihon* 浄土教思想史：インド・中国・朝鮮・日本. Kyoto: Hōzōkan, 2012.

Kanakura, Enshō 金苍円照. *Memyō no Kenkyū* 马鸣の研究. Kyoto: Heiraku-ji Shoten, 1966.

Karsten, Siegfried G. "China's Approach to Social Market Economics: The Chinese Variant of Market Socialism Seeks to Escape from the Difficulties of Central Command Planning," *The American Journal of Economics and Sociology* 47/2 (1988): 129–248.

Kashima, Tetsuden. *Buddhism in America: The Social Organization of an Ethnic Religious Institution*. Westport, CT: Greenwood Press, 1977.

Kashima, Tetsuden. "The Buddhist Churches of America: Challenges for Change in the Twenty-First Century," in Richard K. Payne, ed., *Shin Buddhism: Historical, Textual, and Interpretive Studies*, pp. 321–40. Berkeley, CA: Institute of Buddhist Studies and Numata Center for Buddhist Translation and Research, 2007.

Kazuo, Mabuchi, Kunisaki Fumimaro, and Inagaki Taiichi, eds., *Shinpen Nihon Koten Bungaku Zenshū 38: Konjaku monogatarishū 4*. Tokyo: Shōgakukan, 2002.

Ke, Yun. "Finding Robot Monk Xian'er: Understanding Buddhism in Longquan Animation," *Journal of Visual and Media Anthropology* 2/1 (2016): 7–24.

Ketelaar, James Edward. *Of Heretics and Martyrs in Meiji Japan*. Princeton, NJ: Princeton University Press, 1993.

King, Richard. *Orientalism and Religion: Postcolonial Theory, India, and "The Mystic East."* New York: Routledge, 1999.

Kishida, Hiroshi 岸田裕之, ed. *Hiroshima-ken no rekishi* 広島県の歴史. Tokyo: Yamakawa Shuppan, 1999.

Klautau, Orion. "Against the Ghosts of Recent Past: Meiji Scholarship and the Discourse on Edo-Period Buddhist Decadence," *Japanese Journal of Religious Studies* 35/2 (2008): 263–303.

Klautau, Orion. *Kindai nihon shisō to shite no bukkyō shigaku* 近代日本思想として仏教史学. Kyoto: Hōzōkan, 2012.

Koda, Tara K. "Aloha with Gassho: Buddhism in the Hawaiian Plantations," *Pacific World*, Third Series, No. 5 (2003): 237–54.

Komine, Kazuaki. "Toshiyori zuinō no uta to katari," *Chūsei bungaku kenkyū* 9 (1983): 1–24.

Komine, Kazuaki. *Inseiki bungakuron*. Tokyo: Kasama Shoin, 2006.

Kornfield, Jack. *Modern Buddhist Masters* (1977). Kandy, Sri Lanka: Buddhist Publication Society, 2007, reprint.

Krishnamurti, Jiddhu. *Freedom from the Known*. San Francisco: HarperSanFrancisco, 1975.

Krishnamurti. *Speech on the Dissolution of the Order of the Star*, August 3, 1929. http://www.jkrishnamurti.org/about-krishnamurti/dissolution-speech.php.

Kuroda, Toshio 黒田俊雄. *Nihon chūsei no kokka to shūkyō* 日本中世の国家と宗教. Tokyo: Iwanami Shōten, 1975.

Kuroda, Toshio 黒田俊雄. *Kuroda Toshio chosakushū* 黒田俊雄著作集. Kyoto: Hōzōkan, 1994.

Kushida, Ryōkō 櫛田良洪. "Himitsu nenbutsu shisō no bokkō" 秘密念仏思想の勃興, *Taishō daigaku kenkyū kiyō tsūgō* 大正大学研究紀要 通号 48 (1963): 43–80.

Kyūsojin, Hitaku. "Shunpishō ni tsuite," *Kokugo to kokubungaku* 16/3 (1939): 52–67.

Lang, Karen C. "Canon and Literature," in Charles Prebish and Damien Keown, eds., *Encyclopedia of Buddhism*, pp. 195–205. New York and London: Routledge, 2007.

La Vallée Poussin, Louis de. *L'Abhidharmakośa de Vasubandhu, Tomes I–VI*. Bruxelles: Institut Belge des Hautes Études Chinoises, 1971.

Layman, Emma McCloy. *Buddhism in America*. Chicago: Nelson-Hall, 1976.

Learman, Linda. "Introduction," in Linda Learman, ed., *Buddhist Missionaries in the Era of Globalization*, pp. 1–21. Honolulu: University of Hawai'i Press, 2005.

Levering, Miriam. "Scripture and Its Reception: A Buddhist Case," in Miriam Levering, ed., *Rethinking Scripture: Essays from a Comparative Perspective*, pp. 58–101. Albany, NY: State University of New York (SUNY) Press, 1989.

Lévi, Sylvain, and J. Takakusu. "Bombai," in *Hōbōgirin, Fascicle I: 93–Fascicle II: 112*. Tokyo: Maison Franco-Japonaise, 1929–1930.

Lewis, Lancaster. "Buddhist Canons: Embodiments of Cultural and National Identity," unpublished lecture. https://www.academia.edu/8603537/Buddhist_Canons_Embodiments_of_Cultural_and_National_Identity.

Li, Rongxi. *Buddhist Monastic Traditions of Southern Asia: A Record of the Inner Law Sent Home from the South Seas*. Berkeley, CA: Numata Center for Buddhist Translation and Research, 2000.

Lin, Irene. "Journey to the Far West: Chinese Buddhism in America," in David K. Yoo, ed., *New Spiritual Homes: Religion and Asian Americans*, pp. 134–66. Honolulu: University of Hawai'i Press, 1999.

Lindsay, Ethan. "Pilgrimage to the Sacred Traces of Kōyasan: Place and Devotion in Late Heian Japan," PhD dissertation, Princeton University, 2012.

Lockman, Zachary. *Field Notes: The Making of Middle East Studies in the United States*. Stanford: Stanford University Press, 2016.

Londo, William. "The Other Mountain: The Mt. Kōya Temple Complex in the Heian Era," PhD dissertation, University of Michigan, 2004.

Lopez, Donald S., Jr. "Introduction" in Donald S. Lopez, Jr., ed., *Curators of the Buddha: The Study of Buddhism under Colonialism*, pp. 1–29. Chicago: University of Chicago Press, 1995.

Lopez, Donald S., Jr. "Buddha," in Donald S. Lopez, Jr., ed., *Critical Terms for the Study of Buddhism*, pp. 13–34. Chicago: University of Chicago Press, 2005.

Lopez, Donald S., Jr. *The Scientific Buddha: His Short and Happy Life*. New Haven, CT: Yale University Press, 2012.

Lopez, Donald S., Jr. "Developments in Buddhist Studies, 2015: A Report on the Symposium 'Buddhist Studies Today,' University of British Columbia, Vancouver, July 7–9, 2015," *Canadian Journal of Buddhist Studies* 11 (2016): 5–36.

Lowe, Lisa. *Immigrant Acts: On Asian American Cultural Politics*. Durham, NC: Duke University Press, 1996.

Makransky, John. "The Emergence of Buddhist Critical-Constructive Reflection in the Academy as a Resource for Buddhist Communities and for the Contemporary World," *Journal of Global Buddhism* 9, special issue "Blurred Genres" (2008): 113–53.

Mari, Michael E. *China and the Legacy of Deng Xiaoping: From Communist Revolution to Capitalist Evolution*. Dulles, VA: Potomac Books, 2001.

Masatsugu, Michael K. "'Beyond This World of Transiency and Impermanence': Japanese Americans, Dharma Bums, and the Making of American Buddhism during the Early Cold War Years," *Pacific Historical Review* 77/3 (2008): 423–51.

Masuzawa, Tomoko. *The Invention of World Religions: Or, How Universalism Was Preserved in the Language of Pluralism*. Chicago: University of Chicago Press, 2005.

McAdams, Mindy. "Finding American Buddhism in Blogs," paper presented at the conference "Buddhism without Borders: Contemporary Buddhism in the West," Institute of Buddhist Studies, Berkeley, CA, March 18–21, 2010. http://www.researchgate.net/publication/266557128_Finding_American_Buddhism_in_Blogs.

McGovern, Nathan. "On the Origins of the 32 Marks of the Great Man," *Journal of the International Association of Buddhist Studies* 39 (2016): 207–47.

McLellan, Janet. *Many Petals of the Lotus: Five Asian Buddhist Communities in Toronto*. Toronto: University of Toronto Press, 1999.

McMahan, David. *The Making of Buddhist Modernism*. London: Oxford University Press, 2008.

McNicholl, Adeana. "Buddhism and Race," in Paul Harvey and Kathryn Gin Lum, eds., *The Oxford Handbook of Religion and Race in American History*, pp. 223–40. New York: Oxford University Press, 2018.

Mills, Martin A. *Identity, Ritual, and State in Tibetan Buddhism: The Foundations of Authority in Gelukpa Monasticism*. New York: Routledge, 2003.

Mitchell, Scott A. "Locally Translocal American Shin Buddhism," *Pacific World: Journal of the Institute of Buddhist Studies*, Third Series, No. 12 (2010): 109–26.

Mitchell, Scott A. *Buddhism in America: Global Religion, Local Contexts*. London: Bloomsbury Academic, 2016.

Mitchell, Scott A. "Scrambled Eggs: At the Intersection of Buddhist Economies and Knowledge Economies," paper presented at the American Academy of Religion (AAR) Conference, November 19–22, 2016, San Antonio, TX.

Miura, Shū 三浦周. "Gakushū" sareru bukkyō—Taishō, Showa shoki no shūmon Daigaku ni okeru karikyuramu no hensen to sono tokushitsu『学習』される仏教——大正·昭和初期の宗門大学におけるカリキュラムの変遷とその特質, in Ejima Naotoshi 江島尚俊, Miura Shū 三浦周, and Matsuno Tomoaki 松野智章, eds., *Kindai nihon no daigaku to shūkyō* 近代日本の大学と宗教, pp. 203–50. Kyoto: Hōzōkan, 2014.

Miyasaka, Yūshō. "Kami to hotoke no yūgō: Mikkyō shisō kara no kaishaku," in Ueda Masaaki, Miyasaka Kōshō, Ōbayashi Taryō, Miyasaka Yūshō, and Gorai Shigeru, eds., *Onbashira matsuri to Suwa Taisha* 御柱祭りと諏訪大社. Tokyo: Chikuma Shobō, 1987.

Moran, Peter. "Introduction," in Peter Moran, ed., *Buddhism Observed: Travellers, Exiles and Tibetan Dharma in Kathmandu*, pp. 1–13. New York and London: Curzon Press, 2004.

Morrell, Robert. *Sand and Pebbles (Shasekishū): The Tales of Mujū Ichien, A Voice for Pluralism in Kamakura Buddhism*. Albany, NY: State University of New York (SUNY) Press, 1985.

Mortland, Carol A. *Cambodian Buddhism in the United States*. Albany, NY: State University of New York (SUNY) Press, 2017.

Murthy, Dhiraj. "Digital Ethnography: An Examination of the Use of New Technologies for Social Research," *Sociology* 42/5 (2008): 837–55.

Nagamatsu, Atsushi 永松敦. *Shuryō minzoku kenkyū: Kinsei ryōshi no jitsuzō to denshō* 狩猟民俗研究：近世猟師の実像と伝承. Kyoto: Hozokan, 2005.

Nakamura, Hajime 中村元. *Bukkyōgo Daijiten* 佛教语大辞典. Tokyo: Tōkyō Shoseki Kabushiki Kaisha, 1981.

Nakamura, Honnen 中村本然. "Dōhan no Jōdo kan" 道範の浄土観, *Kōyasan daigaku ronsō* 高野山大学論叢 29 (1994): 149–202.

Ñāṇamoli, Bhikkhu, trans. *Visuddhimagga: The Path of Purification*. Kandy: Buddhist Publication Society, 2010, fourth ed.

Nanjō, Bunyū 南条文雄. *Kaikyūroku: Sansukuritto* 懐旧録. Tokyo: Daiyūkaku, 1927.

Nattier, Jan. "Visible and Invisible: On the Politics of Representation in America," *Tricycle: The Buddhist Review* (Fall 1995): 42–49.

Nattier, Jan. "Who Is a Buddhist? Charting the Landscape of Buddhist America," in Charles S. Prebish and Kenneth K. Tanaka, eds., *The Faces of Buddhism in America*. Berkeley, CA: University of California Press, 1998.

Needleman, Jacob. *The New Religions*. Garden City, NY: Doubleday, 1970.

*Nihon koten bungaku taikei*, ed. Takagi Ichinosuke et al., 102 vols. Tokyo: Iwanami Shoten, 1957–1969.

*Nihon koten zenshū Honzō wamyō*. Tokyo: Gendai shichōsha, 1978.

*Nihon shisō taikei*, ed. Hayashiya Tatsusaburō et al., 67 vols. Tokyo: Iwanami Shoten, 1970–1982.

Nishimura, Ryō. "Tokumon fujaku: Sono shōgai" (1701–1781) 徳門普寂：その生涯 (1701–1781), *Indotetsugaku Bukkyōgaku kenkyū* インド哲学仏教学研究 14 (2007): 87–99.

Numrich, Paul David. *Old Wisdom in the New World: Americanization in Two Immigrant Theravada Buddhist Temples*. Knoxville: University of Tennessee Press, 1996.

Numrich, Paul David. "Two Buddhisms Further Considered," *Contemporary Buddhism* 4/1 (2003): 55–78.

Okada, Mareo. "Toshiyori Mumyōshō no chosha to sono chojutsu nendai ge," *Geimon* 12/7 (1921): 20–37.

Olcott, Henry Steel. *A Buddhist Catechism: According to the Sinhalese Canon*. London: Theosophical Publication Society, 1887.

Olcott, Henry Steel. *The Golden Rules of Buddhism* (1887). Madras: Theosophical Publishing House, 1902.

Oldenberg, Hermann, trans. *Dīpavaṁsa, The Chronicle of the Island: An Ancient Buddhist Historical Record*. London: Williams and Norgate, 1879.

Orzech, Charles D. "A Tang Esoteric Manual for Rebirth in the Pure Land," in Richard K. Payne, ed., *Path of No Path: Contemporary Studies in Pure Land Buddhism Honoring Roger Corless*, pp. 31–55. Berkeley, CA: Institute of Buddhist Studies and Numata Center for Buddhist Translation and Research, 2009.

Orzech, Charles D. "Esoteric Buddhism in the Tang: From Atikūṭa to Amoghavajra (651–780)," in Charles D. Orzech, Henrik H. Sørensen, and Richard K. Payne, eds., *Esoteric Buddhism and the Tantras in East Asia*, pp. 263–85. Leiden: Brill, 2011.

Orzech, Charles D. "On the Subject of Abhiṣeka," *Pacific World: Journal of the Institute of Buddhist Studies*, 3rd Series, No. 13 (Fall 2011): 113–28.

Ostrowski, Ally. "Buddha Browsing: American Buddhism and the Internet," *Contemporary Buddhism* 7/1 (2006): 91–103.

Ōtani daigaku hensan iinkai 大谷大学百年史編纂委員会, ed. *Ōtani daigaku hyakunenshi* 大谷大学百年史. Kyoto: Ōtani daigaku, 2001.

Ōtani, Eiichi 大谷栄一. "'Kindai bukkyō ni naru' to iu monogatari: Kindai nihon bukkyōshi kenkyū no hihanteki keishō no tame no riro"『近代仏教になる』という物語—近代日本仏教史研究の批判的継承のための理路, *Kindai Bukkyō* 近代仏教 16 (2009): 1–26.

Ouyi Zhixu 藕益智旭. "Guan quan Kaishi xueshu Fahua jing ba" 觀泉開士血書法華經跋, in *Ouyi dashi quanji* 藕益大師全集, 18: 11267. Taipei: Fojiao shuju 佛教書局, 1989.

Paramore, Kiri. "Anti-Christian Ideas and National Ideology: Inoue Enryō and Inoue Tetsujiro's Mobilization of Sectarian History in Meiji Japan," *Sungkyun Journal of East Asian Studies* 9/1 (2009): 107–44.

Pas, Julian F. *Visions of Sukhāvatī: Shan-Tao's Commentary on the Kuan Wu-Liang-Shou-Fo ching*. New York: State University of New York Press, 1995.

Payne, Richard K. *The Tantric Ritual of Japan: Feeding the Gods—The Shingon Fire Ritual*. Śata-Pitaka Series no. 365. New Delhi: International Academy of Indian Culture and Aditya Prakashan, 1991.

Payne, Richard K. "Realizing Inherent Enlightenment: Ritual and Self-Transformation in Shingon Buddhism," in Michael B. Aune and Valerie DeMarinis, eds., *Religious and Social Ritual: Interdisciplinary Explorations*, pp. 71–104. New York: State University of New York Press, 1996.

Payne, Richard K. "The Cult of Arya Aparamitayus: Proto-Pure Land Buddhism in the Context of Indian Mahayana," *The Pure Land: Journal of Pure Land Buddhism*, 13–14 (1997): 19–36.

Payne, Richard K. ed. *Re-Visioning "Kamakura" Buddhism*. Honolulu: University of Hawai'i Press, 1998.

Payne, Richard K. "Ajikan: Ritual and Meditation in the Shingon Tradition," in Richard K. Payne, ed., *Re-visioning "Kamakura" Buddhism*, pp. 219–48. Honolulu: University of Hawai'i Press, 1998.

Payne, Richard K. *Language Conducive to Awakening: Categories of Language Use in East Asian Buddhism, with Particular Attention to the Vajrayāna Tradition*. Düsseldorf: Hauses der Japanischen Kulter, 1998.

Payne, Richard K. "The Shingon Ajikan: Diagrammatic Analysis of Ritual Syntax," *Religion* 29 (1999): 215–29.

Payne, Richard K. "Shingon Services for the Dead," in George J. Tanabe, Jr., ed., *Religions of Japan in Practice*, pp. 159–65. Princeton, NJ: Princeton University Press, 1999.

Payne, Richard K. "Introduction," in Richard K. Payne and Kenneth K. Tanaka, eds., *Approaching the Land of Bliss: Religious Praxis in the Cult of Amitābha*, pp. 1–15. Honolulu: University of Hawai'i Press, 2004.

Payne, Richard K. "Individuation and Awakening: Romantic Narrative and the Psychological Interpretation of Buddhism," in Mark Unno, ed., *Buddhism and Psychotherapy: Across Cultures*, pp. 31–51. Boston, MA: Wisdom Publications, 2006.

Payne, Richard K. "The Shingon Subordinating Fire Offering for Amitābha: 'Amida Kei Ai Goma,'" *Pacific World: Journal of the Institute of Buddhist Studies*, 3rd Series, No. 8 (2006): 191–236.

Payne, Richard K. ed. *Tantric Buddhism in East Asia*. Boston, MA: Wisdom Publications, 2006.

Payne, Richard K. "Aparamitāyus: 'Tantra' and 'Pure Land' in Medieval Indian Buddhism?" *Pacific World: Journal of the Institute of Buddhist Studies*, 3rd Series, No. 9 (2007): 273–308.

Payne, Richard K. "Traditionalist Representations of Buddhism," *Pacific World: Journal of the Institute of Buddhist Studies*, Third Series, No. 10 (2008): 177–210.

Payne, Richard K. ed., *Path of No Path: Contemporary Studies in Pure Land Buddhism Honoring Roger Corless*. Honolulu: University of Hawai'i Press, 2009.

Payne, Richard K. "The Fourfold Training in Japanese Esoteric Buddhism," in Charles D. Orzech, Henrik H. Sørensen, and Richard K. Payne, eds., *Esoteric Buddhism and the Tantras in East Asia*, pp. 1024–28. Leiden: Brill, 2011.

Payne, Richard K. "From Vedic India to Buddhist Japan: Continuities and Discontinuities in Esoteric Ritual," in Charles D. Orzech, Henrik H. Sørensen, and Richard K. Payne, eds., *Esoteric Buddhism and the Tantras in East Asia*, pp. 1040–54. Leiden: Brill, 2011.

Payne, Richard K. "Buddhism or Buddhisms? Rhetorical Consequences of Geo-political Categories," *OUPBlog* (2012): https://blog.oup.com/2012/08/buddhism-rhetorical-consequence-geo-political-category/.

Payne, Richard K. "Buddhism and the Powers of the Mind," in David L. McMahan, ed., *Buddhism in the Modern World*, pp. 233–55. New York: Routledge, 2012.

Payne, Richard K. "Why 'Buddhist Theology' Is Not a Good Idea: Keynote Address for the Fifteenth Biennial Conference of the International Association of Shin Buddhist Studies, Kyoto, August 2011," *The Pure Land: Journal of the International Association of Shin Buddhist Studies*, New Series 27 (2012–2013): 37–71.

Payne, Richard K. "Afterword: Buddhism beyond Borders: Beyond the Rhetorics of Rupture," in Scott A. Mitchell and Natalie E. F. Quli, eds., *Buddhism beyond Borders: New Perspectives on Buddhism in the United States*, pp. 217–39. Albany, NY: State University of New York Press, 2015.

Payne, Richard K. *Critical Reflections on Buddhist Thought*, "on not capitalizing (on) the dharma," July 27, 2018, https://rkpayne.wordpress.com/reflections-on-buddhist-thought-posts.

Payne, Richard K., and Kenneth K. Tanaka, eds. *Approaching the Land of Bliss: Religious Praxis in the Cult of Amitābha*. Honolulu: University of Hawai'i Press, 2004.

Payne, Richard K., and Michael Witzel, eds. *Homa Variations: The Study of Ritual Change Across the Longue Durée*. New York: Oxford University Press, 2016.

Pew Research Center. "Asian Americans: A Mosaic of Faiths," Washington, DC, 2012. http://www.pewforum.org/files/2012/07/Asian-Americans-religion-full-report.pdf.

Pierce, Lori. "Buddha Loves Me This I Know: Nisei Buddhists in Christian America, 1889–1942," in Gary Storhoff and John Whalen-Bridge, eds., *American Buddhism as a Way of Life*, pp. 167–82. Albany, NY: State University of New York (SUNY) Press, 2010.

Prebish, Charles S. *American Buddhism*. North Scituate, MA: Duxbury Press, 1979.

Prebish, Charles S. "Two Buddhisms Reconsidered," *Buddhist Studies Review* 10/2 (1993): 187–206.

Prebish, Charles S. *Luminous Passage: The Practice and Study of Buddhism in America*. Berkeley, CA: University of California Press, 1999.

Prebish, Charles S. "Studying the Spread and Histories of Buddhism in the West," in Charles S. Prebish and Martin Baumann, eds., *Westward Dharma: Buddhism beyond Asia*, pp. 66–81. Berkeley and Los Angeles, CA: University of California Press, 2002.

Prebish, Charles S. *An American Buddhist Life: Memoirs of a Modern Dharma Pioneer*. Richmond Hill, Ontario: Sumeru Press, 2011.

Prebish, Charles S. "The Buddhist Sangha: Buddhism's Monastic and Lay Communities," in John Powers, ed., *The Buddhist World*, pp. 399–416. New York: Routledge, 2016.

Proffitt, Aaron. "Kōen the Dragon Bodhisattva: History and Hagiography: A Translation and Analysis of the *Fuso ryūjinden*," MA thesis, University of Colorado-Boulder, 2008.

Proffitt, Aaron. "Mysteries of Speech and Breath: Dōhan's 道範 (1179–1252) *Himitsu nenbutsu shō* 秘密念仏抄 and Esoteric Pure Land Buddhism," PhD dissertation, University of Michigan, 2015.

Proffitt, Aaron. "Multiple Logics and Multiple Paths in Medieval Japanese Deathbed Practice: Review of Jacqueline I. Stone, *Right Thoughts at the Last Moment: Buddhism and Deathbed Practices in Early Medieval Japan.* " *H-Japan, H-Net Reviews*, November 2017. http://www.h-net.org/reviews/showrev.php?id=50791.

Proffitt, Aaron. "Dōhan's (1179–1252) *Himitsu nenbutsu shō* (Fascicle 1)," in Georgios T. Halkias and Richard K. Payne, eds., *Pure Lands in Asian Texts and Contexts: An Anthology*. Honolulu: University of Hawai'i Press, 2019.

Prothero, Stephen. *The White Buddhist: The Asian Odyssey of Henry Steel Olcott*. Bloomington, IN: University of Indiana Press, 1996.

Quli, Natalie E. "Western Self, Asian Other: Modernity, Authenticity, and Nostalgia for 'Tradition' in Buddhist Studies," *Journal of Buddhist Ethics* 16 (2009): 1–38.

Quli, Natalie Fisk. "Laicization in Four Sri Lankan Buddhist Temples in Northern California," PhD dissertation, Graduate Theological Union, Berkeley, CA, 2010.

Rambelli, Fabio. *Buddhist Materiality: A Cultural History of Objects in Japanese Buddhism*. Stanford: Stanford University Press, 2007.

Reader, Ian. "Buddhism and the Perils of Advocacy," *Journal of Global Buddhism* 9, special issue: "Blurred Genres" (2008): 83–112.

Reitan, Richard M. *Making a Moral Society: Ethics and the State in Meiji Japan*. Honolulu: University of Hawai'i Press, 2010.

Rhodes, Robert F. "Introduction to 'A Translation of "Otani Daigaku's Founding Spirit" by Sasaski Gessho,'" Michael Conway, Takami Inoue, and Robert F. Rhodes, trans., *Shinshū Sōgō Kenkyūjo Kenkyūkiyō* 真宗総合研究所研究紀要 30 (2011): 1–31.

Roberts, Jon H. and James Turner. *The Sacred and the Secular University*. Princeton, NJ: Princeton University Press, 2000. Kindle Edition.

Rodrigues, Hillary. "An Instance of Dependent Origination: Are Krishnamurti's Teachings Buddhadharma?" *Pacific World: Journal of Institute of Buddhist Studies*, Third Series, No. 9 (2007): 85–102.

Rowe, Mark. *Bonds of the Dead: Temples, Burial, and the Transformation of Contemporary Japanese Buddhism*. Chicago: University of Chicago Press, 2011.

Rozenberg, Guillaume. *The Immortals: Faces of the Incredible in Buddhist Burma*. Ward Keeler, trans. Honolulu: University of Hawai'i Press, 2015.

Ruppert, Brian. "Review of Henny van der Veere, *A Study into the Thought of Kōgyō Daishi Kakuban: With a Translation of His Gorin kuji myō himitsushaku*," *Monumenta Nipponica* 56/3 (2001): 422–24.

Ruppert, Brian. "Review of Thomas Conlan, *From Sovereign to Symbol: An Age of Ritual Determinism in Fourteenth Century Japan*," *Japanese Journal of Religious Studies* 40/2 (2013): 386–93.

Sadana, Rashmi. "Reading Delhi, Writing Delhi: An Ethnography of Literature," in Shalini Puri and Debra A. Castillo, eds., *Theorizing Fieldwork in the Humanities*, pp. 151–63. New York: Palgrave Macmillan US, 2016.

Said, Edward. *Orientalism*. New York: Pantheon, 1978.

Salgado, Nirmala S. *Buddhist Nuns and Gendered Practice: In Search of the Female Renunciant*. New York: Oxford University Press, 2013.

Sanderson, Alexis. "The Śaiva Age: The Rise and Dominance of Śaivism during the Early Medieval Period," in S. Einoo, ed., *Genesis and Development of Tantrism*, pp. 41–350. Tokyo: Institute of Oriental Culture, 2009.

Sanford, James H. "Amida's Secret Life: Kakuban's Amida hisaku," in Richard K. Payne and Kenneth K. Tanaka, eds., *Approaching the Land of Bliss: Religious Praxis in the Cult of Amitābha*, pp. 120–39. Honolulu: University of Hawai'i Press, 2004.

Sanford, James H. "Breath of Life: The Esoteric Nembutsu," in Richard K. Payne, ed., *Tantric Buddhism in East Asia*, pp. 161–90. Boston, MA: Wisdom Publications, 2006.

Sasaki, Kyōgo 佐佐木教悟. "Komponsetsuissaiu-bu to Sankei Mujōkyō ni tsuite" 根本说一切有部と三启无常经について, *Indogaku Bukkyōgaku Kenkyū* 印度学佛教学研究 19/2 (1970–1971): 570–677.

Sasaki, Shoten. "Shinshu and Folk Religion: Toward a Post-modern 'Shinshu Theology,'" *Bulletin of the Nanzan Institute for Religion and Culture* 12 (Spring 1988): 13–35.

Satō, Mona 佐藤もな. "Chūsei Shingonshū ni okeru jōdo shisō kaishaku: Dōhan Himitsu nenbutsu shō o megutte" 中世真言宗における浄土思想解釈--道範『秘密念仏抄』をめぐって, *Indo tetsugaku bukkyōgaku kenkyū* インド哲学仏教学研究 9 (2002): 80–92.

Sawada, Janine Anderson. *Practical Pursuits: Religion, Politics, and Personal Cultivation in Nineteenth-century Japan*. Honolulu: University of Hawaiʻi Press, 2004.

Schedneck, Brooke. *Thailand's International Meditation Centers: Tourism and the Global Commodification of Religious Practices*. New York: Routledge, 2015.

Schopen, Gregory. "Archaeology and Protestant Presuppositions in the Study of Indian Buddhism," in *Bones, Stones, and Buddhist Monks: Collected Papers on the Archaeology, Epigraphy, and Texts of Monastic Buddhism in India*, pp. 1–22. Honolulu: University of Hawai'i Press, 1997.

Seager, Richard Hughes. *Buddhism in America*. New York: Columbia University Press, 1999.

Semmens, Justine. "Ten-Precept Mothers in the Buddhist Revival of Sri Lanka," in John Holt, ed., *The Sri Lanka Reader: History, Culture, Politics*, pp. 364–75. Durham, NC: Duke University Press, 2011.

Sharf, Robert. "The Rhetoric of Experience and the Study of Religion," *Journal of Consciousness Studies* 7/11–12 (2000): 267–87.

Sharf, Robert. *Coming to Terms with Chinese Buddhism: A Reading of the Treasure Store Treatise*. Honolulu: University of Hawaiʻi Press, 2002.

Sharf, Robert. "Thinking through Shingon Ritual," *Journal of the International Association of Buddhist Studies* 26/1 (2003): 59–86.

Shi Huikong. 2016. *Stories of Ven. Master Xuecheng*. Beijing: China Fortune Press, 2016.

Shingen, Takagi, and Thomas Eijo Dreitlein. *Kukai on the Philosophy of Language*. Tokyo: Keio University Press, 2010.

Shinohara, Koichi. *Spells, Images and Maṇḍalas: Tracing the Evolution of Esoteric Buddhist Rituals*. New York: Columbia University Press, 2014.

Shinohara, Koichi. "Rethinking the Category of Chinese Buddhist Apocrypha," *Studies in Chinese Religions* 1/1 (2015): 70–81.

*Shinpen nihon koten bungaku zenshū*, ed. Kubota Keiichi et al., 88 vols. Tokyo: Shōgakkan, 1994–2002.

Shintei zōho, Kokushi taikei, ed. Kuroita Katsumi et al., 62 vols. Tokyo: Yoshikawa Kōbunkan, Shōwa 4, 1929–1964.

Shintei zōho, Kokushi taikei, *Nihon kiryaku*, ed. Kuroita Katsumi et al., 3 vols. Tokyo: Yoshikawa Kōbunkan, 1979–1980.

Shōshin, Moriyama. *Tachikawa jakyō to sono shakaiteki haikei no kenkyū*. Tokyo: Kanōen, 1965.

Silk, Jonathan A. "The Composition of the '*Guan Wuliangshoufo-jing*': Some Buddhist and Jaina Parallels to Its Narrative Frame," *Journal of Indian Philosophy* 25/2 (1997): 181–256.

Silk, Jonathan A. "What, if Anything, is Mahāyāna Buddhism? Problems of Definitions and Classifications," *Numen* 49/4 (2002): 355–405.

Skilling, Peter. "Scriptural Authenticity and the Śrāvaka Schools: An Essay toward an Indian Perspective," *The Eastern Buddhist*, New Series 41/2 (2010): 1–48.

Small, Mario Luis. "'How Many Cases Do I Need?': On Science and the Logic of Case Selection in Field-Based Research," *Ethnography* 10/1 (2009): 5–38.

Smith, Fredrick M. *The Self Possessed: Deity and Spirit Possession in South Asian Literature and Civilization*. New York: Columbia University Press, 2006.

Smith, Jonathan Z. *Map Is Not Territory: Studies in the History of Religions*. Chicago: University of Chicago Press, 1978.

Smith, Jonathan Z. "Canons, Catalogues, and Classics," in Arie van der Kooij and Karel van der Toorn, eds., *Canonization and Decanonization: Papers Presented to the International Conference of the Leiden Institute for the Study of Religions*, pp. 295–311. Leiden: Brill, 1998.

Smith, Wilfred Cantwell. "Scripture as Form and Concept: Their Emergence for the Western World," in Miriam Levering, ed., *Rethinking Scripture: Essays from a Comparative Perspective*, pp. 29–57. Albany, NY: State University of New York (SUNY) Press, 1989.

Snodgrass, Judith. *Presenting Japanese Buddhism to the West: Orientalism, Occidentalism, and the Columbian Exposition*. Chapel Hill, NC: University of North Carolina Press, 2003.

Soucy, Alexander. *The Buddha Side: Gender, Power, and Buddhist Practice in Vietnam*. Honolulu: University of Hawai'i Press, 2012.

Spencer, Anne C. "Diversification in the Buddhist Churches of America: Demographic Trends and Their Implications for the Future Study of U.S. Buddhist Groups," *Journal of Global Buddhism* 15 (2014): 35–61.

Spencer, Anne C. and Scott Draper. "Introducing the Sort-of Buddhist: Or, 'If There Is No "I" to Have a Religious Identity, Then How Do I Fill Out This Survey?'" *Interdisciplinary Journal of Research on Religion* 14 (2018): 1–34.

Spiro, Melford E. *Buddhism and Society: A Great Tradition and Its Burmese Vicissitudes*. Berkeley, CA: University of California Press, 1982, second ed.

Staggs, Kathleen M. "'Defend the Nation and Love the Truth.' Inoue Enryō and the Revival of Meiji Buddhism," *Monumenta Nipponica* 38/3 (1983): 251–81.

Stark, Rodney and William Sims Bainbridge. *The Future of Religion: Secularization, Revival and Cult Formation*. Berkeley, CA: University of California Press, 1985.

Stark, Rodney and William Sims Bainbridge. *A Theory of Religion*. New York: P. Lang, 1987.

Stone, Jacqueline. "A Vast and Grave Task: Interwar Buddhist Studies as an Expression of Japan's Envisioned Global Role," in J. Thomas Rimer, ed., *Culture and Identity: Japanese Intellectuals During the Interwar Years*, pp. 217–33. Princeton, NJ: Princeton University Press, 1990.

Stone, Jacqueline. *Original Enlightenment and the Transformation of Medieval Japanese Buddhism*. Honolulu: University of Hawaii Press, 1999.

Stone, Jacqueline. "By the Power of One's Last Nenbutsu: Deathbed Practices in Early Medieval Japan," in Richard K. Payne and Kenneth K. Tanaka, eds., *Approaching the Land of Bliss: Religious Praxis in the Cult of Amitābha*, pp. 77–120. Honolulu: University of Hawai'i Press, 2004.

Stone, Jacqueline. "The Secret Art of Dying: Esoteric Deathbed Practices in Heian Japan," in Bryan J. Cuevas and Jacqueline I. Stone, eds., *The Buddhist Dead: Practices, Discourses, Representations*, pp. 134–74. Honolulu: University of Hawai'i Press, 2007.

Stone, Jacqueline. *Right Thoughts at the Last Moment: Buddhism and Deathbed Practices in Early Medieval Japan*. Honolulu: University of Hawai'i Press, 2016.

Storch, Tanya. *The History of Chinese Buddhist Bibliography*. Amherst: Cambria Press, 2014.

Strickmann, Michel. "The Consecration Sūtra: A Buddhist Book of Spells," in Robert E. Buswell, Jr., ed., *Chinese Buddhist Apocrypha*, pp. 75–118. Honolulu: University of Hawai'i Press, 1990.

Strickmann, Michel. *Mantras et mandarins: Le bouddhisme tantrique en Chine*. Paris: Gallimard, 1996.

Sueki, Fumihiko 末木文美士. *Kamakura bukkyō keiseiron: Shisōshi no tachibakara* 鎌倉仏教形成論——思想史の立場から. Kyoto: Hōzōkan, 1998.

Sueki, Fumihiko 末木文美士. *Meiji shisōka ron* 明治思想家論. Tokyo: Transview, 2004.

Sueki, Fumihiko 末木文美士. "Kōzanjibon juhōyōjinshū ni tsuite," *Kōzanji tenseki bunsho sōgō chōsadan kenkyū hōkoku ronshū*, ed. Kōzanji tenseki bunsho chōsadan (2007): 5–11.

Suh, Sharon A. *Being Buddhist in a Christian World: Gender and Community in a Korean American Temple*. Seattle: University of Washington Press, 2004.

Suh, Sharon A. *Silver Screen Buddha: Buddhism in Asian and Western Film*. New York: Bloomsbury, 2015.

Tachibana, Kenji. "Konjaku monogatari to Toshiyori zuinō tono kankei," *Kenkyūkiyō: Nara joshidaigaku bungakubu fuzoku chūgakkō kōtōgakkō* 5 (1962): 1–8.

Taga, Munehaya. *Eisai*. Tokyo: Yoshikawa Kōbunkan, 1965.

*Taishō shinshū Daizōkyō*, ed. Junjirō Takakusu and Kaigyoku Watanabe, 100 vols. Tokyo: Taisho Issaikyo Kankokai, 1924–1934.

Takanose, Keiko. *Minamoto no Toshiyori*. Tokyo: Kasama Shoin, 2012.

Tambiah, S. J. *Buddhism and the Spirit Cults in North-East Thailand*. Cambridge: Cambridge University Press, 1970.

Tanabe, George J., Jr., "Kōyasan in the Countryside: The Rise of Shingon in the Kamakura Period," in Richard K. Payne, ed., *Re-visioning "Kamakura" Buddhism*, pp. 43–55. Honolulu: University of Hawai'i Press, 1998.

Tanaka, Kenneth K. "Epilogue: The Colors and Contours of American Buddhism," in Charles S. Prebish and Kenneth K. Tanaka, eds., *The Faces of Buddhism in America*, pp. 287–98. Berkeley, CA: University of California Press, 1998.

Tanaka, Kenneth K. "Issues of Ethnicity in the Buddhist Churches of America," in Duncan Ryuken Williams and Christopher S. Queen, eds., *American Buddhism: Methods and Findings in Recent Scholarship*, pp. 3–19. Surrey: Curzon Press, 1999.

Tanaka, Kenneth K. "The Individual in Relation to the Sangha in American Buddhism: An Examination of 'Privatized Religion,'" *Buddhist-Christian Studies* 27/1 (2007): 115–27.

Tanigawa, Yutaka 谷川豊. *Meiji zenki no kyōiku, kyōka, bukkyō* 明治前期の教育・教化・仏教. Kyoto: Shinbunkaku, 2008.

Tanigawa, Yutaka 谷川豊. "'Kyō' no jidai—Kindai nihon keiseiki no bukkyō to minshū kyōka, sōryo yōse, zokujin kyōiku" 「教」の時代—近代日本形成期の仏教と民衆教化・僧侶養成・俗人教育, *Kikan Nihon Shisōshi* 季刊日本思想史 1/75 (2009): 36–53.

Terasaki, Keidō 寺崎敬道. "Komponsetsuissaiu-bu ni tsuite no ichikōsatsu. Sankei Mujōkyō no shūkyōteki imi" 根本说一切有部についての一考察. 三启无常经の宗教的义味, *Indogaku Bukkyōgaku Kenkyū* 印度学佛教学研究 39/2 (1990–1991): 566–68.

Thomassen, Einar. "Some Notes on the Development of Christian Ideas about a Canon," in Einar Thomassen, ed., *Canon and Canonicity: The Formation and Use of Scripture*, pp. 9–28. Copenhagen: Museum Tusculanum Press, 2010.

Tillakaratne, Mihiri Uthpala. "Multiculturalism, Ethnicity, Religious Identity and the 1.5 and Second Generation in Two Los Angeles-Area Sri Lankan Buddhist Temples," MA thesis, University of California Los Angeles, 2012.

Tokiya, Kōki/Yukinori 释舍幸纪. "Komponsetsuissaiu-bu ni in'yō sareru Mujōkyō" 根本说一切有部 に引用される无常经, *Indogaku Bukkyōgaku Kenkyū* 印度学佛教学研究 34/1 (1985–1986): 168–73.

Travagnin, Stefania. "The Mādhyamika Dimension of Yinshun: A Restatement of the School of Nāgārjuna in 20th Century Chinese Buddhism," PhD dissertation, SOAS University of London, 2009.

Tweed, Thomas A. *The American Encounter with Buddhism, 1844–1912*. Bloomington, IN: University of Indiana Press, 1992.

Tweed, Thomas A. "Nightstand Buddhists and Other Creatures: Sympathizers, Adherents, and the Study of Religion," in Christopher Queen and Duncan Ryuken Williams, eds., *American Buddhism: Methods and Findings in Recent Scholarship*, pp. 71–90. London: Routledge, 1998.

Tweed, Thomas A. "Between the Living and the Dead: Fieldwork, History, and the Interpreter's Position," in James V. Spickard, J. Shawn Landres, and Meredith B. McGuire, eds., *Personal Knowledge and beyond: Reshaping the Ethnography of Religion*, pp. 63–74. New York: New York University Press, 2002.

Tweed, Thomas A. *Crossing and Dwelling: A Theory of Religion*. Cambridge, MA: Harvard University Press, 2008.

Tweed, Thomas A. "Crabs, Crustaceans, Crabiness, and Outrage: A Response," *Journal of the American Academy of Religion* 77/2 (2009): 445–59.

Tweed, Thomas A. "Theory and Method in the Study of Buddhism: Toward 'Translocative' Analysis," *Journal of Global Buddhism* 12 (2011): 17–32.

Tweed, Thomas A. "Theory and Method in the Study of Buddhism: Toward a 'Translocative' Analysis," in Scott Mitchell and Natalie Quli, eds., *Buddhism beyond Borders: New Perspectives on Buddhism in the United States*, pp. 3–20. Albany, NY: State University of New York (SUNY) Press, 2015.

Unno, Mark T. "Recommending Faith in the Sand of the Mantra of Light," in Richard K. Payne, ed., *Re-visioning "Kamakura" Buddhism*, pp. 167–218. Honolulu: University of Hawai'i Press, 1998.

Usuki, Patricia Kanaya. "American Women in Jodo Shin Buddhism Today: Tradition and Transition," *Pacific World: Journal of the Institute of Buddhist Studies*, Third Series, No. 7 (2005): 159–75.

Van der Veere, Hendrick. *A Study into the Thought of Kōgyo Daishi Kakuban*. Leiden: Hotei Publishing, 2000.

Van Esterik, Penny. *Taking Refuge: Lao Buddhists in North America*. Tempe, AZ: Program for Southeast Asian Studies, Arizona State University, 2003.

Villero, Ofelia, Natalie Fisk (Quli), and Emily Wu. "New Religious Movements Project Report: For the Area of Cultural and Historical Studies of Religions," unpublished report, September 2006.

Vinītā, Bhikṣuṇī. *A Unique Collection of Twenty Sūtras in a Sanskrit Manuscript from the Potala, Vol. I, 1. Editions and Translations: 5. Anityatāsūtra*, pp. 169–206. Beijing and Vienna: China Tibetology Publishing House and Austrian Academy of Sciences Press, 2010.

Walsh, Michael J. *Sacred Economies: Buddhist Monasticism and Territoriality in Medieval China*. Sheng Yen Series in Chinese Buddhist Studies. New York: Columbia University Press, 2010.

Walters, Christine L. "American Buddhism as Identity and Practice: Scholarly Classifications of Buddhists in the United States," Master's thesis, University of Hawai'i, 2009.

Wang, Bangwei 王邦维. *Nanhai jigui neifa zhuan jiaozhu* 南海寄归内法传校注. Beijing: Zhonghua Shuju, 1995.

Weber, Max. "Part II. 'Objectivity' in Social Science and Social Policy," in Edward Shils and Henry Finch, eds. and trans., *Max Weber: The Methodology of the Social Sciences*, pp. 49–112. New York: Free Press, 1949.

Welch, Holmes. *The Practice of Chinese Buddhism 1900–1950*. Harvard East Asian Studies 26. Cambridge, MA: Harvard University Press, 1967.

Willemen, Charles. *The Essence of Scholasticism. Abhidharmahṛdaya. T. 1550*. Delhi: Motilal Banarsidass, 2006.

Willemen, Charles. *Buddhacarita: In Praise of Buddha's Acts*. Berkeley, CA: Numata Center for Buddhist Translation and Research, 2009.

Willemen, Charles. *A Collection of Important Odes of the Law: The Chinese Udānavarga*. Berkeley, CA: Institute of Buddhist Studies and BDK America, 2013.

Willemen, Charles. "Early Yogācāra and Visualization (Bhāvanā)," in Sarah F. Haynes and Michelle J. Sorensen, eds., *Wading into the Stream of Wisdom: Essays in Honor of*

*Leslie Kawamura*, pp. 209–25. Berkeley, CA: Institute of Buddhist Studies and BDK America, 2013.

Willemen, Charles. "Remarks about the History of Sarvāstivāda Buddhism," *Journal of Buddhist Studies* 11 (2013): 129–45.

Williams, Duncan Ryuken. "Camp Dharma: Japanese-American Buddhist Identity and the Interment Experience of World War II," in Charles S. Prebish and Martin Baumann, eds., *Westward Dharma: Buddhism beyond Asia*, pp. 191–200. Berkeley, CA: University of California Press, 2002.

Williams, Duncan Ryuken and Tomoe Moriya, eds. *Issei Buddhism in the Americas*. Urbana, IL: University of Illinois Press, 2010.

Wilson, Jeff. "Review of *Heartwood: The First Generation of Theravada Buddhism in America* by Wendy Cadge (Chicago: University of Chicago Press, 2004)," *Journal of Global Buddhism* 6 (2005): 7–11.

Wilson, Jeff. "Mapping the American Buddhist Terrain: Paths Taken and Possible Itineraries," *Religions Compass* 3/5 (2009): 836–46.

Wilson, Jeff. "'All Beings Are Equally Embraced by Amida Buddha': Jodo Shinshu Buddhism and Same-Sex Marriage in the United States," *Journal of Global Buddhism* 13 (2012): 31–59.

Wilson, Jeff. *Dixie Dharma: Inside a Buddhist Temple in the American South*. Chapel Hill, NC: University of North Carolina Press, 2012.

Wogihara, Unrai. *The Sanskrit-Chinese Dictionary of Buddhist Technical Terms: Based on the Mahāvyutpatti*. Tokyo: Sankibo, 1959.

Wu, Jiang. "From the 'Cult of the Book' to the 'Cult of the Canon': A Neglected Tradition in Chinese Buddhism," in Jiang Wu and Lucille Chia, eds., *Spreading Buddha's Word in East Asia: The Formation and Transformation of the Chinese Buddhist Canon*, pp. 46–78. New York: Columbia University Press, 2016.

Wu, Jiang and Lucille Chia, eds. *Spreading Buddha's Word in East Asia: The Formation and Transformation of the Chinese Buddhist Canon*. New York: Columbia University Press, 2016.

Xuecheng. "Zhongguo fojiao xianzhuang" ("Current State of Chinese Buddhism"), *Voice of Longquan*, June 18, 2017. http://eng.longquanzs.org/xuecheng/writings/77389.htm.

Xuecheng. "On the Belt and Road: The Spiritual Footprints of Buddhism and the Construction of a New World Civilization," *Voice of Longquan*, June 29, 2017. http://eng.longquanzs.org/xuecheng/writings/76775.htm.

Yamabe, Nobumi. "The Paths of Śrāvakas and Bodhisattvas in Meditative Practices," Meditative Buddhism: Its Origins and Reality, special issue, *Acta Asiatica* 96 (2009): 47–75.

Yang, Fenggang. "The Growing Literature of Asian American Religions: A Review of the Field, with Special Attention to Three New Books," *Journal of Asian American Studies* 3/2 (2000): 251–56.

Yang, Piaowei. *A Roaming AI Xian'er, the Robot Monk*. Beijing: Zhanlu Culture, 2006.

Yong, Amos. "Review Essay: Asian American Religions," *Nova Religio: The Journal of Alternative and Emergent Religions* 9/3 (2006): 92–107.

Yoo, David K. "Enlightened Identities: Buddhism and Japanese Americans of California, 1924–1941," *The Western Historical Quarterly* 27/3 (1996): 281–301.

Yoo, David K. "Introduction: Reframing the U.S. Religious Landscape," in David K. Yoo, ed., *New Spiritual Homes: Religion and Asian Americans*, pp. 1–15. Honolulu: University of Hawai'i Press, 1999.

Yoo, David K. and Ruth H. Chung, eds. *Religion and Spirituality in Korean America*. Urbana, IL: University of Illinois Press, 2008.

Yoshino, Tomomi. "Oni no shikogusa setsuwa wo megutte: Tokyo daigaku kokubungaku kenkyūshitsuzō Oni no shikogusa no shōkai to kōsatsu," *Tokyo daigaku kokubungaku ronshū* 1 (2006): 17–31.

Zacchetti, Stefano. "Notions and Visions of the Canon in Early Chinese Buddhism," in Jiang Wu and Lucille Chia, eds., *Spreading Buddha's Word in East Asia: The Formation and Transformation of the Chinese Buddhist Canon*, pp. 81–108. New York: Columbia University Press, 2016.

Zysk, Kenneth. *The Indian System of Human Marks*. Leiden: E. J. Brill, 2016.

# Index